Street of Dreams –
Boulevard of Broken Hearts

Other Books by Howard M. Wachtel

The Money Mandarins: The Making of a New Supranational Economic Order

Labor and the Economy

Workers' Management and Workers' Wages in Yugoslavia:
The Theory and Practice of Participatory Socialism

Street of Dreams – Boulevard of Broken Hearts

Wall Street's First Century

Howard M. Wachtel

Pluto Press

LONDON • STERLING, VIRGINIA

First published 2003 by Pluto Press
345 Archway Road, London N6 5AA
and 22883 Quicksilver Drive,
Sterling, VA 20166–2012, USA

www.plutobooks.com

British Library Cataloguing in Publication Data
A catalogue record for this book is available from the British Library

ISBN 0 7453 1925 4 hardback

Library of Congress Cataloging in Publication Data
Wachtel, Howard M.
  Street of dreams—boulevard of broken hearts : Wall Street's first century / Howard M. Wachtel.
    p. cm.
  Includes bibliographical references.
  ISBN 0–7453–1925–4
    1. Wall Street—History—19th century. 2. Stock exchanges—United States—History—19th century. I. Title.

HG4572 .W23 2003
332.64'273'09034—dc21

                                                                      2002192595

10   9   8   7   6   5   4   3   2   1

Designed and produced for Pluto Press by
Chase Publishing Services, Sidmouth EX10 9QG, England
Typeset from disk by Stanford DTP Services, Towcester
Printed in the United States of America by Phoenix Color

To Lukas who will inherit this past

Contents

List of Illustrations   ix
Preface and Acknowledgements   xi

1 THE BIG BANG: ALEXANDER HAMILTON AND THE ORIGINS
   OF WALL STREET   1
   Alexander Hamilton's Wall Street   4
   The Hamilton Project   6
   The Street's Origins   8
   Controversy and Scandal   12
   The Congressional Debate   14
   Did Hamilton Collude with Wall Street?   16
   The National Bank, William Duer and Financial Crisis   20
   The Invention of Wall Street   27

2 *LEX MERCATORIA*   31
   The Arcadian Republic Versus the Law of Commerce   31
   Hamilton's Fatal Flaw   33
   Financial Regeneration on Wall Street   36
   Wall Street's Financing of the War of 1812   38
   The New York Stock & Exchange Board   39
   Nathaniel Prime   40
   The Erie Canal   42
   Leveraging Erie's Success   46
   Cultural Improvements   49

3 JACKSON AND THE 1830s BANK WAR   52
   The Second National Bank and Nicholas Biddle   53
   James Hamilton   57
   Jackson's Message to Congress   59
   Framing the Language of Financial Politics   61
   Miscalculations   65
   The Ensuing Financial Crisis   67

4 THE NEW METROPOLIS   71
   The Stock Brokering Profession and Wall Street Innovations   75
   The Telegraph   78

The Clash of Classes   81
Planning for the New Metropolis   86
Evangelicals Confront Mammon   89

5 WALL STREET AND THE CIVIL WAR   93
A Divided Wall Street   94
Country Versus Profits   100
Wartime Financial Measures   102
The Cookes of Philadelphia   104
Wall Street Fights Back   107
Unifying the Nation's Finances   110

6 WARS, OTHER THAN CIVIL   113
Railroad Wars   115
Round Two   118
The Gold War   124
The Aftermath   131

7 TRUSTEE OVER THE NATION'S ECONOMY   135
J.P. Morgan   138
Jacob Schiff and Edward Harriman   142
De Facto Central Banker   144
NYSE's Transformation   146
Women on Wall Street   149
Technological Alterations   157
Pennsylvania Avenue Responds   159

8 THE AMERICAN CENTURY   162
Morgan's Last Hurrah   164
The Pujo Hearings   168
The Money Question   173
The Great Crash and Its Aftermath   177
A New and Better Deal   181
The Era of Global Finance   187
Street of Dreams – Boulevard of Broken Hearts   190

Notes   194
Bibliography   217
Index   225

List of Illustrations

1 The Brushwood Barrier That Became Wall Street, Frederick Trevor Hill, *The Story of a Street*, first published (N.Y.: Harper & Brothers, 1908) — 3

2 The Tontine Coffee House, Library of Congress (LC-USZ62–098020) — 11

3 Under The Buttonwood Tree, Library of Congress (LC-USZ62–39544) — 28

4 Erie Canal Lock, Library of Congress (LC-USZ62–32385) — 44

5 The Panic of 1837, Library of Congress (LC-USZ62–8844) — 64

6 The Sub-Treasury, Library of Congress (LC-USZ62–19196) — 69

7 Wall Street as Sacred Site, Library of Congress (LC-USZC4–2461) — 73

8 The Semaphore Alphabet, Library of Congress (LC-USZ62–050382) — 80

9 Edwin Forrest as Macbeth, Library of Congress (LC-USZ62–095776) — 85

10 Civil War Draft Riots, Library of Congress (LC-USZ62–127304) — 99

11 J.P. Morgan and Colleagues, Library of Congress (LC-USZ62–092327) — 139

12 The Curb Market, Library of Congress (LC-USZ62–19392) — 148

13 Hetty Green, Library of Congress (LC-USZ62–086005) — 156

14 The 'Money Question,' Library of Congress (LC-cai2a14507) — 176

15 Bombing, Library of Congress (LC-USZ262–067516) — 178

16 Anticipating the Crash of 1929, Library of Congress (LC-USZ62–099863) — 180

Preface

This is a history of 'The Street,' as Wall Street came to be known. It is a story of a place and its people that is part history, part mythology and part metaphor all converging at an intersection of reality and imagination out of which emerges a meaning for how Wall Street defines itself and how those on other streets define it. It recounts The Street's evolution in the nineteenth century, its people, symbols, practices and ideology that shaped modern Wall Street in the twentieth century. It is a narrative about the contradictions of a financial culture whose dream of the possible founders on the banality of its realization.

From its modest origin in the late eighteenth century to twentieth-century American icon, Wall Street's history has been indistinguishable from the nation's. It has been both a shaper of that history and molded by it. As creator of image and builder of financial reality, The Street's evolution in the nineteenth century placed its footprint on what Henry Luce – the founding publisher of *Time*, *Life* and *Fortune* – christened 'the American Century' (the twentieth). Alongside specific realities that build a history of Wall Street, there is the *idea* of Wall Street: the impressions, dreams and illusions projected onto it by everyone who encounters The Street.

Wall Street in the twentieth century has been adequately covered in a multitude of books that would fill substantial linear feet of shelf space. This is not the case with The Street's formative years in the nineteenth century. Understanding today's and tomorrow's news emanating from Wall Street is limited without a context which only history can provide: 'the act of endowing ... silent witnesses with a voice.' Consequently, says A.C. Grayling, 'a large part of the historian's task is interpretation. Without interpretation ... documents are mute; until the historian gives them one, they have no meaning.'[1]

The objective of *Street of Dreams – Boulevard of Broken Hearts* is to provide that interpretive context and to offer a hearing to those older voices that shaped modern Wall Street. It is a window into how The Street's accomplishments and excesses, practices and ideology inform the present; how individuals and their eccentricities establish a texture to the characters that built The Street; and how Wall Street influences politics as it is being challenged by larger political forces around it. Histories of The Street frequently have air-brushed out of its past certain controversies that warrant a new look. 'History is not a list of facts,' argues Grayling. 'It is a story that we can draw from them. And many different stories, all equally good, can be drawn from the same facts. Hence disagreement.'[2]

At each juncture in the transformation of the United States, Wall Street was there: at the beginning with the new nation's first Treasury Secretary, Alexander Hamilton, and his financial program; in the underwriting of such great nineteenth-century building projects as the Erie Canal and the railroads, in the battle with Andrew Jackson over the national bank and whether Wall Street or Pennsylvania Avenue would control financial policy; financing the Union side in the Civil War; inventing the *fin de siècle* financial trust; and on into the next century as a primal force in the creation of the American Century. Wall Street placed its imprint on these historical events and took away formative influences on its own development from two other streets: Pennsylvania Avenue and Main Street.

Wall Street is at once a place and in another sense a symbolic roadway that periodically joins with Pennsylvania Avenue and Main Street in a clover leaf pattern, merging separate paths into one intersection for a time before each street proceeds along its own course. As both place and symbol, its surveying and mapping is constructed within a triangular set of political, cultural and financial markers.

The binding together of three streets in the nation's financial evolution occurs in particular ways. The invention of American finance is found at the addresses of the great financial houses on The Street, and the New York Stock Exchange at Broad and Wall is its most famous address. Residents in homes on a composite Main Street from time to time are swept up in the allure of Wall Street, caught in a cycle of infatuation and betrayal that leaves a recurring storyline of fortune and tragedy. Three addresses on Pennsylvania Avenue house the public governors of finance: the White House, the Treasury and the Congress.

The love–hate relationship between Wall Street and the other streets derives from the idealization of The Street, which contributes to Wall Street's dilemma. The Street celebrates its success but is victimized by it too, when its proclivity toward speculative excess is neither effectively questioned by Pennsylvania Avenue nor tempered by Main Street caution. Too many people on Pennsylvania Avenue and Main Street come to believe literally in the ideology of Wall Street, award it an exclusive financial franchise, and bestow on it trusteeship over the nation's wealth and economic culture. At these moments the public governors of finance abandon their role as rule-making referees for the public interest and rally Main Street to The Street's cause as cheerleaders on the sidelines.

The interpretation offered here is of a Wall Street as the outcome of tensions among these three streets, responding to political and financial forces that buffet The Street. In less turbulent times, argue its defenders, Wall Street is seen as the repository of financial wisdom and wizardry, hindered by a meddlesome Pennsylvania Avenue and harassed by an untutored Main Street that complains too loudly when things go wrong. Critics view Wall Street as the repository of greed, seducing a naive Main Street into its version of 'the dream,' and coopting a compliant Pennsylvania Avenue into its financial schemes and ideology. Then infatuation turns to betrayal when The Street's excesses convert to financial crisis.

The analysis I propose for this fluctuation in attitudes is layered and complex. It grants Wall Street the prominence it deserves for its financial creativity and contribution to nation-building, cautions Main Street against the temptation of an unsustainable infatuation with Wall Street, and promotes a minimalist rule-making and refereeing Pennsylvania Avenue that provides space for the game to be played but does not allow it to get out of control. If Wall Street strays off course into excess, it is as much a failure of the other two streets to play their appointed roles as it is The Street's responsibility. The well-known phenomenon of recurrent financial crises, aptly characterized by the title of Charles Mackay's 1841 book as *Extraordinary Popular Delusions and the Madness of Crowds*, yields its own cycle of personal euphoria and despair for the individuals who buy into The Street's myths.[3]

This theme for interpreting Wall Street presents a problem and an opportunity. The problem is how to separate reality from illusion. The opportunity is to use new historical methodology, not yet applied to Wall Street, that challenges the solidity of most 'facts,' looks at historical evidence as not susceptible to a de-coupling from its source, and gives as much weight to perceptions of events – the play of surfaces – as it does to the event itself.

Such a matrix of historical method suits a Wall Street that is itself a wonder of attitudes about a contested reality and competing interpretation of facts, each contingent upon the orientation and reputation of the presenter. Wall Street's first great personage and the nation's first Secretary of the Treasury, Alexander Hamilton, was himself aware of this when he said that 'in nothing are appearances of greater moment, than in whatever regards credit. Opinion is the soul of it, and this is affected by appearances, as well as realities.'[4]

The study of three streets, independent yet interacting and each having a moderating influence on the other, surfaces for only a portion of the more than 200-year history of Wall Street. The obvious question the book seeks to answer is why. The counter-story of an innovative Wall Street, in league with a cooperative government and enticing Main Street into its financial schemes, appears as early as the first two years of Wall Street as a financial center and is most representative of its history. To illustrate this consider The Street's origins in 1792.

The first formal agreement to establish rules for trading among financial brokers – the 1792 Buttonwood Agreement – occurred in the wake of allegations of what today would be called an 'insider' trading scandal, with accompanying attempts at cornering a market and highly leveraged borrowing from an unsuspecting public. When the New York legislature was considering stringent regulation of financial brokering as an aftermath to financial crisis, the 24 Buttonwood signers countered with the idea of self-regulation for an exclusive private club of brokers. This, in fact, is the defining characteristic of the New York Stock Exchange that traces its unbroken lineage to that 1792 accord. With a change of names and in the magnitude of the sums involved, all of the players in the 1790–92 drama would readily recognize Ivan Boesky's and Michael Milken's Wall Street of the 1980s, or the dot.com mania of the 1990s, or the fallen financial idols of the first decade of the twenty-first century. This decade-by-decade recidivism is merely the norm for Wall Street, going back to 1792.

The 1790–92 financial crisis involved The Street's most famous resident, Treasury Secretary Alexander Hamilton, and his 1790 scheme to place the new republic on a firm financial footing. From its origins Wall Street's fortunes and misfortunes, therefore, involve the government, the private investor on Main Street and The Street's financial broker.

After this initial burst of financial innovation, fortune-making and crisis, financial brokering lapsed into dormancy until the War of 1812 and the aftermath of public improvements propelled it once again into the maelstrom of national affairs. These events settled an argument over the character of the new nation, between Thomas Jefferson's ideal of a republic attuned to the rhythms of a rural arcadia and motivated by civic virtue as against Hamilton's understanding of private interest motivated by the law of commerce – *Lex Mercatoria* – in which the governing principle was the metaphor of exchange bound by contract.

With bumps and detours along the way, the course of the nation was set. Wall Street became the preeminent nineteenth-century financial locus for the country and came to dominate twentieth-century global finance.

At each juncture – the battles with President Andrew Jackson for control of financial policy, the Civil War and skirmishes over railroads – Wall Street strengthened its financial and ideological dominance. Its invention of the trust in the late nineteenth century and subsequent reaction in the progressive-era regulatory reform forced a temporary detour but did not derail it. The financing of World War I, and the boom of the 1920s followed by collapse into depression, brought forward an aggressive Pennsylvania Avenue during Roosevelt's New Deal, which finally placed an effective regulatory envelope around The Street. Main Street was now able to dally in Wall Street but on a more level playing field than before or since. This arrangement, whereby the three streets had independent yet cooperating functions, lasted for nearly a half-century, only to be undone by the technological and deregulatory vigor of contemporary globalization.

Now it is time to take a walk down The Street to view its institutional evolution, the characters that left their footprints behind, its architectural statements, the idea behind it and the constellation of forces that emerges as it engages with Pennsylvania Avenue and Main Street.

ACKNOWLEDGMENTS

Part of the book was written in Fall 1999 when I was a Distinguished Visiting Scholar at the American Academy in Berlin. My thanks to its Executive Director, Gary Smith, and to the staff for making this residency along the Wannsee so productive and intellectually stimulating. A grant from the Mellon Fund of American University's College of Arts and Sciences assisted in the manuscript's preparation for which I thank the Dean, Kay J. Mussell. Virginia Myers Kelly consulted on the search for and selection of illustrations. Marie Tyler-McGraw provided a careful and thorough reading, which led to significant improvements in the structure of the manuscript. I am most grateful to Roger Van Zwanenberg, Publisher and Managing Director of Pluto Press, for allowing me to write the book I wanted to write. An author cannot ask for more from a publisher.

Howard M. Wachtel
Washington, D.C. 2002

1 The Big Bang: Alexander Hamilton and the Origins of Wall Street

Wall Street began in the seventeenth century as a heap of untrimmed trees, hauled from the nearby forest and made into a brushwood barrier that extended along the southern tip of the Dutch colony of New Amsterdam.[1] Designed to keep Indians from the Lenape territory out and livestock in, it was only the first of many walls erected to protect the street, some physical and others political.[2] Wall Street received this name from the British in 1685. It had its origins as a financial center in the 1792 Buttonwood Agreement among brokers who traded in the bonds that the nation's first Treasury Secretary, Alexander Hamilton, floated to replace Revolutionary War debt. This accord established rules and commission rates for buying and selling financial paper in order to protect The Street – as it came to be called – from an invasive regulation by the states of the new American republic.

Almost immediately after its launch in 1790, the Treasury scheme was followed by speculation, scandal, profiteering and a subsequent financial crisis that provoked proposals for intrusive regulation of Wall Street brokerage business by the New York state legislature. The Buttonwood Agreement was Wall Street's response. It established a precedent that continues into the twentieth century: the alternative of self-regulation to public regulation with rules and fixed commissions among brokers dealing in financial instruments. In its first financial decade Wall Street faced all of the dilemmas that would plague finance for the next 200 years in America. It responded by walling itself off from government intruders, much as the Dutch did when the street was a dirt path near a brushy barrier erected to prevent Indian incursion.

The brushwood barrier of the 1640s was replaced a decade later by a triangular palisade fence at the northern frontier of New Amsterdam that ran for a thousand yards from the East River along the present Wall Street, past Broadway, south to Pearl Street where it turned and extended north back to Wall Street. Fixed deep in the ground with foundation stones and rising twelve feet to sharpened peaks, it was designed to deter a new enemy: the British.[3] It was 'deemed essentially necessary,' said the 1653 proclamation from Governor Peter Stuyvesant to the 800 or so inhabitants, 'to enclose the greater part of the city with upright palisades ... so that in case of necessity all the inhabitants may retire therein ... and defend themselves and their property against attack.'[4] Built by Dutch contractors, the wall was financed by an unsecured loan, because a dispute over who should pay for the wall – the colony or the home government – was not settled before it was built.[5]

It is fitting that a street that would become synonymous with international finance should find its lineage in a Dutch colony, because the Dutch originated the idea of a limited-liability stock issue in Amsterdam with arguably the first international trading enterprise, the *Verenigde Oost-Indische Compagnie* (Dutch East India Company) in 1602. Its cousin, the Dutch West India Company, was chartered in 1621 and capitalized at 7.5 million guilders. It financed settlements in New Amsterdam with capital in the world's first building devoted to stock transactions, which opened in Amsterdam in 1611.[6]

Located on the tip of an island between two easily navigable rivers, the deep natural harbor made this spot an obvious choice for the Dutch maritime nation wedged between British colonies.[7] New Amsterdam, however, was not always the quaint and bustling little town depicted by later lithographers and local historians. One such retrospective 1895 romanticization imagined 'fair-haired, red-cheeked Dutch maidens who, tripping down the foot-path to the water, bearing the household linen to the wash, gave their name to Maiden Lane; or the jolly old burghers, clad in baggy knee-breeches and smoking long pipes, who ... played their game of bowls upon the smooth turf of Bowling Green.'[8] Reality is captured by this appeal sent back to the Netherlands in 1644 by the burghers of New Amsterdam, which describes the aftermath of an Indian attack and their fear for the future:

Our fields lie fallow and waste; our dwellings and other buildings are burnt. We are burdened with heavy families; have no means to provide necessaries any longer for our wives and children.[9]

The home government responded by sending Peter Stuyvesant as Governor in 1647, who brought some stability and secured minimal economic improvement.

Stuyvesant's wall did not prevent the British from taking the colony by invasion from the sea in 1664, toward the end of an extended naval conflict between the Netherlands and England. It was a conquest with no casualties, in which the Dutch inhabitants, according to an early Wall

1. The Brushwood Barrier that Became Wall Street
The 'Cattle-Guard of 1644' is a 1908 representation of the brushwood barrier that eventually became the alignment of Wall Street. The year of its publication happened at a moment when Wall Street was under challenge from Main Street and coincides with other aspects of The Street's 'myth-making origins.' (From Frederick Trevor Hill, *The Story of a Street*, first published N.Y.: Harper & Brothers, 1908.)

Street history, 'virtually welcom[ed] the invaders.'[10] The Dutch and the British settlers had already established commercial ties among themselves that transcended the distant quarrels of their home governments. Stuyvesant was given safe passage back to Amsterdam by the British, where he was rudely greeted by the Dutch West India Company for what the Company saw as his management failures in New Amsterdam. He returned to the renamed colony of New York to live out the remainder of his life, where he established a fruit-tree farm with cuttings from Holland near what is now Thirteenth Street and Third Avenue.[11] British surveyors retained the contours of Stuyvesant's wall when they mapped out a new street in 1685 which they named *Wall Street*.[12]

The strategic placement of Wall Street alongside New York's deep and natural harbor has always lent it a special claim on the city's commercial and financial life, first with the Dutch, then the British and finally with the American nation. Under the British, Wall Street became the center of a rapidly growing port city, populated by merchants' homes and offices, coffee shops and insurance brokers. The British and the Dutch, along with

French Huguenots, Sephardic Jews, Africans and others inhabited lower Manhattan in what would become New York's trademark image of a city of many nationalities.

The decision to center so much of British colonial life on Wall Street was influenced by the Governor of New York appointed by the British, Thomas Dongan, who had secretly purchased rights to the land adjacent to the wall before it was paved and then subdivided his holdings into lots which he sold in 1686.[13] He was joined in this land speculation by two of The Street's early great names: Nicholas Bayard and Abraham DePeyster. They bought property near Wall Street before it was improved, proposed a site for Trinity Church and donated the land on which the City Hall was built.[14] In the last decade of the 1600s the old wooden palisade wall was demolished and its foundation stones used in the construction of City Hall, Wall Street was paved and the first Trinity Church was built.[15] Dongan, Bayard and DePeyster fared well in their land deals, the first but by no means the last episode in this aspect of Wall Street's story.

Colonial Wall Street in the 1700s kept pace with the growth of New York City as a trade center and port city. During the American Revolution it was content to view the battles from some distance. New York was still a modest third to Philadelphia and Boston in finance and patriotic fervor. The majority of loans to the American revolutionary cause came from Philadelphia merchants, and New York spent much of the Revolutionary Era occupied by the British. With the city's population standing at over 31,000, a rebuilt Trinity Church was consecrated in 1791 and towered over a street that housed 54 merchant businesses, a schoolteacher, a clockmaker, a snuff and tobacco manufacturer, a grocer, bookseller, milliner, printer, upholsterer, two tailors, three auctioneers, a tavern, a porter house and a fashionable boarding house.[16]

ALEXANDER HAMILTON'S WALL STREET

The most prominent of all these residents in the early republic was Alexander Hamilton. He had a small house at the corner of Wall and Water Streets near the Coffee House Slip on the East River, which he frequently visited.[17] Hamilton was one of those great designers of American society who set in motion political and economic forces that not only shaped the new nation but influenced its culture and clarified its future. Hamilton pursued his mission through finance and commerce, confident that the character of the new nation would be defined as much by the system that produced and distributed articles of commerce as by articles in the

Constitution. Hamilton saw his role, according to one observer, as closer to that of a prime minister in George Washington's presidency than simply that of a treasury secretary.[18]

Hamilton was born in 1755 on the Danish island of St. Croix, came to New York at the age of 17, and was only in his mid-thirties when he took over the dismal finances of the new nation as Treasury Secretary. A handsome man of average height, Hamilton's slimness and grace set him apart from the more portly male figures of the time as his quick mind had set him apart from other young Revolutionary War officers and led to him becoming a valued *aide-de-camp* to General Washington. He established a home and business at number 57 Wall Street in 1783, where he wrote 63 of the 85 essays for the *Federalist Papers*, those essential arguments for the ratification of the new nation's constitution.[19] Over the next decade, these writings on politics and finance, and his actions as Treasury Secretary, set the tone for subsequent generations of financial leaders.

As a Wall Street habitué, Hamilton has been implicated by some historians and defended by others for his role in the financial crisis that followed on his plan to fund the Revolutionary War debt. What was his role in the financial speculation and its subsequent cycle of public infatuation and betrayal? Did he pass information, knowingly or unknowingly, to some of his closest friends, associates and neighbors – and in one instance possibly to his deputy in the treasury – who used privileged knowledge about the funding scheme to enrich themselves at the public's expense and seduce an unsuspecting Main Street into Wall Street's first financial scandal? After two centuries of off-and-on debate about Hamilton's involvement, there is still no direct evidence that can resolve this debate. It is, however, worth looking at this question in light of new letters found in Hamilton's accumulated and published papers and new historical methodology that allows a revisit to a long festering historical argument. This reexamination of the origins of The Street challenges some of the celebratory writings that accompanied its 200th anniversary a decade ago.[20]

The contemporary historical methodology is associated with a new historiography that challenges the solidity of most 'facts,' looks at historical evidence as not subject to a de-coupling from its source, and gives as much weight to perceptions about events – the play of surfaces – as it does to the multiple interpretations of the event itself. It relies less on direct evidence, the 'smoking gun' which is rarely available, and instead focuses on the cumulative weight of evidence, much as a jury would in coming to a decision in most trials that are built on just such a foundation. Such a matrix of historical method suits a Wall Street that is itself a wonderland of attitudes about a contested reality and competing interpretation of facts, each contingent upon the orientation and reputation of the presenter. Alexander Hamilton was himself aware of this when he said that 'in nothing are appearances of greater moment, than in whatever regards credit. Opinion is the soul of it, and this is affected by appearances, as well as realities.'[21]

Wall Street's emergence as a financial center was initiated by Hamilton's actions as Treasury Secretary. What he did was simply to rid the new nation of its Revolutionary War debts with the aid of his Wall Street compatriots, and by so doing he established a set of premises on which the development of a new economy could begin. In 1790 he submitted to the Congress his now-famous *Report ... for the Support of the Public Credit* in which he laid out a subtle means for establishing the new nation's credit in national and world financial markets with a deftness that even by today's standards would be impressive.

THE HAMILTON PROJECT

As a legacy of the Revolutionary War, the country had accumulated debts totaling more than $54 million in the form of foreign and domestic debts, almost worthless paper money (Continental currency, valued at $40 million), and outstanding state borrowing ($25 million).[22] Annual federal tax receipts could not even cover the $4 million interest owed on the debt.[23] The currency had become virtually worthless after the war, yet it remained in circulation where it competed with newly issued state currencies, falling in value and creating price inflation. Financial confusion reigned as the value of some states' currencies fell at varying rates while others rose, reflecting different levels of war debts. European backers of the Revolution, including Dutch bankers and the French government, awaited payment on loans and domestic investors awaited assurances of monetary stability.

Hamilton's remedy, outlined in his *Report*, contained two essentials: first, redemption of the Continentals at face value even though they were worth a fraction of face value on the current market. For this he proposed to swap a new currency for the Continentals; second, he proposed that the federal government assume all the outstanding state debts. Together, these measures became known as the *funding and assumption* policies of the new federal treasury. Then he borrowed money for the new federal treasury by issuing bonds to support his vision of economic development led by government investment and underwriting of private investment. The end result, Hamilton argued, would be old bad debt wiped off the books and worthless currency removed from circulation, and a new currency with stable value and money to finance the new government. This took some sleight of hand, to say the least, and perhaps some privileged information passed to brokers who were essential in executing the project.

To implement this policy Hamilton first issued a new currency which replaced the old Continental currency. A considerable amount of the Continentals were held by Wall Street brokers who had been buying them at a deep discount on the speculation that just such a redemption would occur. Secondly, Hamilton obtained funds to finance the country by selling some $80 million in federal government bonds, which were sold for the new currency primarily to merchants and brokers in the coastal towns that were the commercial centers of the new nation. These brokers bought the interest-bearing bonds with the new currency they had swapped for the Continentals. In essence he created a revolving door: out went new currency notes from the Treasury, replacing the Continentals, and back in came the new currency to the Treasury in exchange for bonds which were disbursed from the Treasury to many of the same people who had exchanged the worthless Continentals for the new currency at a handsome profit. The brokers on Wall Street started with Continentals, obtained the new currency for a short time, and then exchanged this money for interest-bearing bonds. The net effect was an exchange of bonds for Continentals. The low-value Continentals were transformed into bonds with intermediate broker holdings of Hamilton's new currency. Hamilton had a treasury to work with, the worthless Continentals were off the street and brokers held bonds.

This is precisely where the conjecture surfaces about private information passed by or through Hamilton to his friends and neighbors on Wall Street who were critical to the success of his project. Did they know Hamilton was going to support the assumption of state debts and did they know he would support the purchase of Continentals at full face value, instead of their much lower spot market value? And would he allow the final holder to be the recipient of the purchase rather than, as some advocated, establishing a sequential line of owners who would share in the purchase? The bonds were sold to the same merchant-brokers who had bought the Revolutionary War notes on speculation after the war, anticipating a government funding and assumption plan that would turn the venture into a profit for them. A significant cluster of such merchant-brokers were located on Wall Street. Buying the Continentals at a severe discount, the speculators turned around and sold them at face value to the Treasury, successfully executing a classic arbitrage strategy by profiting on the difference between the purchase and sale prices. Bonds sold to the broker-speculators were bought with the new currency. Speculation in Continentals and state debt was concentrated in lower Manhattan, and it was on Wall Street that the first arrangement was conceived among brokers for the sale and purchase of financial instruments. In one year alone – 1789 – $2.7 million of southern debt, denominated in Continentals, was purchased on Wall Street, nearly two-thirds of their total outstanding debt.[24]

THE STREET'S ORIGINS

According to the story Wall Street tells about itself, an agreement was reached among 24 brokers on 17 May 1792 under a buttonwood tree at 68 Wall Street to provide a market for the purchase and sale of these new securities. The buttonwood is a majestic tree, known more commonly as a sycamore. It is a tall, leafy tree that can grow to 150 feet, spread its girth to as much as a 15-foot diameter, and takes its name from the hard brown fruit that looks like a button. The largest hardwood in the eastern United States, the buttonwood is a loner – a solitary giant that often grows in isolation from other trees, even those of its own kind. The Wall Street specimen was all the more compelling as a singular and sheltering meeting place, because during the Revolutionary War years of 1779–80 most of Manhattan's trees had been cut down for firewood.[25] With many of Manhattan's streets devoid of trees, this towering buttonwood and its story has retained a special place in the iconography of Wall Street. The tree survived until 14 June 1865 when at eight in the morning it succumbed to a storm.

We know there was a Buttonwood Agreement, but the historical validity of a meeting under the shade of this tree is in doubt. It may have been the only outdoor site large enough to accommodate a meeting of all the brokers who normally operated from small individual offices where they held daily bond auctions. The agreement was in the nature of a medieval guild organization. It provided that the 24 signers grant preference in transactions to each other at a fixed and uniform commission rate. With immaculate brevity, in contrast to subsequent stock exchange constitutions, the Buttonwood Agreement simply read in total:

We, the Subscribers, Brokers for the Purchase and Sale of Public Stock, do hereby solemnly promise and pledge ourselves to each other, that we will not buy or sell from this day for any person whatsoever, any kind of Public Stock, at a less rate than one quarter per cent commission on the Specie value, and that we will give a preference to each other in our Negotiations.[26]

Exclusivity of membership and a fixed minimum price are traditions that continued on the later Exchanges until well into the twentieth century. The Buttonwood signers were doing what all market-makers try to do: monopolize the market by placing a wall between themselves and others and permitting entrance only at the market's convenience and discretion.[27]

The original 24 brokers came from a lower Manhattan that was increasingly peopled with risk-taking merchants of diverse origins, unlike the more homogeneous and sedate Puritans of Boston or Quakers of Philadelphia. The Dutch colony of New Amsterdam that the British took over in 1664 was the most multi-ethnic of all the American colonies. Only half of New Netherland – the Dutch colony that today takes in the states of Delaware, New Jersey, New York, and parts of eastern Pennsylvania and western Connecticut – were Dutch.[28] Wall Street was then viewed as something of a cultural backwater and a *mélange* of financial operatives lacking the clubbiness that accompanies homogeneity. Rebecca Franks, who moved from Philadelphia with her husband David Franks – the compiler of New York's first postal directory – complained that the women of Philadelphia 'have more cleverness in the turn of an eye than those of New York have in their whole composition. ... I don't know a woman [in New York] who can chat above half an hour, and that only on the form of a cap, the color of a ribbon, or the set of a hoop.'[29]

Many of the older, more established Dutch and English families had moved north of lower Manhattan where they exercised social and cultural leadership, leaving southern sections of the city to clusters of their own rural cousins, French Huguenots, Swedes, Sephardic Jews and Africans. The Buttonwood signers were a mixture of older Dutch and British merchants and newer merchants from these other groups. The first name to appear on the Buttonwood Agreement is that of Leonard Bleecker, a friend of George Washington, and one of six escorts that accompanied his carriage on 30 April 1789 to the first President's inauguration at Pierre L'Enfant's newly designed Federal Hall on Wall Street.[30] Descended from Dutch settlers and later intermarrying with the British, the Bleeckers were established pillars of Wall Street life: active in Trinity Church affairs, major financiers and confidants of New York and national political leaders.

At least three Buttonwood signers – Bernard Hart, Isaac M. Gomez and Benjamin Seixas – were members of the city's first synagogue:

Congregation Shearith Israel, founded in 1654 and located at what is today 22–24 South William Street.[31] Seixas was descended from the synagogue's first Rabbi, Gershon Mendes Seixas, and Hart married Rebecca Seixas, a member of the Seixas family. Bernard Hart had a long and distinguished career on Wall Street. He was born in England in 1764 and came to New York in 1780, after living six years in Canada. It was Hart who preserved the only extant copy of the Buttonwood Agreement, which he turned over to its successor organization in 1840.[32]

A representative of the British and Anglican tradition among the Buttonwood signers was Augustus H. Lawrence, described as a 'prince of a man ... large figure, fine full face, hair nicely powdered, a queue and white top-boots ... a good representative of the New York merchant of the olden time.'[33] He was noted for splendid dinners at his residence at 23 Park Place and the equipage that made up his stable of horses and carriages. Thin as the documentary record of this period is, names on the Buttonwood Agreement will appear again and again in the financial machinations that define this brief Big Bang period of 1790–92: Leonard Bleecker, Bernard Hart, Benjamin Seixas, Samuel Beebe, Isaac M. Gomez and Peter Anspach, among others.[34]

Wall Street prospered in its early days and quickly erected important structures to house its merchant and financial activities. The first of these, the Tontine Coffee House, was completed at the corner of Wall and Water Streets in 1794, some 100 feet from the buttonwood tree, on land owned by the Gomez family whose Isaac Gomez was one of the 24 Buttonwood signatories.[35] Borrowing from the British tradition, the Georgian-inspired Tontine contained a hotel and coffee house along with a gathering place for merchants. Sited almost at the mid-point of a Wall Street that was anchored on one end by Trinity Church and on the other by Federal Hall, the architecture of the Tontine Coffee House combined the agora with that of a religious and civic institution. This imposing edifice continued the British tradition of mingling large merchant exchanges with coffee houses. The first use of the words 'Stock Exchange,' for example, appeared in London where merchants gathered in small byways and alleys – between Lombard and Cornhill Streets and Exchange and Sweeting Alleys, stopping at Jonathan's Coffee House, their favorite meeting place to transact business. After being burnt down in 1748 and rebuilt a year later, with financing arranged by some of the London brokers, Jonathan's Coffee House changed its name in 1773 to 'The Stock Exchange.'[36]

The Tontine is important in the history of Wall Street, for it was there that the Buttonwood brokers set up offices to conduct their exchange

2. The Tontine Coffee House
This retrospective 1910 engraving of the Tontine Coffee House (the largest building on the left with flag) contrasts the well-dressed brokers with a display of merchant activity at Wall and Water streets as it was imagined to appear in 1797. (From a 1910 painting by Walter Monteith Aikman and published by Society of Iconophiles. Library of Congress, Prints and Photographs Division.)

auctions. No mere café, the Wall Street Tontine Coffee House was a carefully designed investment vehicle that took its name from an investment structure named after Tonti, an Italian banker of the seventeenth century who set up companies to provide their investors with a life annuity that could be passed on to one survivor. Much like a lottery, each investor gambles that his designated survivor can outlive the other designees. This particular tontine was financed by 203 merchants and brokers, with each assigning his investment to one other person. In the New York investment vehicle ultimate ownership went to the seven surviving assignees who then had to liquidate the investment. In this instance, the surviving assignees divided up the Tontine assets in 1876, even though the original structure had been demolished in 1855.[37]

The backbone of an emerging Wall Street financial edifice was the broker. The idea of a broker was not new to merchant businesses that would trade in anything from furs to slaves. He serves as a middleman, buying from a purveyor of merchandise, and selling it to someone else. It comes from the French, *brochier*, which refers to an individual who 'broached' or tapped a wine keg in medieval France. The *brochier* would buy a wine keg, tap it and then sell its contents by the cup to purchasers – presumably covering costs and making a profit.[38] Wall Street was the direct inheritor of this practice as it evolved over nearly two centuries, starting first in Holland with the Dutch East India Company in 1602, then in the trading companies of the City of London in the eighteenth century and emerging in lower Manhattan at the century's end.

CONTROVERSY AND SCANDAL

In the two years prior to the 1792 Buttonwood Agreement, scandal erupted on Wall Street and threw into sharp relief four recurring archetypes who operate in the world of finance. One was the public policymaker in the person of Alexander Hamilton and another the financier, seeking always to maintain internal controls, as represented by the 24 Buttonwood signatories. Perhaps most interesting were the impresario of civic works, John Pintard, and the fallen speculator, William Duer. The fate of all of these types is entwined in Wall Street's first financial scandal.

The scandal originates in Hamilton's funding and assumption measures, which were controversial on several counts. Why should the holders of Continentals, who purchased on speculation from their original owners at considerably less than face value, be paid at face value? Many of the original holders of Continentals had dumped them for whatever they could get. They were soldiers who had been paid in Continentals, or farmers and tradesmen who had sold goods to the army. The buyers of these apparently worthless Continentals were often rich and powerful merchants who snuggled along the coastlines of the port cities and dabbled in whatever could be bought at a low price and sold at a higher price. The sellers were individuals such as the veteran who wrote this letter to the Massachusetts *Centinel* on 20 March 1790, describing the plight of his fellow soldiers who had not received full compensation for their war duties:

They must dispose of their ... pay, or they must go hungry. What was the encouragement when they offered their paper for sale? That government would never be able to pay it, and that it was not worth more than 2s. for 20s. This was the language of all the purchasers.[39]

The speculative perspective was captured by an early historian of Wall Street: 'The wily hastened to the highways and byways and bought up, at remarkably low prices, the Government "stock" held by ignorant men who did not dream that it could be redeemed at par.'[40] These 'ignorant men,' it turns out, faced many bureaucratic obstacles in establishing their back claims to the Continentals.

New York's treasurer, Gerard Bancker, has left a record of how he handled claims of soldiers who had not received full compensation for their war duties. It sheds some light on these two competing interpretations. His papers show a draft of a document (1792) in which he first wrote, then crossed out, some words pertaining to certificates of payment due to the 'troops who served in the late War and which he was by law directed to deliver ... on their application at the Treasury Office of the State.' He replaced this simple formulation – that the soldier need only apply for his Continentals, now potentially worth a considerable sum in 1792 with the surfacing of Hamilton's plan – with a bureaucratic nightmare. The individual soldier not only had to apply for back payment, according to the revised rules, but now also had to produce a document from an officer with whom the soldier had served, proving his identity. But even that was not enough. When 22 such statements were presented and signed by one officer, several claims were turned down on the basis of the individual soldier having served in a different regiment; or claims for dead soldiers, upon investigation, showed the individual alive and well. All this points to a general confusion over who had title to back pay claims and how they were to be awarded, not to mention the difficulties an individual faced when confronting a government that was prepared to place such a bureaucratic maze in his way.[41] It also reveals how Bancker went through considerable contortions to deny claims of soldiers who presented themselves for back payment.

This leads to a question: was information concerning his scheme to fund and assume Continentals and debts at face value passed on through or by Hamilton to his merchant friends ? How did the buyers of the Continentals know they would be redeemed at par? There are no definitive answers to these questions, but the evidentiary record points toward the conclusion that the first market for government securities was created by interested parties with special information. One observer, for example, attributed speculators' acquisition of Continentals to 'smart gentlemen [who] purchased in anticipation of a federal refunding loan. Residing in the East,' he says, 'where affairs of state originated and were known to the "inner circle," they had a great advantage over the general public.'[42]

Alexander Hamilton lived in the center of this merchant-broker neighborhood of lower Manhattan. He conversed daily with his compatriots, drank coffee at the places where business was transacted, and conceivably talked about his ideas for the financing report he was preparing for Congress. He shared with merchant-brokers a commercial outlook that went beyond the technical financing of debts to cultural and political concepts of nation-building. He may have received ideas from them as much as passing on his own, testing proposals to see if they would work.[43] All this occurs at a time when sensibilities about the exchange of information between private traders and government officials were vastly different from today. No illegality was associated with such contacts, although political opposition to such arrangements was important in the new republic as it sought to distance itself from precisely a type of behavior that had plagued England in the eighteenth century.

One of the original 24 brokers who signed the Buttonwood Agreement was Peter Anspach, and he has left a documentary record that sheds some light on this conjecture. Between 1789 and 1792 there were some 900 bills and receipts that Anspach handled, dealing with the sale and purchase of Continentals and state debts – mostly those of New Jersey. Typically, the state debt notes were bought at a discount of 50 per cent. Another New York broker advertised on 22 June 1791, that 'any person willing to have their North Carolina debt funded, may have it done on reasonable terms by applying to William Boyd.'[44] By the end of 1789 around 70 New Yorkers owned $2.7 million worth of debt from such states as North and South Carolina, about one-third of all the outstanding state obligations. Two prominent names that surface later in speculation and scandal are Andrew Craigie and four others in his syndicate (over $100,000) and William Bayard in partnership with Herman LeRoy ($580,000).[45]

THE CONGRESSIONAL DEBATE

Hamilton's plans prevailed over the opposition of such eminent political voices as Thomas Jefferson and James Madison, who sought a way to diminish the rewards from speculation. As leaders of the Virginia delegation in Congress, they represented a state that had paid off virtually all its war debts, were on the other side of many debates with Hamilton over the character of the new nation, and saw his program as a wedge into a strengthening of the commercial principle and a diminishing of their cherished idea of civic virtue rooted in a rural arcadia. Madison proposed, for example, that secondary holders of Continentals receive their purchase price and the original holders receive the difference between their sale price and face value – what came to be called 'discrimination.' Aside from the practical problem of sorting out the chain of ownership, Hamilton's supporters then and now mounted a stout defense of his full funding policy based on the sanctity of contracts and the fact that future financial transactions between government and the public would be hampered if the face value of government obligations were not protected. But this misses the point. It was not a question of full funding or partial funding of the state debt and Continentals, or honoring contracts or not honoring contracts. It was a question of who would receive funding and which contract would be honored.

To overcome Jefferson's opposition, Hamilton struck a deal with him during a half-hour walk that started in front of President George Washington's house just beyond Wall Street and continued along lower Broadway. Hamilton agreed to support moving the capital out of New York to a new 'federal city' on the Maryland–Virginia border – after a ten-year detour to Philadelphia to secure Pennsylvania's support for the funding and assumption scheme – in exchange for Jefferson's support for his financial plan.[46] This was crucial to the success of Hamilton's project, because the funding and assumption proposal had been defeated in the House of Representatives and his only chance of victory was in the Senate where the Virginia delegation was absolutely essential. Jefferson's motivation was to separate the capital from the 'moneyed men' he associated with New York.[47]

The path to Hamiltonian financial policy was further smoothed by certain members of Congress who directly or indirectly stood to benefit from the purchase of Continentals at face value or from the assumption of state debt. Some members of Congress hired agents to roam the country-side and buy up Continentals and state debt. There was Elbridge Gerry of Massachusetts, $33,000 in Continentals and $16,000 in state debt; Roger Sherman and Jeremiah Wadsworth of Connecticut, a total of nearly $8,000 and $21,500 respectively; Elias Boudinot of New Jersey, $49,500; and George Clymer of Pennsylvania, $12,500.[48] With great solemnity these and other lesser holders of now-valuable assets spoke in favor of Hamilton's plan on the floor and voted against James Madison, who wrote to Thomas Jefferson in July, 1791: 'of all the shameful circumstances of this business, it is among the greatest to see the members of this legislature who were most active in pushing this job openly grasping its emoluments.'[49]

With Jefferson's acquiescence to the Hamilton plan assured by the deal that moved the political capital south, the separate financial capital remained in the north. Wall Street and Pennsylvania Avenue became two thoroughfares with distinct cultures and missions that sometimes collided and at other times colluded.

DID HAMILTON COLLUDE WITH WALL STREET?

Central to the funding and assumption scheme was Hamilton's understanding that it relied on confidence and wealth: the creation of a group of wealth-holders who shared his vision of a commercial, investment-based culture and their confidence in the federal government's financial stability. His funding-assumption plan provided both, he thought. Capital would be concentrated in the hands of a merchant-broker class who would become risk-takers in investing in the nation's future. To acquire the confidence of these nascent capitalists, Hamilton knew he had to purchase their support in advance and he had done so through the funding-assumption scheme.

As with all programs for financial stabilization, the director is as much a conjurer as a financial genius. Hamilton believed that the public interest could best be constructed by steering individual private interests into an aggregate public interest, rejecting Jefferson's notion of building a collective 'public' from individual civic virtue. 'Men will pursue their interests,' said Hamilton to the New York ratifying convention for the Constitution. 'It is as easy to change human nature, as to oppose the strong current of selfish passions. A wise legislator will gently divert the channel, and direct it, if possible, to the public good.'[50] Whether viewed as a magician creating illusions about the value of American paper money or as a cynical manipulator whose reforms began as a piece of financial chicanery, Hamilton succeeded.[51] Four decades passed before his system was seriously challenged.

Two months before Hamilton's report to Congress, William Constable – a Wall Street merchant-broker, client of Hamilton's, occasional dinner guest and financial adviser to Hamilton, who figures prominently in the eventual scandal – wrote to his colleague Andrew Craigie, whose syndicate held over $100,000 in state debt:

> I dined with Hamilton on Saturday. He is strong in the faith on maintaining public Credit ... I tried him on the subject ... 'they must no doubt be funded tho it cannot be done immediately,' was his remark, 'they must be put upon a footing,' meaning these as well as the funded Debt. In short am more & more of the opinion that they are the best object at present.[52]

Hamilton frequently called on Constable for advice, as in their exchange of letters about estimates for revenue that could be raised with new customs duties. The 'subject' Constable refers to are 'indents,' certificates of interest due on the public debt. Although this is only a part of Hamilton's financial concerns, it does reveal his willingness to discuss specifics about his funding and assumption plan with Wall Street brokers who had a direct speculative interest in his plans, if Constable is credible. There is considerable evidence that Hamilton relied on Constable for ongoing advice and counsel. The editors of Hamilton's collected papers in a footnote to this exchange about issues surrounding interest on public debt note that 'Perhaps H. requested the data supplied by Constable in connection with "Report ... for the Support of Public Credit," Jan. 9, 1790.'[53]

This communication from Constable to Craigie occurs after Craigie had expressed the view that he knew of 'no way of making safe speculations but by being associated with people who from their official situation know all the present & can aid future arrangements either for or against the funds.'[54] Incriminating as these communications are, defenders of Hamilton point to his letter to Henry ('Light Horse Harry') Lee of Virginia who was rebuffed when he sought information on debt funding. Wrote Hamilton, 'I am sure you are sincere when you say you would not subject me to an impropriety ... But you remember the saying in regard to Caesar's wife. I think the spirit of it applicable to every man concerned in the administration of finance of a country.'[55] Hamilton was responding to Lee's direct and rather crude overture in which Lee said:

> From your situation you must be able to form with some certainty an opinion concerning the domestic debt. Will it speedily rise, with the interest accruing command specie ... what will become of the indents already issued? These queries are asked for my private information, perhaps they may be improper, I do not think them so.[56]

A breeder of horses, 'Light Horse Harry' Lee coupled this inquiry with an offer to Hamilton of a gift of a 'grand riding horse,' in August 1791, later modified in October of the same year to a 'gentle horse ... less addicted to starting and stumbling.'[57]

To Hamilton's defenders the 'Caesar's wife' reference suffices.[58] But does it? Because of Hamilton's geographic proximity and cultural affinity to Wall Street, he would be much more likely to converse candidly about his financial plans with someone like Constable or Craigie than with Lee, a Virginian whose Congressional delegation constituted the most formidable opposition to his plans. Lee was also known neither for his personal reliability nor for his complete support of Hamilton's project.[59] Lee is simply not someone Hamilton would be expected to take into his confidence. Hamilton did not share the same world view as the Virginia planters and saw them as his principal adversaries in the debate over how the country should be developed. The 'Caesar's wife' defense is, therefore, built on a very shaky foundation.

In the context of the period, it is easy to see how Hamilton would protect himself and divert Lee. Yet this colloquy is cited again and again as definitive.[60] The Lee correspondence raises another question in the form of a false negative: why isn't there correspondence between Hamilton and his Wall Street friends that can corroborate charges of 'insider trading,' while there is a clear rebuff to Lee in writing? There is no written documentation, because none was needed. Oral communication would have been preferred in such matters, was easier among geographically proximate neighbors and friends, and would likely have taken place in a more casual manner – a chat over coffee or at dinners together. This is confirmed by William Constable who notes that, 'I cannot commit to paper my reasons, nor explain from whence I have my information, but I would not deceive you [and] my opinion is founded on the best information.'[61]

A second line of defense by Hamilton's supporters dwells on allegations that can be more readily dismissed. One involves an affair he had with Maria Reynolds and an attempt at blackmail by her jailed husband, James, in which he claimed he had evidence of Hamilton's passing confidential information. The notorious scandal-mongering pamphleteer, J.T. Callender, used the Reynolds case, along with another charge against Hamilton instigated by James Reynolds's cellmate, to attack him in 1797. Hamilton's curious confessional response to the affair, in which he revealed more about his love affair with Maria than had Callender, has been frequently cited by his defenders:

> Merely because I retained an opinion once common to me and the most influential of those who opposed me, that the public debt ought to be provided for on the basis of the contract upon which it was created, I have been wickedly accused with wantonly increasing the public burthen many millions in order to promote a stock-jobbing interest of myself and friends.[62]

A more serious charge against Hamilton involves William Bingham, a respected Philadelphia merchant and speculator, who wrote to Hamilton spelling out his views on full funding of the debts and asked him 'how far any of my Sentiments coincide with yours.' Thomas Willing, Bingham's father-in-law, claimed to have seen Hamilton's response in which he states his support for 'whole price' funding.[63]

Hamilton's sagacity has never been challenged. Nor is there a trail of money that can be traced back to him. He lived a life of modest means. However, no one contests the fact that he had an abiding obsession with influence and power and with seeing his view of the nation's development realized, all of which could be found in a successful alliance with such like-minded men of stature as the Wall Street broker. A more plausible explanation for Hamilton's actions, therefore, is that he never thought twice about testing his ideas and sharing information with people who were his neighbors and allies in the contentious arguments with the Virginians over the form of the new republic. To one of the editors of his collected papers, and a sympathetic biographer, Hamilton 'believed that winning and keeping the confidence of men with money to bestow or withhold was essential to the fiscal operations of the new government.'[64] A less generous interpretation from a critic says 'Those who assume that the Secretary of the Treasury could have carried out his enormous reorganization of the finances without conferring with the leading financiers of the time have only an elementary knowledge of Treasury administration.'[65]

As to his knowledge of financial affairs, Hamilton had few, if any peers, then or at any time since. He was concerned about speculative panic because of the historical memory of such proximate financial panics and manias as Holland's Tulipomania (1637) and the South Sea Bubble (1720).[66] He wanted to take every precaution to avoid their recurrence. One way to do this would be to prepare for contingencies in advance, for example, by limiting speculation largely to a relatively small, trusted group inside a wall of privileged information. To put the question in the negative: how could Hamilton not know that the gambles of private speculators would make or break his project, depending on whether they 'guessed' correctly about a policy whose success he valued at whatever the cost?

Hamilton's mistake was to be blind to what many of his contemporaneous critics saw as a violation of republican sensibilities, best summed up in this 1792 New York *Journal* commentary in which 'this great minister' is taken to task for:

Plans that have tended ... to meliorate the pockets, and not the heads and hearts of the people. ... liberty and independence ... have been struck out from the American vocabulary, and the hieroglyphs of money inserted in their stead. ... the ordinary walks of industry begin to be loathed and are about to be abandoned for the *golden* dreams of speculation.[67]

THE NATIONAL BANK, WILLIAM DUER AND FINANCIAL CRISIS

A year after Hamilton's Report on credit to the Congress and his successful completion of the funding and assumption project, he turned to building a second complementary financial institution: a National Bank, which passed the Congress in February 1791, again overcoming the opposition of Jefferson and Madison. If the funding and assumption plan aroused suspicions of interest conflicts, Hamilton's National Bank led to a financial crisis that further compounded his reputation for probity and came to cause him much grief. Echoing a refrain that would be repeated by many subsequent central bankers, Hamilton opined that 'there should be a line of separation between honest men and knaves, between respectable stock-holders and mere unprincipled gamblers.'[68]

The National Bank was endowed with capital supplied partly by the new government and partly by private investors who paid with the same government bonds that Hamilton had issued for funding and assumption, primarily by swapping them for shares in the National Bank. Added to the sequence described earlier, brokers now owned shares in a new national bank, having parlayed their initial holding of discounted Continentals into this favorable ownership position. Starting with low value script, passing through new currency on which considerable profit was made, trans-forming the new money into government-backed bonds, and finally converting them into ownership in a bank, brokers seemed to have discovered a financial holy grail. All of this was accomplished with Hamilton's assistance, and he fulfilled his objective of setting the new nation on a reasonably stable financial course. The cleverness by which money passed through a revolving door impressed financiers not only in the United States but across the Atlantic, as well, attracting investors from Europe. Hamilton issued government bonds to sponge up bad paper and then recaptured those same notes to fund a new bank that would help finance his scheme for national development. He packaged old debt in a new wrapper and sold this new financial product to Wall Street.

While Hamilton was suspected by his political opponents of too great an intimacy with his merchant friends, he was also ill-served by his closest associate, William Duer, Hamilton's Assistant Treasury Secretary and Wall Street resident. Duer used his close association with Hamilton to profit from and ultimately destabilize Hamilton's financial plans, thereby leading to the very speculative panic he had sought so much to avoid. Even prior to the National Bank operation, Duer had enriched himself on the earlier funding and assumption phase, accumulating as early as 1786 about $67,000 in Continentals in his private account and another $200,000 in partnership with a half dozen other speculators.[69] Born in England in 1747, Duer served as Secretary of the Board of the Treasury from 1786 to 1789, was a member of the Continental and Confederation Congresses, found a house for Washington and prepared for its occupancy when he moved to New York, and speculated in anything and everything – Continental scrip, stock of the Bank of the United States, and land in Ohio and Maine.

When the Treasury Department was created in September, 1789 Duer was appointed Assistant Secretary by his friend, Alexander Hamilton. He served in this position only about seven months, when he resigned in April of 1790. In his letter accepting Duer's resignation, Hamilton tells his 'dear friend' that he 'is sensible of the force of motives' behind his decision. Indeed, Duer's extensive investment in public securities made his position in the Treasury Department politically embarrassing to Hamilton, even by the relaxed standards of the time.[70] In December 1790 Duer sent subsequent Buttonwood signer, Leonard Bleecker, to South Carolina as his agent to purchase Continental securities. There is evidence that Duer began his buying even before Bleecker's trip, perhaps when he was still Assistant Treasury Secretary and that Duer's close business associates received advance information from him on Hamilton's proposals enabling them to purchase large amounts of securities at low rates.[71] It may be fair to say that William Duer was the first in the new United States to use a public office for private enrichment. Duer became one of the richest men in the new republic, living like a minor Rothschild in the former Philipse mansion, hosting with his wife, the former Kitty Alexander, dinner parties described by the Rev. Manasseh Cutler as consisting of 'not less than fifteen different sorts of wine at dinner, and after the cloth was removed, besides most excellent bottled cider, porter, and several other kinds of strong beer.'[72]

Not satisfied with his speculation on Continentals, Duer entered into a secret partnership to attempt a corner on the market for securities of the Bank of New York, a state-chartered commercial bank that Hamilton had initiated to handle transactions of the National Bank. The Bank of New York was an essential ingredient in the financial stew Hamilton was preparing. Because the National Bank was not a commercial bank and could not accept deposits or engage in the sort of commercial bank activity that conducts financial transactions, Hamilton needed a faithful commercial bank through which he could manage financial stability and conduct necessary government transactions. For this a reliable bank was needed by Hamilton, and his promotion of the Bank of New York was his instrument. Duer saw this as an opportunity for profit, and he began his corner maneuver toward the end of 1791 with prominent Wall Street names that always seem to be around when financial activities are reported: Alexander Macomb, Walter Livingston, Benjamin Walker and William Constable – the same individual whose correspondence figures in Hamilton's support for underwriting accrued interest on the bad debts of states. Duer is the forerunner of the common trait of greed that pervades The Street's history and informs at least part of its present-day character.

This is the first attempt to corner a market in Wall Street's history but certainly not the last. The strategy behind such a maneuver is to buy up as much of the stock of an institution as possible at a price that has been driven down, remove the factors that drove down the stock's price, then sell the stock once the price has risen. With ownership concentrated, the cornerers hope to be able to manipulate the stock's price to their advantage. The problem is that market forces, energized by the cornerers' purchases, should push up the price, which is precisely what the cornerers seek to avoid until they execute their sell strategy. The trick is to keep the stock price low, at the same time as the cornerers are raising its demand by buying more. For this they have to find a device at the outset to drive the stock price down and be able to keep it low enough and long enough for the corner to be profitably secured. In the Duer corner the mechanism involved a clever ruse that was designed to convince financiers a new bank was being created to compete with the Bank of New York, thereby deflating the price of that bank's securities.

The consortium that Duer put together called this the 'Million Bank' and to their delight other financiers copied the idea in January, 1792 and floated proposals for two other banks: the Merchants Bank and the Tammany Bank. Within a short time all three folded into the original Million Bank, but the start-up of several banks had accomplished its purpose and the price of securities for the Bank of New York fell.[73] Duer bought up Bank of New York shares by borrowing against anything he could find and, when he ran out of collateral, he borrowed from Main Street New York citizenry at interest rates of from 2 to 4 per cent per month. As his principal agent he employed an inexperienced Wall Street broker, named John Pintard.

Pintard's family had been engaged in various merchant activities. He was established in business with the aid of his uncle, Lewis Pintard, who had raised the young, orphaned John Pintard. He first surfaced on Wall

Street in a partnership with the eminently estimable Leonard Bleecker in December, 1790.[74] This partnership was short-lived, and one month after it dissolved in October 1791, Pintard was employed by Duer as his agent. Pintard first went into the brokerage business for himself, with Duer as a major client, and then with four others opened an office at 22 Wall Street – 'a large convenient room for the accommodation of dealers in stock,' said the public announcement on 6 February 1792.[75] In the five months between November 1791 and March 1792, Pintard signed notes for Duer worth nearly $700,000.[76]

To obtain a broker's license, the recipient had to take an oath that was supposed to prevent shadowy practices. A stockbroker's license was awarded to John Pintard, for example, on 25 November 1790 by the city's mayor, Richard Varrick, that specifies his title as 'Stock Broker in the Funds of the United States of America.' It obligated Pintard to conduct his affairs without 'Fraud or Collusion according to the best of his skill and understanding and that he will not directly or indirectly be in any-wise concerned or interested on his own private account in the purchase or sale of Funds of the United States of America.'[77] The next day he placed an ad in the New York *Daily Advertiser* in which he said, 'The opinion of many respectable characters has confirmed his own idea [about] the advantages of negotiating through the medium of an agent, no ways interested in purchases and sales on his own account.'[78] Such lofty verbiage in the license and proclamations of neutrality by Pintard and his sort, however, did nothing to prevent financial misdeeds by Pintard even as he rationalized his Hamiltonian vision of the new nation alongside his questionable financial practices. This apparent contradiction in ethics was not uncommon for the time and is one that surfaces frequently on Wall Street.

Pintard was the visionary American of the Federal era who saw vast possibilities in the future of the new nation. The United States embodied the ideas of the eighteenth-century European Enlightenment not only in its form of government, but also in a generation of men who believed that all branches of knowledge could be mastered by the public-spirited citizen for the benefit of the republic. Such a man of parts was Pintard. In him, as in others, this honorable goal was flawed by an occasional inability to separate his private gain from the public interest.

Descended from French Huguenots, he was born in 1759 and graduated from Princeton College in 1776 where he was a classmate of Aaron Burr, subsequently served in the New York Assembly, and was an Assistant Alderman for New York's east ward. Later as a trustee of the New York Society library, Pintard was a major contributor to its collection. He was the principal force behind the founding of the American Museum, which aimed at educating and elevating the public while demonstrating to a skeptical Europe that the new American republic had not only abundant varieties of natural history, but the art and science to portray and classify them. For Pintard, Wall Street, too, could work to prove the cultural superiority of American institutions while, happily, compensating its investors well. But the effort failed, as did others like it in the new nation. The building that housed the American Museum was subsequently bought by P.T. Barnum, who displayed circus-type, sideshow curiosities in the 1840s, around the same time as Wall Street was about to become dominated by the ex-circus roustabouts, Jim Fisk and Daniel Drew. Barnum's museum burned down on 13 July 1865, leaving a 'dead whale ... in the streets for two days after the fire, and a marble statue of Queen Victoria perched blithely among the blackened ruins.'[79]

By August 1791, Hamilton began to have doubts about his friend William Duer and cautioned him against undue speculation, to which Duer proffered an indignant reply. Hamilton then wrote:

> I think I know you too well to ... harbor the most distant thought that you would wander from the path either of public good or private integrity. But I will honestly own, I had serious fears for you – for your *purse* and for your *reputation*.[80]

Upon subsequently learning of the Duer scheme to add a competitive bank to his Bank of New York, Hamilton was enraged both for reasons of pride and his concern that another bank would lead to an overextension of credit, thereby jeopardizing his grand plan for establishing the creditworthiness of the new nation. He collaborated with William Seton, cashier of the Bank of New York, to deprive Duer and his accomplices of access to the bank by refusing to accept their deposits. The Bank of New York tightened credit and curtailed the discounting of paper, which had the effect of retarding Duer's scheme to buy up bank securities but also brought on the very financial panic Hamilton had wanted to avoid.

With interest payable at from 2 to 4 per cent per month, any interruption of a cash flow is deadly, which is precisely what happened as a result of Hamilton's pressure on the Bank of New York to withhold further credit to Duer and his accomplices. Almost immediately after Hamilton's counterattack through the Bank of New York, Duer and Pintard were forced to default. Once the word got out, they were besieged by creditors wanting to be paid off while they still could, but it was too late. On 9 March 1792

Duer stopped payment on the notes. In an effort to deflect responsibility away from himself and toward Pintard, he said they were 'issued by my Agent during my absence, under Circumstances which require Investigation.'[81] As panic took over the city and angry mobs demanded retribution, Duer was fortunate to be placed in jail. The turmoil was captured in this account:

> There is scarcely anything but Noise and Racket last night and the night before we had a Mob Raised and nothing would satisfy them but the father of Speculation, the great W. [Duer] who is confined in gaol at present and who they blame for carrying off all the money from this city, and the cause of many failures that has happened. Lately, the Mob has endeavored to get him out of gaol, but the Mayor & city officers have prevented them as yet – almost one half of this city is turned Bankrupt, owing to the Cursed Speculation.[82]

Said his colleague William Constable of Duer: His 'talents are confessed and his information and resource superior to any Man I ever knew but he cannot go straight.'[83]

Duer and Pintard each blamed the other for the financial crisis and for inducing innocent people to depart with their savings. Alexander Macomb, a Duer defender, has written that Pintard took the life savings of 'shop-keepers, widows, orphans, Butchers, Carmen, Gardners, market women & even the noted Bawd, Mrs. Macarty.' On 24 March 1792 from his prison cell, Duer published a handbill in which he claimed that he was the victim of the 'malice of open enemies and the insidious insinuations of pretended friends' and offered to make 'prompt arrangements for the reimbursement of all advances made by distressed widows, or orphans, mechanics or tradesmen.'[84] Duer never made good his pledge. A few days later, Duer's allies rallied to his defense and further implicated Pintard. Here is what Alexander Macomb said about Pintard, about a month before Macomb joined Duer in jail. Duer, he claims, had 'entrusted Pintard with his signature to Blank notes [and] Pintard had gone off ... with a very considerable amount of a man's property whose agent he had been.'[85] Alexander Macomb, commenting on his beloved New York, lamented:

> Three months past in this city every face was blythe, everything seemed to flourish, all had favourable prospects and everything look'd well. At present every countenance is gloomy, all confidence between individuals is lost, credit at a stand, and distress and general

Bankruptcy to be daily expected – for everyone gambled more or less in these cursed Speculations.[86]

Pintard, in the meantime, was avoiding creditors and retreated to Newark, New Jersey in May of 1792, only three months after opening his office. Just before Duer's arrest, his endorsed notes were selling at half of their face value. On 14 May he sent an open letter from Newark addressed to the 'creditors of William Duer and John Pintard' in which he appealed to them to allow him to return to New York from his New Jersey exile. 'His only error,' he pleaded, 'has been the unfounded confidence in Mr. Duer, while acting as his agent.'[87] On 15 May the letter was read at the City Tavern at a meeting of Pintard's creditors, and he was granted a three-month reprieve to return to New York.[88] Before he could return, however, Pintard was arrested in Newark upon a creditors' suit brought by Elizabeth Graham, Michael D. Henry and Henry Cruger. Left with bankruptcy as his only option, he could not follow through on his public promise to make due on some of his debts.

The bankruptcy option at this time was not available to Pintard, however, because bankruptcy law was a state prerogative, granted to a specific individual on a case-by-case basis. New York was in no mood to award this privilege to Pintard during the aftermath of a financial crisis, even one as short as this one, which ended by the summer of 1792 but did not replace the lost savings of creditors. The atmosphere was too incendiary, as witnessed by H.M. Colden who wrote to J. Wadsworth on 18 April 1792 that 'a few Persons about 4 or 5 hund[red] in Number assembled round the Jail last night – threw Stones ... & broke some of the Prison windows and Lamps ... but were soon dispersed.'[89] Pintard remained in Newark for eight years, of which 14 months was spent in jail between 1797 and 1798. These reverses and his confinement may have made him introspective. As a self-professed rational man, he was able to separate his personal financial disaster from his observations of nature and politics. As horticulturalist and diarist, he produced the most detailed record of daily life from the period that has been preserved.[90]

Out of jail in 1798, but still unable to return to New York, he took a trip south to Washington, D.C. and saw in the new capital going up the 'future metropolis of the western world.' His questionable legal status did not disqualify him from dining with the likes of President George Washington, Chief Justice John Marshall and Thomas Jefferson, where he talked about grand schemes for the opening of the 'west.'[91] If finance would not project him into the role he wanted, some other American stage would.

Finally, in September 1800 the Congress passed the law for which Pintard had been waiting: a uniform system of bankruptcy that permitted him to return to New York and get on with a new life. He applied for a discharge from his financial obligations on 17 September 1800. His former partner Leonard Bleecker carried a petition signed by 14 of his creditors supporting his appeal – 'an adequate number and value,' Pintard comments in his diary. When Judge Hobart signed the order granting him bankruptcy relief, Pintard notes in his diary at '¼ past 11 – Liberated thank God after Mr. Duer failed 8 years, 6 months and eight days.'[92] By contrast, William Duer never recovered from his financial collapse and spent his remaining years in prison where he died on 7 May 1799.

THE INVENTION OF WALL STREET

The Duer–Pintard financial scandal was one of the proximate events that led to the Buttonwood Agreement, as brokers sought to pacify an angry public by devising rules for securities markets that preempted public regulation and left self-regulation of financial markets under their control. It was partially an effort to hold off government intervention after the New York state legislature had made securities auctions illegal on 2 April 1792, and further bills had been introduced in the New York and Pennsylvania legislatures to address the 1792 financial crisis and scandal.[93]

A week after Duer's arrest and about two months before the Buttonwood signing, a group of brokers met on 21 March at Corre's hotel where, as reported in the *Gazette of the U.S.*, the 'merchants and dealers in stocks ... appointed a committee to report such regulations relative to the mode of transacting their business, as in their opinion may be proper.'[94] Here is the true origin of the Buttonwood Agreement, which produced a self-regulated Wall Street securities industry that invents itself in response to the first financial scandal on The Street in order to wall itself off from more aggressive government regulations. At least four of the 24 Buttonwood signers had been directly involved with Duer, most prominently Leonard Bleecker and Benjamin Seixas.

From this point forward Wall Street develops the case for its being a private membership association that authenticates the integrity of its members, polices itself and provides physical facilities for a closed club.[95] Looked at this way, it is not a business and, therefore, not susceptible to public regulation. This argument prevailed until the New Deal financial reforms corrected the Wall Street excesses that had contributed to the Great Depression of the 1930s.

The initial meeting at Corre's Hotel frames a more accurate portrait of Wall Street's origins in repairing the damage incurred after its first financial crisis. Meeting in a stuffy hotel room, however, does not satisfy the need for a soothing cultural icon, such as the buttonwood tree which conjures up an image of the airy outdoors, imagery that can be painted, reproduced as prints, framed and hung in scores of brokers' offices.[96] Nor does it lend itself to the sort of myth-making found in the 1892 centennial remarks of the New York Stock Exchange's President in which he borrowed an elysian, pastoral imagery to enshrine a legend of a group of 'unconscious founders of the great Stock Exchange,' who found themselves 'in the shade of the spring mantled limbs, with the birds chirping in the leaves overhead and village gamins playing about.'[97]

3. Under the Buttonwood Tree
Gathering 'in the shade of the spring mantled limbs' of the Buttonwood, this early twentieth century iconography of Wall Street places it in the imagery of the nation's founding fathers, while the contemporaneous evidentiary record locates the meeting in Corre's Hotel. (Library of Congress, Prints and Photographs Division.)

Wall Street, in just two years as a financial center, wrote and enacted a script that would be reenacted over the next two centuries. Between 1790 and 1792 it witnessed a brilliant financial scheme by Alexander Hamilton to establish the new nation's credit by marrying public and private interests. The first formal brokers' agreement among securities dealers was created in response to a financial crisis to bring some order and respectability to an institution in disrepute after the Duer scandal. While Wall Street produced early financiers who saw themselves as responsible and benevolent, it also gave rise to frenzied speculation orchestrated by schemers and scoundrels who anticipated many of the *mea culpas* of fallen financial angels that will be encountered over and over again in the next 200 years. And, finally, it threw forth a great cultural interpreter whose efforts at preserving and sponsoring American art and literacy are another Wall Street reality.

That cultural impresario was John Pintard, who went on to have a remarkable career – one of the most significant among the merchants of lower Manhattan in the early years of the republic. After his release from financial obligations, he used his contacts with political luminaries – Princeton classmate Aaron Burr, Thomas Jefferson, James Madison, John Marshall and George Washington – hoping to receive an appointment to a foreign capital or some post in New Orleans. When none bore fruit, he noted in his diary:

> Thus ends my prospects of preferment. I am in no wise disappointed. …
> I must rely on my own exertions solely to remount in life. If a post in
> New York City could be obtained, that would enable me to live & attend
> to some collateral objects, it would answer, but to accept a station the
> duties of which would exact the whole of my time & its emoluments
> barely support me, would be absurd and degrading.[98]

Pintard returned to New York where he was to live out a significant second life. When his uncle Lewis purchased the New York *Daily Advertiser*, he gave John Pintard a one-fourth share and installed him as editor, but this did not last long. The 'collateral objects' to which he was drawn were the collection and preservation of data about life in New York. In 1804 he was appointed Clerk and City Inspector of New York where he established a registry of births and deaths. He left this post in 1809 to become Secretary of the Mutual Insurance Company and held that post until 1829.

This employment permitted him to assist in the formation of a variety of historical and cultural institutions for the city. In 1805 he and eleven others started the first New York 'free school' for poor children, a forerunner of the public education system. His greatest achievement was the establishment of the New York Historical Society in 1804 where his papers, letters and diaries reside. His death at age 86 in 1844 ended a career that is best described by an 1870 profile of him:

> He could ignite a handbill that would inflame the minds of people for any good work. He could call a meeting with the pen of a poet, and before the people met, he would have arranged the doings for a perfect success. He knew the weak point of every man, and he would gratify the vanity of men and get their money, and accomplish his good purpose, without any of them suspecting they were merely the respectable names and moneyed tools that Mr. Pintard required.[99]

The basic character of an institution is often established in its infancy. Such is the case during the early years of Wall Street. The cycle of euphoria, followed by speculation and panic, followed by reform and redemption happens in its first two years. Hamilton demonstrates how Wall Street can prosper from a tidy relationship with Treasury policy, only to have it sundered by speculation. Then Wall Street has to defend itself from that same government, which transforms itself into potential regulator. To the two streets – Wall Street and Pennsylvania Avenue under construction – that created a uniquely American-style confluence of finance and politics, a third was added: the Main Streets of America where the typical citizen lives who is swept up in the prospects of quick gain from a financial gamble or who simply feels the impact of Wall Street without participating directly. This three-act play has been restaged periodically in The Street's history without much alteration except for names, context and particular triggering mechanisms.

Between the big-bang years of 1790 and 1792, Wall Street established itself as an emerging center for finance; the political capital began to take shape on Pennsylvania Avenue, surveyed and laid out as a result of Hamilton's political compromise to obtain his funding and assumption scheme; and investors across the new republic on what will become many Main Streets became swept up in the allure of finance.

President George Washington departed by barge where the Hudson River ends in lower Manhattan on 30 August 1790, never to return to the city, two weeks after the last meeting of Congress in Wall Street's Federal Hall. New York relinquished its temporary home as capital city of the United States as it was inventing itself to become the permanent city of capital.

2 *Lex Mercatoria*

After the turbulent and inventive years of 1790–92, Wall Street securities markets were dormant for two decades until the War of 1812 spawned a new burst of government borrowing and revived securities brokering on The Street. By the 1830s the commercial culture that Alexander Hamilton had promoted was clearly in the ascendant in the country and its locus was New York. *Lex Mercatoria* – the law of commerce – began to assert its governing principles over what remained of the Jeffersonian republican ideal of a nation governed by the rhythms of a rural arcadia and small-scale artisanal production. Wall Street was at the center of these changes. It affirmed its place as the nation's emerging hub for the financing of the War of 1812, underwriter of bonds during the great canal-building era, financial pivot for a rapidly growing transatlantic trade, and broker of securities for newly chartered manufacturing corporations. At the end of this period Wall Street was poised not only to pass Philadelphia and become the financial fulcrum of the nation but to play a principal role in defining the essence of the uniqueness of the United States. This did not happen immediately, but the foundations were laid, gradually refined and perfected over the remainder of the nineteenth century.

The ascendancy of merchants and commerce in the fledgling United States was neither altogether welcome nor universally accepted in the nascent nation, until the War of 1812 and its aftermath of 'public improvements' resolved the debate between Jefferson's idea of republican civic virtue as the nation's adhesive and Hamilton's federalist ideas of commerce, markets and contracts as the glue that would hold the country together. Jefferson's reliance upon what one writer describes as an 'elysium of contented, prosperous, and largely self-sufficient farmers,' periodically replenished by the country's abundant land, was no match for the revolutionary potential of the market and its Wall Street legions.[1]

THE ARCADIAN REPUBLIC VERSUS THE LAW OF COMMERCE

The ideas of Jefferson (the arcadian republic) and Hamilton (the law of commerce) derive from different philosophical traditions that competed in the early American republic. From the French enlightenment, Jefferson chose to emphasize what is described as the 'conception of human perfectibility and ... equalitarian democracy in which the political state should function as the servant of the common well-being ... .' From the Anglo-Saxon market tradition came Hamilton's 'assumed universality of the acquisitive instinct and ... a social order answering to the needs of an abstract "economic man," in which the state should function in the interest of trade.'[2]

This debate was not solely a theoretical discussion among elites. It seeped down to the common laborer as in this testimonial from an ordinary English workman in the textile trades, John Petheram, who emigrated to New York in the 1830s, ready to try out his ideas on a new land which he thought was ready for them. He was surprised to find how little Adam Smith's ideas about the division of labor had penetrated into the consciousness of American manufacturers and how a republican sensibility prevailed that was alien to him. He describes an encounter with a drug manufacturer in New York, John Morrison, in which he says he 'tried to make the old fool Morrison believe that by dividing the labour, which was not done here as it [is] in England, more work could be done. ... [He] had never read Adam Smith,' he remarks. To which Morrison replied that 'we want no one person over another which would be the case if you divided the labour,' and Petheram complained: 'They were all alike ... I have heard this over again.'[3]

Looking back on the sharpness of the debates and the slash-and-burn rhetoric employed, one is hard-pressed to find great differences between the antagonists. In one recent historical treatment the comment is made that 'in the early nineteenth century, to be an American was by definition to be a republican, the inheritor of a revolutionary legacy in a world ruled by aristocrats and kings.' While everyone might define themselves as a republican, however, 'what it meant to be an American republican ... was by no means self-evident.'[4]

For the American political debate, Hamilton adapted the political writings of David Hume, the economic ideas of Adam Smith and the three-volume memoir by the French Minister of Finance, Jacques Necker. Hume provided Hamilton with a rationale for distrusting republican virtue, while Smith offered a justification for the natural human instinct associated with the market. From Necker, Hamilton saw how a finance minister could meld politics with financial policy. Rounding out these intellectual influences on Hamilton's thinking was Wyndham Beawes' *Lex Mercatoria*. From this work Hamilton began to understand, according to one of his biographers, how the established rules and customs governing commercial exchanges were 'consistent with [his] notions about liberty, industry, justice and honor, because it was built upon free contractual relationships.'[5] The contract, in Hamiltonian federalist thinking, would replace the reliance on custom and tradition that so dominated English commerce. It was not only a more flexible and dynamic instrument on which to build a robust economy but also a more effective way to attain the republican values of a personal independence that merged with civic responsibility.

HAMILTON'S FATAL FLAW

At the apogee of his achievements in his mid-thirties as Treasury Secretary in the early 1790s, Hamilton was described as the 'dashing young aide of the revolution ... slender, his bearing ... erect, he stood out in any group, particularly among official colleagues such as the portly Henry Knox, the rotund John Adams, and the angular Thomas Jefferson.' From the moment of Hamilton's arrival in New York from St. Croix in October, 1772 at the age of 17, he was 'excited by its crowded streets, its many countinghouses, its attractive shops with their adjoining residences.' This characterization by a Hamilton biographer, who worked on the editing of his collected papers, describes how the Wall Street area of Manhattan struck Hamilton as a 'metropolis and its cobbled streets the pathway to his own success,' which was always associated with the commercial world he was sent to learn about. Seven acts of Congress between 1789 and 1792, initiated by Hamilton in his five historic reports, shaped the early federalist era. While accepting a democratic form of government for a republic, Hamilton was intellectually and socially a patrician public citizen who believed governance should accrue to that combination of wealth and intelligence he found among fellow federalists. It is fair to say that both Hamilton and Jefferson believed in a plutocracy but disagreed over its make-up. Not born into wealth, Hamilton's success says a biographer was the 'reward of calculated charm, hard work, individual study, determination, and discrete deference,' with a dash of 'shrewd self-promotion.'[6]

By the end of the 1790s and the turn of the century, however, Hamilton's star had begun to wane. Besieged by enemies and critics, and goaded by his own failings, Hamilton had become a broken man by his early forties. He carried on bitter feuds with a gallery of notables and unknowns, from Presidents Thomas Jefferson and John Adams to lesser New York politicians. He was simply not capable of separating political argument from the personal, which not only prevented him from attaining the higher offices he deserved but exposed a character flaw that eventually led to his death.

With no one was Hamilton's quarrel more emphatic and tragic than with his New York republican rival, Aaron Burr. Whatever Burr tried to do, there was Hamilton trying to impede his way. The political differences between Burr and Hamilton were heightened by their contrasting lineage and personal styles: the one born to wealth and power, the other an immigrant persistently battling against an established elite he thought of inferior intelligence whose access to power descended from a holdover of British custom. More than a personal demon for Hamilton, Burr represented everything he sought to replace in his meritocracy of achievement through commerce and contract. The confident *bon vivant* Burr was a descendant of Puritan ministers and a college president. His charm and lineage often made it possible for him to evade the consequences of his failed grand schemes. While Hamilton desired many of the high prizes that Burr sought, his lack of background, he thought, prevented him from attaining them. His distaste for the profligate and meddlesome Burr caused him to persuade the New York delegation to support his political opponent – the republican Jefferson – for president in 1800 in order to block Burr and relegate him to the vice presidency. To carry his point of view on virtually every national and state issue that came up, he started the New York *Evening Post* in 1801, the nation's oldest, continually published daily newspaper.

Burr, for his part, was not bashful about destabilizing Hamilton's financial project. For example, he wanted to start a New York bank to challenge Hamilton's cherished Bank of New York. Thwarted at every turn in these efforts, Burr obtained a charter in 1799 from the New York City Council for a system of water purification and delivery that would relieve Manhattan of its periodic epidemics spread through the water system. The enterprise was called the Manhattan Company, and its charter contained a clause cleverly inserted by Burr that allowed surplus capital from the waterworks to be used 'in anything not inconsistent with the laws and constitutions of the United States or the State of New York.' Armed with surplus capital and making use of this clause, Burr started his rival bank, the Bank of the Manhattan Company, forerunner of the Chase Manhattan Bank.[7] This challenge was aimed at one of Hamilton's prize accomplishments and was the very same affront that Duer had launched, only to see Hamilton retaliate and produce Wall Street's first financial crisis. In a paradox of history, this water charter was the loophole that created a merged bank in the 1950s, the Chase Manhattan Company, that was permitted at a time when bank mergers were illegal, because a clever lawyer argued successfully that combining the Chase Bank and the Manhattan Company was not a merger of two banks but of a water company and a bank.[8]

Burr and his associates had little interest in ameliorating Manhattan's water problems. They were more interested in their bank. The exclusive charter granted by the City Council to the Manhattan Company had little to justify itself. By 1800 only six miles of pipe had been laid, serving only 400 residences. Quality was ignored in order to shave surpluses for the bank. Hollowed-out logs were used instead of iron pipes. A promised reservoir of 1 million gallons was never realized and one holding only 132,000 gallons was built. The reservoir's structure, however, was spared no expense. Its four Doric columns and statue of Oceanus conveyed a grandeur designed to fool the public and satisfy the builders.[9] None of this was lost on a fuming Hamilton. The rivals ended up challenging each other to a duel.

A bullet from Burr's pistol killed Hamilton on 11 July 1804 on a dueling field in Weehawken, New Jersey on the west bank of the Hudson River. The proximate dispute over bank rivalry that led to the duel was just part of the accumulated animosities and insults between the two that fit the purposes of the *code duello* of the time. This was not the first time Hamilton had tempted fate in a duel. Ten years earlier, for example, he had challenged James Nicholson, a commodore who once commanded a vessel named after Hamilton, only to be saved by their seconds who worked out a face-saving accommodation.[10] Hamilton suffered the same fate as his son Philip, who had been killed on the identical Weehawken field less than three years earlier at the age of 20 in a duel with George I. Eacker, a Jeffersonian opponent of the elder Hamilton. It was instigated by the younger Hamilton's defense of his father's reputation when he encountered Eacker sitting next to his box at the Park Theater in New York. Some biographers have noted the similarity and wonder whether his son's death in his defense had mortally wounded Hamilton's spirit and led to his own demise and death as he sought, tragically, to emulate his son's false notion of pride.[11]

After he was wounded, Hamilton's seconds took him to the house in lower Manhattan of William Boyd who had figured prominently in the speculations over Revolutionary War debt 20 years earlier. Hamilton died the next day.[12] Following a large and impressive funeral cortege along Wall Street, he was buried in the courtyard of Wall Street's Trinity Church. Burr's career was over. Facing a charge of murdering the first citizen of Wall Street, he slipped out of town.

FINANCIAL REGENERATION ON WALL STREET

If political high drama consumed Wall Street's attention in the first decade of the new century, the more familiar and comfortable world of finance dominated the second. The War of 1812 was the initial stimulus for financial regeneration. Following the French Revolution, European countries were at war almost continuously from 1793 to 1815. The chief combatants, France and England, both turned to the United States for food when either their vessels were used in battles or trade routes were blocked. They also needed American ports as a transshipment point from their West Indies colonies. Initially both honored an agreement that proclaimed American ships neutral. They could transport products from French and British colonies in the West Indies with impunity but only if they first docked at an American port and then re-exported.

No better scheme could have been devised to favor the growth of America's fledgling commercial economy and domestic production. Exports rose from just over $20 million in 1790 to $108 million in 1807. A good portion of this was domestically produced – nearly $50 million in 1807. Because of the preferences given to American-flagged ships, U.S. shipowners' share of trade from the West Indies went from 59 to 92 per cent. Their earnings were $42 million in 1807 compared to around 6 million in 1790.[13] New York merchants, shipowners and exporters fared well in their competition with Baltimore, Philadelphia and ports north during this war-induced, expanded trading opportunity because of Manhattan's ports' deep-water accessibility and relative infrequency of ice clogs in winter. Between the early 1790s and 1807, imports rose from $1.4 million to $7.6 million through the ports of New York and exports grew from $2.5 million to $26 million.[14]

This bonanza was interrupted in 1807 when President Jefferson pushed through Congress his policy of neutrality. Harassed by both the French and the British navies, President Thomas Jefferson retaliated by declaring a trade embargo on American shipping to the combatants in 1807 in order to demonstrate the importance of American shipping to Europe and protect the American fleet by removing it from the Atlantic. What he succeeded in doing, however, was demonstrating just how vulnerable coastal merchants were to any break in trade with Europe. Between 1807 and 1808 New York exports fell by 80 per cent and imports by 60 per cent, leading to 120 bankruptcies.[15] New England towns were particularly hard hit as port cities up and down the Atlantic Coast faced a cessation of business activity and frequent bankruptcies for the two years that the embargo was law. In 1814 representatives from the New England states met in Hartford, Connecticut to consider leaving the union if the war did not end.

Between the passage of the Embargo Act and the 1812 declaration of war against Great Britain, American merchants and state legislators sought ways out of their dilemma. The state of New York provided Wall Street with important new investment opportunities and gave the city of New York a boost with an important law on incorporation, which helped propel it past its traditional rivals of Philadelphia and Boston and its new rival, Baltimore.

In 1811 New York was the first state to ease the laws regulating incorporation, moving the process from the state legislature to an administrative body. Prior to that year states granted corporate charters upon the presentation of a specific proposal to the legislature for a corporation to open a bank, or build a turnpike or start an insurance company. Not only did such applications take time, as they wended their way through the legislative process, but the machinery for incorporation opened the door for corrupt political payoffs, either to start a new enterprise or prevent one from starting. The 1811 law in New York for the first time in the nation eliminated this procedure, substituting an administrative body that would receive applications for corporate charters and expediting the approval process, thereby circumventing the cumbersome legislative process. By 1817, 546 corporate charters were issued in New York.[16]

The constriction of European trade caused merchants to turn inward to the inland American economy, and New York City's site was fortuitous. Better placed than the rock-ribbed New England towns and without the vast distances that separated the south from its interior, New York saw the opportunity to build toll roads into the state's interior. By 1822 some 4,000 miles of turnpikes were in operation in New York alone.[17] The profitable distance for hauling wheat by wagon had increased to 100 miles between 1772 and 1819, and the country's first commercial wheat belt extended from the lower Connecticut River south and west to the lower James River in Virginia, then inland into Virginia's Shenandoah Valley. The decision to start road building turned out to be advantageous, because the War of 1812 drastically reduced America's foreign trade and forced the country into much greater self-reliance. When the War of 1812 reduced exports from a peak of $108 million in 1807 to just 7 million in 1814, and imports from $109 million to 13 million, there was less of an economic impact because of the ability of the nation to turn inward and satisfy its economic needs from its own economy.[18]

WALL STREET'S FINANCING OF THE WAR OF 1812

To finance the War of 1812 with Great Britain, Congress authorized bond issues of $61 million between 1812 and 1814. This was not a very successful financing effort, however. Only some $45 million of the bonds were actually sold. Of that, about 8 million were sold at par – the full price at which the bonds were offered for sale – and the rest at about 80 to 88 cents on the dollar.[19]

This 1812 bond offering was less successful than Hamilton's 20 years earlier for both financial and political reasons. In 1812 the national government faced more competition for finance capital from banks, from some newly chartered manufacturing corporations, and from states that were financing large road-building projects. Political predispositions added to the problems that Treasury Secretary, Albert Gallatin, faced in selling the bonds. Many Wall Street merchant-brokers had strong commercial ties with Great Britain and financial links in the City of London. They tilted towards England and away from France in the foreign policy dispute over how to navigate the currents pushing and pulling the government toward and away from the two powerful European rivals. This was not lost on a Congress and a country divided along a fault line between finance and small-scale artisanal manufacturing, farmer and banker, and north versus south. New York banks with close ties to the treasury were implicated too, and this did not help Gallatin. They were accused of restricting credit to new business, farmers and tradesmen. Much of the capital of New York banks was held in Great Britain, a country that was threatening war and harassing American shipping.

A second problem faced by Gallatin was the absence of a national bank through which federal bonds could be sold and a market made for the resale of the bonds. Hamilton's national bank was given only a 20-year charter, and the Congress refused to re-authorize it in 1811. Foreshadowing a major drama involving the treasury and J.P. Morgan in the first decade of the twentieth century, the Treasury Secretary Albert Gallatin, without a national bank at his disposal, had to go to major financiers of the day – New York's John Jacob Astor and Nathaniel Prime and Steven Girard of Philadelphia – and negotiate directly the terms of war financing. These financiers bought the Gallatin bonds at a discount in a syndicate with others and then resold them in smaller lots, thus inaugurating a new arrangement whereby bank tenders were sold at a discount to intermediaries who then retailed them to the public.[20]

THE NEW YORK STOCK & EXCHANGE BOARD (NYS&EB)

The War of 1812 revived financial brokering activity on Wall Street, and three events after the War's close in 1815 propelled The Street forward: the opening of the Second Bank of the United States upon its re-chartering by Congress in 1816, the first loan flotation for the construction of the Erie Canal, and the formation of the New York Stock & Exchange Board to accommodate these developments. Twenty-eight million of the Second Bank's total capitalization of $35 million was sold to the public. The Erie Canal issued bonds that were authorized by the state of New York in 42 flotations between 1817 and 1825, amounting to some $7 million.[21]

Even though Wall Street's financial institutions were creative and flexible, they were still not adequate to absorb activity on this scale. They were also less reputable than rival Philadelphia's, whose auction markets were seen as less speculative, more carefully policed, and boasted a superior organizational efficiency.[22] It was to Philadelphia that several prominent Wall Street brokers turned when they wanted to establish a new organization. They sent a representative to Philadelphia early in 1817, who reported back about the organization and constitution of the Philadelphia exchange.[23]

On 25 February 1817 an organizational meeting was held among 25 brokers belonging to seven different firms at the office of Samuel Beebe at 47 Wall Street.[24] At that meeting a constitution was adopted that was modeled on Philadelphia's, a name chosen – the New York Stock & Exchange Board – and officers selected. The first president was Nathaniel Prime, and John Benson was named Secretary.[25] This constitution, as amended slightly in 1820, can be said to represent the authentic beginning of the organized New York securities markets – the one that the present New York Stock Exchange can point to as its parent.

The 1817 organization has a connection to the 1792 Buttonwood Agreement, but the link between the two is not as seamless as the oral tradition would have it. The strongest connection is the overlap among some of the participants in both: Leonard Bleecker, Samuel Beebe, Bernard Hart, Augustus H. Lawrence, Hugh Smith and William Robinson.[26] No doubt they carried an institutional memory that informed the 1817 meeting.

The 1817 NYS&EB Constitution was quite distinct from the Buttonwood Agreement in its length and legalisms, however. The Buttonwood contained less than 70 words in presenting itself as a guild-like organization to set fixed commission prices and form an exclusive system of preferences among the members. The NYS&EB Constitution contained over 1,500 words and provided for a detailed legalistic set of rules and procedures that could have been, and was, drawn up by a Philadelphia lawyer. This fits with a recent interpretation of this period in American history as one that elevated the juridical approach to many aspects of life. From its earliest days the country used the law, lawyers and the legal method to specify relationships that in Europe or Great Britain were still defined more by custom.[27]

Befitting a document of such length, the NYS&EB had detailed rules for admission, behavior and participation. The Buttonwood's fixed commissions were present and remained in place as a pillar of The Street for over 150 years, until the exchange adopted reforms in the mid-1970s. The NYS&EB set itself up as a cartel in which it excluded non-members from its auctions, thereby denying them information, and providing prices only after the auctions were concluded. Non-members were charged higher commission prices, and entry for new members was very difficult due to the rule that three 'black balls' were sufficient to deny membership application. The original low initiation fee of $25 hid the fact that gaining membership was virtually impossible because, as in all cartels, there is a logical incentive for the insiders to protect their position by excluding outsiders from entry. The 1820 revisions opened up membership to several new selected large brokers but after that it remained essentially closed until after the Civil War.[28]

Where the NYS&EB differed most from Buttonwood was in its restrictive entry to its twice-daily auctions. In this way the NYS&EB presented itself as an exclusive guild, which established securities prices among a few very large and influential brokers on Wall Street. The history of rivalry and competition on The Street from this point forward is about the tension between the restrictiveness of the 'official' exchange and the challenges from outsiders who assumed functions that could not be fulfilled by the NYS&EB. It took not much more than a decade for the NYS&EB to find itself tested by an aggressive set of contenders who congregated and did business on the sidewalks around Wall Street in what became known as the Curb Market.

NATHANIEL PRIME

Among the names missing from the Buttonwood Agreement but appearing on the small list of charter members of the NYS&EB, one stands out above all the rest: Nathaniel Prime. He was the Board's first President and became one of the great shapers of modern Wall Street. Described with a redundant flourish as 'stout, thick, short, and heavy in person' by a contemporary journalist, Prime was born in Rowley, Massachusetts in 1768 and came to New York to start a securities business in 1795 when demand for such services was very slim in the aftermath of the Duer financial scandal.[29]

Prime was an innovator as a private banker, as an underwriter of new bond issues, and as a conduit into British financial markets. Discreet in the tradition of British merchant banking houses, Prime's late-Federal building where he conducted his business evoked the atmosphere of a safe, comfortable home.[30] He first made his mark and fortune in handling notes of incorporated banks. His papers reveal extensive purchases and sales of shares in Burr's Bank of the Manhattan Company.[31] He was the first to become a 'market maker,' by which is meant someone who controls so much of the activity in a stock, bond or banknote that he or his firm can establish their price. By 1802 Prime was publishing each week the prices of some ten securities in which he made a market.[32]

Prime did this not only in bank shares but in direct lending as well. He was the first of the great private bankers in New York to supplement the financial operations of the chartered banks. The rate of interest he charged on loans was carried in newspapers as 'Prime's rate of interest.' It was known on The Street as the best price for money, because he was careful to trade only in the most secure stocks and bonds and make loans only to the most creditworthy. From this comes the designation, *prime rate of interest*, still in common usage today as the base-line interest rate charged by banks to their most creditworthy borrowers. Prime was also the first to establish direct correspondent relations with British financial enterprises as a result of his pioneering work in establishing investment banking in the new United States.[33]

Prior to 1812 banks, or governments, or insurance companies issued bonds and sold them directly to buyers, using Wall Street brokers as intermediaries and marketers. Prime and some of his colleagues started the practice of buying up large quantities of bond issues and then reselling them in blocks. No longer passively waiting to be approached by states that wanted to float bonds, Prime approached states directly and sold them on the idea of issuing bonds that he would syndicate.

Prime specialized in canal issues – first the Erie then later in bond issues backed by the states of Ohio, Louisiana and Mississippi. In this way Wall Streeters facilitated the flotation of bond issues, because the issuer could now work with a large syndicate that would take a substantial position, hold some and sell the rest. With an agreement in advance to buy a block of new bond issues, risk was reduced and ambitious investment ventures found it easier to see the light of day. It is fair to say that the financing of canals in the 1820s and railroads in the 1840s would not have been as extensive without Prime's investment banking innovation. Some of his best customers for resale were in Great Britain where he established correspondent relations with Baring Brothers and the Rothschilds. Starting with their first canal shares in 1823, Baring owned some $322,000 by the end of 1825.[34]

Following the Treaty of Ghent in 1814, which ended the War of 1812 and established a new era of more amicable British–American foreign relations, British capital became essential in the economic development of the United States. Anticipating this, Prime and his merchant friends in New York greeted the signing of the Treaty with this doggerel: 'Commerce and Plenty attendants in her train/ Again shall flourish through our vast domain.' Starting a tradition that was to become a New York trademark, especially when electric bulbs became available, the Bank of New York posted a sign lit with candles so it could be seen at night as well as day that simply read: 'PROSPERITY.'[35]

Prime predates the Morgans as an investment banker and in paving the way for tight connections between Wall Street and the City of London. Reputed to be the third richest man in New York in 1830, he retired from his firm of Prime, Ward & King in 1832 owning over 20 undeveloped lots and six homes, including a country house with 130 acres on Long Island and a great mansion at the corner of Broadway and the Battery. However, like so many barons of The Street that were to follow him, Prime lived out his later years as a rich man with a troubled spirit and died, it is widely thought, by his own hand. The popular legend was that a 'strange fancy seized upon his mind, that he was becoming poor – that his destiny was to die in an almshouse. Under this singular monomania, and hallucination of mind, he cut his throat with a razor, and died on the instant.'[36]

THE ERIE CANAL

The year 1817 welcomed the launching of two projects befitting the vision of Prime and his colleagues who created the NYS&EB: canal building and the re-chartering by Congress of the Second Bank of the United States. The Second Bank offered $28 million of its $35 million capitalization to the public and much of that went through Wall Street. Between 1816 and 1840, $125 million was invested in some 3,326 miles of canals, with Wall Street playing a major role by providing the market for the state bonds that were used to finance canal building.[37]

The grandest of all canals was New York's Erie, a project of monumental scope and ambition that ran 364 miles from Albany to Buffalo through a largely unsettled wilderness, with engineering challenges that were more formidable than any encountered in canal construction elsewhere in the world. Before the Erie was begun, the longest canal in the nation was only 28 miles. Forty feet wide and four feet deep, rising and falling 660 feet through 88 locks and passing over 18 aqueducts, the Erie was to become the longest canal ever built in any country. In George Rogers Taylor's classic history of transportation, he says, 'the building of the Erie Canal was an act of faith, the demonstration of a spirit of enterprise by an organized government,' which at that time was seen by Wall Streeters as an essential ingredient in the recipe for economic prosperity.[38] It was finished eight years after construction began, two years ahead of schedule, and inaugurated by its promoter, Governor De Witt Clinton, on 26 October 1835 when he boarded a flat-bottomed canal boat, the *Seneca Chief*, in Buffalo east to Albany and then down the Hudson to New York where on 4 November he was greeted by 100,000 at a triumphal celebration and parade. In its first year 42 canal boats carried 100,000 passengers and 435,000 gallons of whiskey, 562,000 bushels of wheat, paying a half-million dollars in tolls that was sufficient to cover debt charges. Shipping costs from Lake Erie fell from $100 a ton to $9. Tolls produced surpluses over loan repayments that were used to build another 600 miles of canals in New York.[39]

The canal was designed to connect the Great Lakes with New York City by building a west–east water linkage between Buffalo on Lake Erie and Albany on the Hudson, then south on the Hudson in steamboats to docks in lower Manhattan.[40] Visionaries looked beyond this to additional canal linkages flowing outwards from the Erie's terminus at Buffalo, southwards to the Ohio River on the Ohio and Erie Canal and the Wabash and Erie Canal. With the Ohio River feeding into the Mississippi River, New York was effectively connected to New Orleans and major cities along the Mississippi. A water pathway was now established between lower Manhattan and New Orleans, using the Hudson River north from Manhattan to Albany, west on the Erie Canal to Buffalo, then onto feeder canals to the Ohio River, down the Mississippi River to New Orleans. The Erie Canal responded to the commercial opportunities created by thousands of settler-farmers who moved to the more hospitable land in the Ohio and Mississippi valleys, America's early New West between the Appalachian mountains and the Mississippi River. By 1840 the vision of connecting the Gulf of Mexico by water to the port of New York was realized.[41] Because the canal route provided transport through a cooler part of the country than south through New Orleans, less wheat and flour rotted or soured. In 1839 New York received three times as much wheat as New Orleans for foreign shipment.[42]

4. Erie Canal Lock
The canal barge (left) and the activities around the *Lockport* exchange, with the lockhouse on left, depicts the many people and occupations needed to move traffic on the Erie Canal. (Library of Congress, Prints and Photographs Division.)

New York was not the only state trying to develop a water route to the west. Virginia, Pennsylvania, Maryland and Massachusetts had competing projects on the drawing board to get there first. Pennsylvania was New York's principal rival and had an advantage in that it was nearer the destination across the Appalachian mountains to the upper Ohio River. But New York had an asset which the Erie engineers exploited. In upstate New York there is a break in the Appalachians at the Mohawk River that lessened the elevation to a maximum of 650 feet above sea level. This is the same route that the New York Central railroad followed when it was built in the middle of the century, and later still that of the New York Thruway of the twentieth century, built by laying concrete over much of the Erie Canal.[43]

When the 364-mile Erie Canal was completed in just eight years in 1825, it had already taken in a half-million dollars in tolls. The cost of moving a ton of freight between Buffalo and New York City had fallen from 20 cents per mile to less than one cent. The Erie was a financial success – perhaps the most profitable financial investment ever made in any transportation project in the nation's history. Within seven years it had recovered its costs. Deepened and widened between 1835 and 1862, the Erie continued to expand its tonnage of freight even in the face of stiff competition from railroads and reached its peak of freight haulage in 1880.[44]

As impressive as the engineering and construction achievements are, the Erie also stands as a monument to another grand achievement – its financing – that is rarely noted, because it cannot compete with the sheer physicality of the canal. Without Wall Street, Erie and the other 3,000 canal miles would not have been built. The financing of the canals with state authorized bonds, that were then sold and resold on financial markets, required innovative Wall Street financial institutions to make it happen.

America's turnpikes and canals also offered several lessons to the nation. The first was that new technology derived from ambitious engineering and construction challenges. Road-surfacing innovations and truss-and-suspension invention in bridge construction, for example, were a direct outcome of the turnpike era that carried over into railroad construction. For the Erie, engineers designed new excavating equipment and a new type of mortar to fortify its 88 locks.[45] Between 1825 and 1830 more than 400 patents a year were issued – many of them for inventions associated one way or another with transportation.[46] This serviced future transportation and manufacturing requirements that built on the Erie's and turnpike's pioneering methods.

A second lesson has to do with the financial viability of large transportation projects. What later became known as 'economies of scale and scope' is the reason for Erie's financial success and others' failure. Undertakings which required large investments had to be of sufficient scale to cover the fixed costs in order for them to be profitable, and their scope had to be vast and linked to other economic structures. The cost of unloading from river boats onto canal boats was so large, compared to the per-mile costs of moving freight once on canal boats, that only a large project such as the Erie was profitable. The savings on the per-mile transport along the canal were needed to cover the large costs of transferring freight from river to canal boats. The Erie could achieve economies of scale and scope where shorter canals, costing less money to build, could not. It was the length of the Erie that allowed savings on per-mile transport to offset larger costs of loading and unloading from river to canal boats.

LEVERAGING ERIE'S SUCCESS

Wall Street and Chestnut Street were the two major financial centers in 1817, but by 1840 lower Manhattan had surpassed downtown Philadelphia as the nation's financial center and it has never relinquished this status. One reason for this was the very success of the Erie Canal which it helped to start. By 1840 the inland water network of canals and rivers and lakes was complete – connecting the west to Atlantic coast ports. New York replaced New Orleans as the principal embarkation point for export products from the west. The Great Lakes became the hub, receiving goods – primarily wheat and other grains – through the finger-like network of feeder canals from the major inland rivers, then on to the Erie, down the Hudson from Albany in steamers, off-loaded in New York, and then packed off to Great Britain in trans-Atlantic ships, like those of the Black Ball Line that had revolutionized Atlantic shipping in 1818 with the first regularly scheduled service from the United States to England.[47] The repeal of the Corn Laws in Great Britain – tariffs on grain imports – opened a vast market for American farmers to exploit through the Erie system.

The invention of the steamboat by Robert S. Fulton, and its commercial application by the time the Erie Canal was ready, combined with an innovation in shipping – regular 'packet' ships that sailed on a schedule rather than when full – to cement New York's preeminent position in transatlantic trade. The Irish-American Fulton was that quintessential curious American of the early Republic. In 1786 he went to London to study painting, dabbled for a while as an artist, then moved in 1797 to the center of the art world, Paris, where he changed his interest to civil engineering and worked on an early version of the torpedo to blow up British ships. He met Wall Street's Walter Livingston in Paris and persuaded him to finance his idea of steam-powered boat construction – a vision to place a water-based vessel on its own power, thereby separating it from the natural and unreliable power of wind and sail. In 1803 Fulton was able to launch a prototype on the Seine.[48] Backed by Livingston, Fulton took his invention to New York and on 17 August 1807 rolled out his invention that was to revolutionize the movement of people and cargo. When Fulton died in 1815 he received The Street's highest honor, a funeral service in Trinity Church and a street named for him a short distance from Wall Street that began at Gold Street and ended at the East River, later immortalized as a New York landmark, the Fulton Fish Market.

Over the next decade more efficient engines supported larger vessels, so that by the time the Erie Canal was functioning steamboats were loaded on the upper Hudson at the eastern Albany terminus of the Erie Canal, sent quickly down river to the port of New York, where the cargo was loaded onto the newly created regular packet lines to such ports as Liverpool in England and Le Havre in France. Packet lines were the ultimate destination of wheat from the western terminus of the Erie in Buffalo, having been loaded onto canal boats from the great grain belt west of the Appalachians, where the wheat was shipped up the Mississippi on Fulton's steamboats – thereby challenging the natural flow of the river's direction – offloaded onto one of the feeder canals into the Erie, and then onto canal barges, bound for the eastern terminus in Albany, from which the cargo went down the Hudson to lower Manhattan. Manufactured goods from the east and from Great Britain retraced the journey westward from ports in New York, up the Hudson to Albany, then onto the Erie Canal destined for farmers and tradesmen west of the Appalachians.

All of this activity brought new business to New York's banks and securities markets and also created an insurance industry to underwrite the safety of all this cargo that was unrivaled by either Boston or Philadelphia. Then there were the natural advantages of New York's port: its harbor was vast, waters deep, close to the ocean, easily accessible from Long Island and the Hudson, and less susceptible to fog and ice than Philadelphia or Boston.

Added to this was the important new innovation of regularly scheduled transatlantic departures. The transplanted English merchant, Jeremiah Thompson, conceived this idea, and in 1818 the first sailing of the Black Ball Line left New York's harbor.[49] By sailing on schedule rather than waiting for a hull to be filled or for weather to clear, transatlantic commerce was revolutionized. The swift, regularly scheduled sailing ships to Liverpool from New York returned not only with cargo but with news from England and Europe that provided Wall Streeters with early information about financial developments abroad and helped it in its competition with Philadelphia's Chestnut Street.[50] By 1840 an average of three sailings a week, on a typical journey of 39 days, carried not only products to and from ports in New York and Liverpool, but people as well – nearly 60,000 in 1837 compared to 3,800 in 1820.[51] Some were travelers, but many were new immigrants from Ireland and Germany to provide a source of labor for the expanding economy. The success of this innovation was also used to support cotton exports from southern ports in what came to be known as 'the Cotton Triangle'. Wall Street brokers financed the shipping of cotton from southern ports up the coast to the port of New York, offloaded onto the packet lines, then across the Atlantic to the textile factories in Liverpool, carrying back manufactured products that were shipped along the Erie system to the west and back down the coast to southern ports, from where the the loading of cotton began again.[52] The port of New York, abutting Wall Street's lower Manhattan, carried half the nation's imports by 1850 and a third of its exports in the 3,000 vessels that came from some 150 ports around the world.[53]

New York's second commercial innovation around the same time was the use of auction markets to sell merchandise imported from England. Previously, a British manufacturer would first sell his products to an exporter, who would then sell the merchandise to an American importer – called a 'factor' – who would buy the goods, take possession and resell them. By consigning his merchandise directly to an American auctioneer, the British manufacturer circumvented this process and reduced costs by eliminating commission charges to one of the middlemen.[54]

This combination of the Erie Canal, Wall Street's financial capacity, New York's harbor, the invention of the steamboat, and the innovation of regularly scheduled transatlantic packet shipping consolidated New York's position as the premier Atlantic port and financial-insurance locus for the nation. Its share of the country's international commerce grew from 38 per cent in 1821 to 62 per cent in 1836.[55] Topping off this impressive display of capital accumulation was the ever-present land speculation that accompanies transportation projects. Such recurrent Wall Street names as William Bayard, who bought over 300,000 acres along Erie's route, appear on land registries. Nathaniel Prime's firm of Prime, Ward & King underwrote Wall Street's biggest Erie land speculator, Isaac Bronson. All of this rebounded onto the value of Manhattan land, which saw a rise of 750 per cent between the Revolution and the aftermath of the War of 1812.[56]

The mortar had barely dried on the last locks of the Erie Canal before a new form of transportation appeared: railroad tracks and ties that would transform the American landscape as they snaked their way across the continent, eventually pushing beyond the canal system's confined reach at the Mississippi River. Construction of the first common carrier between Baltimore and Ellicott Mills, Maryland was started by the Baltimore & Ohio Railroad Company in 1828, and the first train ran over its 13 miles of track on 22 May 1830.[57] In that same year the first railroad stock in the nation was issued for the Mohawk and Hudson and sold on the NYS&EB.

The great canal-building era resolved the debate that had raged between republicanism and federalism in the early days of the republic. A *lex mercatoria* prevailed by creating on the land what could not be settled in verbal discourse. The transformation of the natural environment to accommodate new transport systems fulfilled both the needs of an enlightenment imagination and a commercial culture. Even Jefferson – who had not envisioned this use of the land – became swept up in its grandeur. Predicting this resolution, John Pintard, ever the visionary of commerce and culture, wrote in his diary as early as 1 August 1801: 'President Jefferson has agreeably disappointed the apprehensions of his political enemies who prognosticated the prostration of all public improvements. On the contrary, he furthers everything ... roads, streets, etc.'[58] Paradoxically, 'instead of creating a new benevolence and selflessness,' contends an historian of the early republic, 'enlightened republicanism was breeding social competitiveness and individualism,' the very character and culture it had wanted to avoid.[59]

CULTURAL IMPROVEMENTS

Internal improvements did not stop at the Erie's water's edge; it encompassed a cultural campaign under Wall Street stewardship to make New York into a great capital of culture to go along with its city of capital. As befitted the vision of Wall Street's financial leaders and appropriately for the ambitions of an American enlightenment, The Street's denizens pursued 'cultural improvements' to accompany their support for internal improvements, all underwritten by the great new wealth of the Canal era. Between 1825 and 1830 gas lights were installed on Wall Street. To intermediate savings of ordinary working people, William Bayard, John Pintard and Thomas Eddy created the First Savings Bank, limiting investments to government bonds. Opened in 1819, by 1824 it had some 30,000 depositors, assets of $1.5 million, and was the largest holder of Erie Bonds.[60] New, grand bank buildings were erected, most notably Euclid Thompson's federal-style building for the Wall Street branch of the Second National Bank. A new urban plan was initiated for Manhattan in 1811, consisting of a geometric grid of 50–60-foot-wide north–south streets and twelve east–west avenues intersecting at right angles every 200 feet, with wider streets of 100 feet every half mile or so. In 1820 the new and grander Park Theatre opened; new mansions were built within walking distance of Wall Street; horse-drawn omnibuses borrowed from London and Paris made their appearance around 1829; writers such as William Cullen Bryant and James Fenimore Cooper and artists, Samuel F.B. Morse and Thomas Cole, found patrons among the wealthy; The New York Institute of Learned and Scientific Establishments opened, all spurred on by an 1816 resolution of the City Council promising financial support for cultural institutions because, as one member said, New York had for 'too long been stigmatized as phlegmatic, money making & plodding.'[61]

The most celebrated architectural achievement was the new Merchants' Exchange Building at Wall and Hanover Streets. This housed the NYS&EB, which moved there in 1827 from the older Tontine Coffee House. With this building, Wall Street made an architectural statement; it consciously abandoned Jefferson's Romanesque-Republican style for the iconography of the Greek Temple of fifth-century B.C. Athens, a design borrowed from the headquarters of the Second National Bank on Chestnut Street in Philadelphia. Inspired by the Parthenon, the Greek temple's religious symbolism and its reference to Athenian democracy, combined with an imputation of solidity, fit perfectly America's new self-image. Translated into financial use, this design informed Wall Street's architecture for a half-century and conveniently fulfilled the Merchants' Exchange's functional requirements. To a passing public its massive, columned facade broadcast a message of grandeur, while its spacious interior hall could hold large crowds of buyers and sellers in a bazaar-like setting, with illumination coming from a central dome. Smaller rooms along the window-lighted skin of the building housed ancillary offices.[62]

From a large second-floor room (number 43), designed with the NYS&EB in mind by the architect, Joseph Coppinger, the NYS&EB expanded until trading volume reached 8,500 shares a day in 1835 – a 50 per cent increase from the day it moved into its new quarters.[63] Under an expansive rotunda, the confident members of the NYS&EB conducted their twice-daily stock and bond auctions bathed in light from Coppinger's innovative skylight construction. An 1822 letter from architect Joseph Coppinger to William Bayard of the NYS&EB describes the design of the second-floor exchange room as sitting above first-floor offices with the 'center of the building to receiveth light from the floor' and the ubiquitous 'coffee room to be annexed' to the building. The architect's plans called for the renaming of the street in front of the building as 'Exchange Street', but this was never realized and it remained Wall Street.[64] With its squared-off stone and sheer mass, the architectural rendering of the Merchants' Exchange set the motif for all later designs through the present building that was opened in 1903.[65]

Outside the Merchants' Exchange was the Curb Market, a less genteel mass of humanity of all sorts of dealers in securities shunned by the NYS&EB. These brokers, who could not gain access to the closed club of the NYS&EB, inaugurated a story line that prevails to this day. Many new forms of securities and new enterprises not yet established found a way to raise capital on innovative and 'unofficial' markets, because the more cautious official exchange would not touch them. 'Between ten and three o'clock, Wall Street is crowded with speculators, money-changers, merchants, bank directors, cashiers ... with scenes, incidents, personages, and manners peculiar to New York,' wrote a journalist for the New York *Mirror* in 1836. The *Mirror* commented on how these midday visitors to The Street conveyed a mood of 'anxiety, worry, fretfulness, hurrying to and fro, wrinkled brows, eager eyes, calculating looks, restless gestures, and every indication which follows in the train of grim-visaged care.'[66]

By the 1830s Wall Street was no longer governed by the leisurely rhythm of coffee-house life and was beginning to take on a more modern tempo of frenetic bustle. Allowing for some excess of hyperbole, first-person accounts of the atmosphere in the Tontine and the Merchants' Exchange reveal the evolution of the market's style. Describing the early days of the Tontine at the turn of the century, an observer wrote about how 'sedate old merchants with a piece of thirst-provoking cod fish or a dry cracker in one hand, and a steaming glass of Old Jamaica, oily schnapps, or sound old port in the other, gravely exchanged the courtesies of the day.'[67] By way of contrast, a broker described his colleagues during the Merchants' Exchange period as 'financial commanders [with an] arsenal in which their arms and chariots are stored, the stronghold to be defended or besieged, the field for strategy, battles and plunder.'[68]

On 16 December 1835 a great fire consumed lower Manhattan, virtually destroying it. It started around nine in the evening in the dry goods store of Comstock and Adams on Merchant Street.[69] The Merchants' Exchange was one of 700 buildings destroyed over 13 acres at a total loss that exceeded $18 million. The recorded memory of the NYS&EB was preserved by a heroic watchman, Mr. J.R. Mount, who rescued most of the records and was given a $100 reward by its members.[70]

To a superstitious Wall Street, an omen was transmitted. When the great dome of the Merchants' Exchange fell in, it demolished Ball Hughes's 15-foot statue of Alexander Hamilton that had been placed in the rotunda just eight months before the fire.[71] This marks a punctuation in The Street's history. Hamilton's era ended, to be replaced by a new populist challenge to the moneyed men of Wall Street and their dominance over the nation's economic fortunes. Its leader, Andrew Jackson, came from the new West. He marshaled a constituency that owed its existence and income to Wall Street's Erie Canal era that connected an interior agricultural and artisanal economy to the port of New York and made it possible for the new West's larger population to grow and prosper.

3   Jackson and the 1830s Bank War

A singular meeting between a future president and a Wall Street business-man foreshadowed The Street's financial fortunes in the three decades before the Civil War. The future president was Andrew Jackson and the Wall Street businessman was James Hamilton, son of Alexander Hamilton. The proximate event was the complex struggle surrounding the re-chartering of the Second Bank of the United States. Pennsylvania Avenue, in effect, introduced Wall Street to Main Street via Jackson's populist rep-resentation of the Common Man. For the first time, the three streets staked out clear positions on financial policy in the United States.

Wall Street encountered Jackson in December, 1827 about a year before he was elected president, when James A. Hamilton – a wealthy New York real estate speculator – was invited to meet Andrew Jackson at his Hermitage estate outside Nashville, Tennessee. Hamilton was interested not only in meeting Jackson on his own account but also in scouting him for such New York political allies as Governor Martin Van Buren, who became Jackson's Vice President in 1832 and then succeeded him as president in 1836.

As Hamilton and Jackson traveled together down the Mississippi River, from Nashville toward New Orleans to commemorate Jackson's victory in the Battle of New Orleans, something happened that captured the essence of the differences between an older, northern urban sensibility and the new West. This is how Hamilton described the episode in his *Reminiscences*:

> In the course of the voyage an event occurred, which I repeat, as it is suggestive of character. A steamer of greater speed than ours, going in the same direction, passed us, crossed our bow; then stopped and let us pass her; and then passed us again in triumph. This was repeated again and again, until the General being excited by the offensive course, ordered a rifle to be brought to him; hailed the pilot of the other steamer, and swore that if he did the same thing again he would shoot him. As I believed the General was in earnest, and as such an outrage could not be of service to our cause, I went below and stated to Mrs. Jackson what had occurred; she said mildly, 'Colonel, do me the favor to say to the general I wish to speak to him.' I did so.[1]

Needless to say, the 'outrage' on the Mississippi was averted, but Hamilton's reference to 'our cause' in the face of Jackson's swagger – was it done for Hamilton's benefit as a theatrical gesture to reinforce stereotypes? – summed up the rather odd political relationship between the two that was to continue for the duration of their political lifetimes. The two men represented their respective streets in the convoluted tussle over the re-chartering of the Second Bank due to expire in 1837. The younger Hamilton was an opponent of the Second National Bank, whose 20-year charter had begun in 1817. He became an important advisor to Jackson on his banking policy, although deviating at the end from Jackson's opposition to any form of national bank.

The familial relationship of the Hamiltons to national banking policy in the United States had not escaped Jackson's attention. At that same first meeting Hamilton described Jackson's 'strong opinions against the Bank of the United States; and to my great astonishment said, (when excited), "Colonel, your father was not in favor of the Bank of the United States".' Hamilton remarked in his diary that he was 'confounded, and at a loss what to say, as I did not suppose he spoke from want of knowledge.' However, in order to preserve his and his allies' 'cause,' Hamilton put the necessary interpretation on Jackson's remark by taking his comment to mean a reference to 'this particular bank' and, as he wrote in his notes of the meeting, 'made no reply.'[2]

Wall Street in the person of Alexander Hamilton's son had met the tribune of Main Street's common man: Andrew Jackson. The conflict among the three great streets in American financial politics – Wall Street, Pennsylvania Avenue and Main Street – began to take on clarity and a defined shape as never before.

THE SECOND NATIONAL BANK AND NICHOLAS BIDDLE

The Second National Bank was granted a 20-year charter by Congress in 1816, a lapse of several years after the failure to re-charter the First National Bank, in order to pay off debts from the War of 1812. It opened its doors in Philadelphia on January, 1817 only to be quickly engulfed along with other banks in the Panic of 1819. The Bank's trustees issued loans in excess of its reserves and, when cotton prices suffered a cyclical fall in Europe and Great Britain, a domino effect ricocheted through the banking system. Failed loans forced local banks to call in good loans to accumulate reserves. The National Bank then called in its loans to overextended state banks leading to a classic financial panic that started in 1819 and lasted through several years of deflation and recession which hit the south and west particularly hard. Among those affected was a western planter named Andrew Jackson who never forgot this experience.[3]

The record of the Bank in the first five years or so, therefore, was lackluster at best, leading to the replacement of its first President, Langdon Cheeves, with Nicholas Biddle in January, 1823. A child of the Philadelphia elite and an urbane republican, Biddle was 37 when he took over the leadership of the Bank. He studied law at Princeton after an undergraduate degree from the University of Pennsylvania. Upon receiving his law degree at the age of 17, Biddle first intended to embark on a literary career, working with Joseph Dennie who published *Port Folio*, a highly-regarded literary magazine.

A year after completing his law degree, Biddle was given a position in Paris as Secretary to General John Armstrong, the American Minister to France. There he worked on the Louisiana Purchase, attended the coronation of Napoleon Bonaparte at Notre Dame Cathedral, and went to Greece with an archeological expedition from Cambridge University. He returned to the United States in 1807 and resumed his literary career as an editor at *Port Folio*. Among other projects, he was the co-author of the Lewis and Clark expedition report. 'So skillfully was the work done,' says Reueben Gold Thwaites, himself an expert on western exploration, 'that probably few readers have realized that they had not before them the veritable journals of the explorers themselves, written upon the spot.' He was prescient in remarking that 'the result will remain one of the best digested and most interesting books of American travel.'[4]

One of Biddle's sympathetic chroniclers looks at him as part of an earlier American tradition that included people like fellow-Philadelphian, Benjamin Franklin, in which the 'man of affairs and the man of letters were one,' unlike his literary contemporaries for whom the pursuit of wealth and public affairs was anathema. 'Literature and affairs had parted company, and a man was supposed henceforth to belong to one or the other. Nicholas Biddle belonged to both.'[5] He had one foot comfortably set in the inquiries common to the Age of Reason and the other rather uncomfortably planted in the raucous America of the 1830s.

In 1824, a year after he became President of the Bank, Biddle proudly presided over the dedication of its new headquarters building on the south side of Chestnut Street, between Fourth and Fifth streets. Designed by William Strickland, and patterned after the Parthenon in the reassuring solidity of the Greek revival style that was in vogue for financial edifices, the building must have satisfied Biddle, because his own estate – called

Andalusia and built around the same time – was in the same classical revival style he had studied during his archeological digs in Greece.[6] The design specifications for the Second Bank called for a 'chaste imitation of Grecian architecture in its simplest and least expensive form.' When Biddle assumed presidency of the Bank, he had already been influenced by his youthful archeological work in Greece and by an 1814 article by George Tuckerman he had edited for *Port Folio*, which advocated the use of Greek architectural forms as a way to convey American political ideals, asserting the congruence of American with Athenian democracy. Strickland published an article in *Port Folio*, after completing the building of the Bank, in which he discussed specifically the problems of adapting the Parthenon to a bank's requirements.[7]

The Second National Bank was established by statute as a bank for the federal government. Not yet a central bank such as the Bank of England or the twentieth-century U.S. Federal Reserve, the Bank was the depository for the federal government's tax receipts, paid its bills, and received deposits from private state-chartered banks, known colloquially as 'state banks.' These state banks deposited funds with the National Bank, because it was the most secure place to hold reserves. Under Biddle the Bank took on the functions of a regulatory authority and embryonic central bank, which were never explicitly specified in the Congressional chartering statute. It extended lines of credit to state banks if their operations were sound and loans creditworthy. If not, it withheld lines of credit or required larger amounts of specie – gold and silver – to be deposited in the National Bank as a reserve against loans.

This discrimination in policy toward state banks was attacked by Biddle's critics as revelatory of his favoritism toward certain banks that were either part of an elite network or were in states such as Pennsylvania or New York and part of a financial oligarchy. However, there need not be anything sinister, conspiratorial or mysterious about this practice. Standard banking practice affords different individuals or institutions varying lines of credit, depending upon an assessment of creditworthiness. Financial institutions require varying amounts of collateral against loans after evaluating credit risk today as Biddle did by adjusting the specie reserves he demanded from the private state banks. Where the Second National Bank was vulnerable was in its methodology for assigning creditworthiness. Suspicions arose – probably justified – that it was based on who you knew and from what social class you came from rather than derived from any objective criteria.

This function of the National Bank evolved organically out of conventional banking practices between the National Bank and state banks. It is easy to see how this happened without resorting to a Jacksonian, moneyed-oligarchy conspiracy theory used to attack Biddle and his banking associates for appropriating financial power and extending the Bank's authority beyond its Congressional charter. State banks wanted to use the National Bank as a safe and secure depository, but the National Bank had to decide on its own policies with the state banks when it came to extending loans to them or assessing the portfolio structure of their deposits. None of this resonated with the Jacksonians – a new class of wealth-holders who, paradoxically, owed their existence to Wall Street's sponsored Erie Canal and the subsequent development of a vibrant interior economy west of the Appalachians that took advantage of all the opportunities produced by the booming transatlantic trade.

At its peak the National Bank controlled one-fifth of all bank notes in the country and one-third of the bank deposits and specie in the nation. To service this complex operation, Biddle extended the reach of the National Bank by establishing 29 branches in the country and expanded its financial influence to the private business community by direct lending and investments in company securities. The business historian, Alfred Chandler, writing about the history of management in the nineteenth century, has said that the Bank was the most complex of all business institutions in the first half of that century – the 'first prototype of modern business enterprise in American commerce.'[8] Through its ability to extend credit to state banks and directly to businesses, it effectively regulated the rate of growth of the money supply.[9] With the Bank's exclusive and privileged relationship to the treasury and its ability to conduct banking on a nationwide basis, Biddle adroitly calibrated the expansion of credit, minimized bank failures, and managed a rather stable growth of the economy without severe financial crisis or inflation.[10] In Biddle, however, no more inviting target for Jackson's denunciation of a moneyed aristocracy could have been constructed by central casting. While the Jacksonians saw Biddle as a past master at intrigue and devious strategies, he actually was quite clumsy in his political calculations – precisely the opposite of his shrewd financial maneuvers. Jackson lost no time in exploiting these vulnerabilities in Biddle.

While the Bank was venerated among Chestnut Street financial elites, it had a different resonance to Jackson and the Jacksonian alliance of a western 'frontier politics' with southern, anti-Whig (Federalist remnants) sentiment, northern financiers who wanted to elevate their state banks in importance, a new entrepreneurial class that was cut off from credit, and farmers in the new territories. To them the Bank represented a concentration of money and power that was sanctioned by the government but outside its influence or control. Without the federal charter and its use as a treasury depository, the Bank could not wield the power it did. But it was responsible only to wealthy investors in its bonds and not to any public authority. While it effectively operated as a public central bank, where was the public? Such a conundrum was caused by an imperfect statute that one would have thought could be corrected by changing the Bank's governing structure and prescribing in more detail what it could and could not do. But this managerial solution had little support from either Biddle's or Jackson's camp. As Jackson said to Biddle much later, when political skirmish had degenerated into metaphorical war: 'I do not dislike your Bank any more than all banks. But ever since I read the history of the South Sea Bubble I have been afraid of banks.'[11] Biddle, for his part, never reckoned the consequences that would accrue from his taking on Jackson over the re-chartering of the Bank.

JAMES HAMILTON

Shortly after the 1828 election of President Andrew Jackson, James Hamilton began to take more interest in the future of banking policy under the newly-elected president. So did Martin Van Buren, then Governor of New York. In a long memo to Van Buren in December of 1828, Hamilton staked out a position that was broadly representative of Wall Street's views. While not committing himself one way or the other on the utility of a national bank, Hamilton outlined an argument for a narrow concept of banking, summed up by his formulation of a banking system in which banks serve as a '*medium* of trade, and not the *capital* necessary for carrying it on.'[12] By this he meant a banking system that neither made loans for investment nor calibrated the rate of growth of the money supply, thereby avoiding the Second Bank's stop-go policies of over- and under-extension of credit. This somewhat naive view leaves unsaid how investment occurs without bank loans, except through financial markets such as Wall Street. Such a concept of narrow banking confines banks to receiving deposits and acting solely as a lubricant for carrying on market exchange but not expanding it through investment loans. The limitation of Hamilton's concept was not understood by him or his compatriots. Armed with this memo, Van Buren proceeded to try to exert his influence over Jackson's bank policy.

The general consensus is that Jackson's initial feints at the Bank were less a move to destroy it than to bring it under his control. Van Buren's motives were fuzzy, but one of the most powerful was to remove New York and Wall Street from the shadow of Philadelphia and locate the center of financial influence on The Street where financial and commercial realities dictated it belonged. Eliminating the Second Bank, therefore, need not necessarily imply the absence of a national bank in Hamilton's scheme. A new one based on Wall Street was a distinct possibility. Jackson's acceptance of Wall Street's arguments for eliminating the Second Bank, however, carried no commitment as to what, if anything, would replace Biddle's bank.

As the clock ticked on the preparation of Jackson's first message to Congress on banking and other policies, Hamilton became the chief conduit between the Albany–Wall Street axis and Pennsylvania Avenue. At the urging of Van Buren, he used his influence with the President to manufacture an invitation to the White House in the fall of 1829 to examine and comment on the draft sections pertaining to the Bank. Hamilton wrote in his diary that the draft attacked the Bank of the United States 'in a loose, newspaper, slashing style.' Working until about four in the morning on the document, he retired at five, awoke at eight, and went to Jackson's room 'to inform him that the work was finished. The President asked, "what have you said about the Bank?" I replied, "Very little".' Hamilton did not want to promote a simple up or down decision on the re-chartering of the Bank at that time. His 125 words pointed out the problems with the existing Bank, talked about the 'constitutionality and the expediency of the law [and how] it must be admitted by all that it has failed in the great end of establishing a uniform and sound currency.' Hamilton sought to buy time and create space for future consideration of alternatives to a straightforward elimination of the Second Bank.

After receiving this response from Jackson: 'Oh! My friend, I am pledged against the bank, but if you think that is enough, so let it be,' Hamilton immediately went to see Van Buren who had been awaiting him in a Washington hotel. At breakfast Van Buren asked: 'Well, Hamilton, what is done? I replied, "the work is finished. I could not induce him to let me omit everything as to the bank, and here is what he agrees to".'[13]

These diary representations suggest a divergence of views between Jackson and Hamilton that began to emerge over the possible repercussions of anti-Bank policy. Hamilton must have begun to have doubts about whether he could dissuade Jackson from the bold anti-bank position on which he had campaigned for the presidency. It is at this time that the politically attuned and highly ambitious Van Buren probably began to have second thoughts about his aggressive stance against outright re-chartering, once he intuited that Jackson was not about to be persuaded to accept a new national bank on Wall Street. Jackson may have drawn an unintended conclusion – deliberately or otherwise – that he had Wall Street's support for a no-national-bank policy. Wall Street's interests, however, were to slow down the process, to buy more time so that they could build a case for a new national bank on The Street. Jackson liked to refer to the Bank as 'that Monster,' but perhaps the New York schemers should have begun to wonder about the monster they had birthed in their tactical maneuvers with the military hero of the Indian Wars.

JACKSON'S MESSAGE TO CONGRESS

Jackson's first message to Congress on 10 December 1829 contained much more than the limited criticism Hamilton had written for him. Jackson let it be known that he would veto a re-chartering of the Bank, that if there were to be a national bank it should be under the direction of the treasury and, using Hamilton's formulation, that it should simply be a bank of deposit without the power to extend credit. The influential New York *Commercial Advertiser* reflected upon the message and five days later concluded their editorial by saying 'The more we study it, the more we are convinced of its unsoundness.'[14]

The Albany–Wall Street axis was taken aback by the detailed criticism and uncompromising posture revealed by Jackson in his December 1829 message to Congress. Less than a month later on 4 January 1830 Hamilton dispatched a detailed 3,000-word memorandum to Jackson on national banking issues. This document was a tactical maneuver in the contest over Jackson's subsequent bank policy. It defended the idea of a national bank by setting forth the reasons why the federal government needed a national financial policy and its own bank to implement it, lest the economy drift into cyclical contortions. Jackson responded some months later on 3 June 1830, probably after other contacts with Hamilton and his ideas, saying that he supported a narrow, Hamilton-type deposit bank and 'if the Federal Government should have anything to do in banking establishments ... then it should belong to the nation exclusively ... and not to a few moneyed capitalists.'[15] On the surface it would appear that none of these national bank principles were objectionable to Hamilton or Van Buren. Each side, however, was speaking in its own coded language and seeing the other's through a prism of its own construction.

Jackson's specific complaints were: first, that the National Bank caused financial crises by overextending credit; second, by favoring coastal as opposed to interior borrowers and state banks, the Bank discriminated against his constituency. Both these objections were presumably addressed by a narrow bank concept. Wall Street was more interested in where the Bank was sited than it was in particular Bank policies.

While there were differing opinions on Wall Street about the National Bank, there was little genuine support for Jackson's program writ large. As inheritors of a Hamiltonian-Federalist tradition, Wall Street found scant merit in Jackson's policies, except insofar as his desire to rid the nation of the Chestnut Street Bank would also conveniently rid Wall Street of its principal rival for financial supremacy. Aside from a handful of prominent wealth-holders, such as John Jacob Astor who was the first president of the Manhattan branch of the Second National Bank, Wall Street aligned itself with the strategy to use Jackson's hostility to the Philadelphia Bank to destroy it and put in its place a national bank on Wall Street. To prepare for this eventuality, Van Buren established a bank insurance fund to organize Wall Street for the takeover of national finance. Under this legislation a Safety Fund was established for banks – the first system for insuring bank deposit liabilities to customers. Through this measure, the New York banks would demonstrate their soundness in anticipation of a new national bank in their midst. A century before the country had a similar national insurance system in the form of Federal Deposit Insurance, the New York program effectively supported its banks through 1866, when the last of these chartered banks was folded into another bank security structure.[16]

Wall Street's brief for relocation of the national bank was based on its size and importance to the nation's finances. The Port of New York took in more customs revenues – the government's principal source of tax receipts – than all the other ports in the country combined. These tax payments by New York merchants, however, were deposited in the Philadelphia Bank and went to enhance Biddle's power and influence over national finance. 'It was the Bank in Chestnut Street,' according to one of the first comprehensive histories of banking in America, 'whose constant regulatory action restrained the freedom of Wall Street's banks to lend what they considered to be their own money [and raised the] lively question of whose pockets the profits were going into.'[17]

Shortly after Jackson announced he would veto any Congressional legislation that re-chartered the Bank, a formal proposal was put forward on 12 February 1832 under the authorship of Elisha Tibbets for a national bank on Wall Street capitalized at $35 million. It never saw the light of day but reflects Wall Street's own misreading of Jackson's intentions. Jackson had become more convinced than ever of the folly of a national bank in any form. Aligned with him were private, state-chartered banking interests around the country that wanted more control over the financial conditions in their states. Jackson's voting constituency of disgruntled farmers, emerging speculative entrepreneurs, and skilled urban workers were his foot soldiers in the battle with Biddle and his bank.

Wall Street was part of this coalition but had a different agenda which eventually got lost in the passions of Jacksonian politics. Each side, it should be noted, represented itself in the politics of the day as the tribune of Main Street in this contest for popular support. This is an important development that presages future contests among the three streets in the quest to forge an ideology and political language for public loyalties. 'Wall Street, the state banks, and speculative borrowers dress[ed] up ... in the rags of the poor and parad[ed] with outcries against oppression by the aristocratic Mr. Biddle's hydra of corruption, whose nest they aspired to occupy themselves,' was an editorial comment offered by the bank historian, Bray Hammond.[18]

Nicholas Biddle, for his part, misread Wall Street's strategy, and, as assessed by Hammond, 'thought capitalists are supposed to stick together, whether in New York or Philadelphia, and to cut the throats of the poor only, not one another's.'[19] Jackson, however, saw the unlikely alliance of Wall Street and Main Street as an opportunity for a popular revolt of the composite common man against privilege.

The net result of the destruction of the National Bank was indeed to move the center of financial power to Wall Street but to place it in private hands without any public oversight until early in the next century when the Federal Reserve system was established. The demise of the Second Bank, therefore, did not lessen the power of the banks but made private bankers preeminent without any public counterweight. Jackson's 'common man' on Main Street continued to feel mistreated, but now by private bankers. The weight of financial markets shredded Jackson's goals even though he probably never grasped that, in applying his skills as a military tactician in this theater of financial conflict, he could win the battle but lose the war.

FRAMING THE LANGUAGE OF FINANCIAL POLITICS

Jackson's 10 July 1832 veto statement of Congress's re-chartering of the Second Bank framed the language of American financial politics for a century and beyond. 'Grants of monopolies and special privileges,' wrote Jackson, had 'arrayed section against section, interest against interest, and man against man, in a fearful commotion which threatens to shake the foundations of the Union.' In an idle threat, Biddle answered by saying,

'This worthy President thinks that because he scalped Indians and imprisoned judges, he is to have his way with the Bank. He is mistaken.'[20]

The eventual showdown on the re-chartering of the National Bank was forced by Biddle's allies in the Senate. Senators Henry Clay (Kentucky) and Daniel Webster (New Hampshire), who was on the payroll of the Second Bank, sought to corner Jackson by forcing through a vote on re-chartering in the Congress four years before it needed re-chartering but coincidentally just several months before the 1832 presidential election. If the re-chartering succeeded, Jackson would be embarrassed and weakened, they thought. If his veto was upheld, then it would become an issue for the electorate to decide. They miscalculated on both counts. The veto was upheld by Congress and Jackson was given his best political issue in his successful 1832 election campaign against Clay.

Biddle had not distinguished himself in the interval between Jackson's 1829 legislative message to Congress and his veto of the re-chartering bill in 1832. He paid newspapers for favorable articles; used Bank funds to print and circulate widely a House of Representatives report about the virtues of the Bank; tightened credit and demanded higher specie reserves from state banks to frighten Congressional leaders into supporting the Bank; and paid members of Congress on retainer. Senator Daniel Webster, for example, was widely known as a supporter of the Bank, as well as a borrower from the Bank and paid legal adviser. Brashly he wrote to Biddle: 'I believe my retainer has not been renewed or *refreshed* as usual. If it be wished that my relation to the Bank should be continued, it may be well to send me the usual retainer.'[21]

New York was suffering from one of the worst of its periodic epidemics of cholera in July 1832; the newspapers of the day reported daily cholera deaths alongside stock reports, using a tabular form for both. When Jackson's veto message reached The Street in July, the *Commercial Advertiser* could not resist making the connection with the cholera epidemic: 'It is most unfortunate, that just at the crisis of this great providential affliction, the evil should have been aggravated by the folly and wickedness of the National Executive.' Now free from the delusion that a blow to Philadelphia would quickly become a benefit to Wall Street, the editors of the New York *Commercial Advertiser* published the full text of Jackson's veto message, followed by an editorial which said in part: 'The back-stairs Cabinet has prevailed ... by signing the veto prepared for him against the re-chartering of that great public institution, so essential to the soundness of our currency, and the commercial credit and business of the nation.' The paper weighed in the next day with a sharper tone and wrote about its 'profound contempt for his sophistry.'[22] The *American Daily Advertiser* used blunter language: 'the reasons for the veto ... disgrace the country [and are a] libel on our country's intelligence.' And the *U.S. Gazette* engaged in a bit of sophistry of its own when it opined that the 're-chartering of the Bank will, of course, aid the stockholders, among whom are widows and orphans, and aged citizens, who look to their dividends for daily bread. The veto has taken from these the means of their support.'[23]

Wall Street's plaintive presentation of the claim, that the ordinary American is the investor whose interests are protected by The Street, emerged to compete with Jackson's embrace of the Common Man. Wall Street and Pennsylvania Avenue struggled to construct and control the symbols that would capture the allegiance of Main Street. This is revealed in the *Commercial Advertiser*'s rejection of the 'rant about monopolies, which is all founded on the notion that a few favored citizens only can procure stock; as if any one, with money enough in his pocket, might not go into the market, and buy at the market price as much as he could pay for.'[24] This statement about the fairness and neutrality of Wall Street's securities markets, while juridically correct, ignores the concentration of wealth that precluded most citizens from investing in stocks or bonds in the early 1830s. The best estimates indicate that in 1828 4 per cent of the individuals in New York controlled about half of all the wealth in the city.[25] Nevertheless, The Street's attempts to fashion what later came to be called 'people's capitalism' originates in this Wall Street campaign to coopt the popular politics of the moment and offer itself as protector of Main Street.

The veto was a setback for Biddle's campaign to re-charter the Bank but did not represent any real diminution in Bank power, because it had four more years to operate under its charter. Biddle schemed energetically to try and elect his Senate Bank supporter, Henry Clay, as president, but Jackson's victory in the 1832 presidential election ensured the end of the Bank. To add to his victory in the ongoing campaign against Biddle's bank, on 26 September 1833 Jackson announced through his Treasury Secretary, Roger Taney, that the government would henceforth withdraw its deposits from Biddle's National Bank and redeploy its existing deposits and future receipts in certain private, state-chartered banks, dubbed Jackson's 'pet banks.' Three of the first seven banks named were in New York.[26] This struck at the heart of Biddle's financial influence and signaled the end of the Second Bank's power.

Biddle tried to counter Jackson's move by calling in loans and contracting credit. Such a step could have been justified on grounds of prudent banking but was trumpeted by Biddle as demonstrating the financial consequences of Jackson's policies to Wall Street's financial community in the hope they would rally to his defense and force another vote in Congress to renew the Bank's charter. This showed again Biddle's misjudgment, which continued to plague him, because as one financial historian has written: 'Nicholas Biddle believed that the charter fight was a contest between Wall Street and Chestnut Street rather than, as the Jacksonians implied, a contest between the humble agrarians and the moneyed aristocracy.'[27] Jackson was able to place the blame on Biddle for the subsequent economic slump in 1834 that was brought on by this contraction of credit and use it as one more instance of the flaunting of power by an unelected financial oligarchy. Biddle not only played into Jackson's hands but lost the confidence of some of his most powerful Wall Street supporters, among them Albert Gallatin, the elder statesman of American finance, successor to Alexander Hamilton as Treasury Secretary, and inheritor of his prestige on Wall Street.[28]

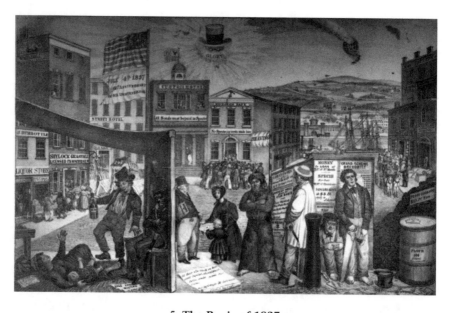

5. The Panic of 1837
This 1837 lithograph, called 'The Times,' by Edward Williams Clay, is a kaleidoscope of images of New York during that year's financial chaos that derived from President Andrew Jackson's bank policies. His hat, spectacles and clay pipe are in the center with the word 'Glory' above an idle Custom's House declaring 'All Bonds must be paid in Specie,' while next to it thronged with people is the Mechanics' Bank with a sign, 'No Specie payments made here,' – indicating no one has Specie. In the foreground are Main Street's melange of 'victims': a banker or landlord encountering a begging widow (center), an intoxicated street family (on left), and an unemployed carpenter (right). (Published by H.R. Robinson, Library of Congress, Prints and Photographs Division.)

Biddle and Jackson, by this time, were engaged in a grand game of chicken: 'All the other Banks and all the merchants may break,' Biddle declared, 'but the Bank of the United States shall not break.' When delegations from Wall Street descended on Pennsylvania Avenue, Jackson thundered, 'brokers and stock speculators and all [who] were doing business on borrowed capital ... ought to break,' and if they were not satisfied, 'go to Nicholas Biddle.'[29]

MISCALCULATIONS

The prospective removal of deposits from the National Bank and their dispersal to private state banks alarmed James Hamilton. In a letter to a 'Discrete Friend' on 19 March 1833 – about six months before Jackson removed the deposits – he explained that Louis McClane, who had just been moved from Secretary of Treasury to Secretary of State because he disagreed with Jackson's policy, had asked him to 'obtain the opinions, in writing, of distinguished bankers in New York on this subject.' Hamilton consulted with Albert Gallatin – Wall Street's most respected financial authority – who was startled by Jackson's proposal, and received a long written response to queries from another Wall Street financial authority, Isaac Bronson, the successful speculator in land along the route of the Erie Canal. All this orchestration of informed opinion did nothing to dissuade Jackson. To the dismay of both Hamilton and McClane, Van Buren, now the Vice President, did not join them in their appeal. Hamilton recounts how McClane asked Van Buren whether 'you now advocate the removal in obedience to the wishes of the President.' Van Buren answered: 'I found the President was so determined that I could not oppose him' – a response McClane found 'painful,' according to Hamilton.[30]

A few weeks prior to his order, Jackson approached Hamilton and asked him to go through his father's papers to find support for his actions. By this time Hamilton must have thought himself trapped in a spider's web of his own design. He delayed taking action on Jackson's specific request but took the opportunity to write back to Jackson on 13 September 1833 and say that 'I have conversed with several disinterested men well acquainted with the subject.' After yet another long discourse on banking in this letter, Hamilton tried to steer Jackson toward a new national bank but did not challenge the inevitable and concluded 'that as the present Bank is to be wound up, and as no other is created to supply its place, the Treasury *must* make the attempt to use the State Banks as its agents, and that without delay.'[31] Resigned finally to Jackson's unswerving opposition to a national bank, Hamilton provided him with a letter from his father in which the elder Hamilton had directed the Collector of New York customs revenues to deposit 'public moneys' in the Bank of New York rather than in the first National Bank. Although the letter could be interpreted as support for Jackson's redeployment of federal deposits into state banks, recall, however, that this was a tactical move by Alexander Hamilton in his dispute with Duer over Duer's attempt to establish a rival bank to the Bank of New York.[32] It did not necessarily condone using state banks for federal deposits as a deliberate circumvention of the depository function of the First National Bank.

Thus ended one of the most peculiar and misbegotten alliances of the early American republic. Outmaneuvered at every turn by what they thought was an untutored blusterer, the financial sophisticates on Wall Street became the used not the users. Those on Chestnut Street were simply subdued. To test his support where it was thinnest, Jackson toured the Northeast in May and June of 1833 and was greeted by a boisterous crowd of some 100,000 in New York. The 1834 New York mayoralty election was contested over Jackson's bank policy between a coalition of workers, artisans and small businesses who identified with Jackson's campaign and bankers who opposed Biddle. Their standard-bearer and Democrat candidate, Cornelius Lawrence, was himself a banker. Opponents of Jackson's bank policy were drawn from the older Federalist groupings who nominated the venerable Wall Streeter, Giulian Verplank under the newly-formed Whig party. So inflamed was popular discourse, it was necessary to position military guards around the Merchants' Exchange and the Wall Street branch of the National Bank on election day. The anti-Bank forces behind Lawrence won by 150 votes out of 35,000 cast but the pro-Bank Whigs captured the City Council, reflecting a city equally divided between pro- and anti-Bank sentiment.[33]

Jackson's removal of deposits enlarged the divisions on Wall Street between its earlier Federalist traditions and the new breed who thought they could outflank Jackson by supporting his attack on the Bank and then resurrect a new national bank on The Street. The older Federalist remnants on Wall Street – now Whigs – had always stood solidly behind Biddle and the Bank. Wall Street merchant and diarist, Philip Hone, for example, was a firm supporter of Biddle and the Bank. He wanted nothing to do with the Machiavellian political maneuvering of the younger Hamilton and worked to mobilize Wall Street opinion in outright support of Biddle. On 31 January 1834 in the midst of financial panic Hone wrote in his diary that:

If General Jackson had visited Wall Street this morning he might have been regaled with a sight similar to that of the field of battle at New Orleans. His killed and wounded were to be seen in every direction, and men enquiring with anxious solitude, 'Who is to fall next.'[34]

A week later on 7 February a petition drive resulted in an anti-Jackson rally at a nearby park, and a few days later Hone recounted how several thousand gathered at another demonstration to protest against Jackson's actions.

THE ENSUING FINANCIAL CRISIS

The momentous events of 1832–3 did not resolve the problems of bank policy in the United States. They merely brought on the very financial chaos feared by wiser heads. There would be two more epoch-making measures adopted by Jackson in response to the confusion in financial markets that produced episodic crises between 1833 and 1837. With Biddle and the National Bank effectively out of the way, the growing number of state-chartered banks liberally sprinkled loans and credits on a borrowing public that speculated aggressively in federal land sales. The dollar value of land sales increased from 5 million in 1834, to 15 million in 1835, and 25 million in 1836.[35] Debts of state governments, largely for popular trans-portation projects, increased by $150 million between 1830 and 1838. Much of the capital for this speculation in western land sales originated on Wall Street. The largest financial institution in the West, for example, was the Ohio Life Insurance and Trust Company, but 70 per cent of its stock was controlled by easterners, primarily Wall Street financial houses, and its charter was written by Wall Street's Isaac Bronson, among others. Its officers were selected by him as well. This was not lost on Ohioans who decried the 'Wall St. Gentry of New York,' in their newspapers.[36]

To calm the rising land speculation in the nation, Jackson issued his *Specie Circular* in March, 1836 that required specie – gold or silver – in payment for all federal land sales, instead of bank notes or a combination of bank notes and specie. This caused the dollar-value of land sales to plummet by 72 per cent between 1836 and 1837, a deflation in unit land prices of 15 per cent, and a financial panic that led to a depression which lasted until the mid-1840s.[37]

In 1836 the legislature of New York responded to the financial panic on Wall Street in a familiar way, as it did previously after Wall Street's first Duer-inspired financial crisis in 1792, by initiating a statute to regulate the sale of securities. The NYS&EB opposed the legislation, offered the defense of self-regulation, and added another argument that now acknowledged the question of where the locus of financial power will reside in the United States: 'Any unnecessary restrictions imposed upon this branch of business, would be calculated to divert it to other places, where a greater spirit of liberality prevails.'[38] Competition among states, based upon regulatory aggressiveness, appears in the language of political argument for the first time.

To Jackson and his bank-policy managers on Pennsylvania Avenue, a principal source of the financial chaos was located in the state banks that had been receiving federal government deposits and then leveraging those deposits into an excessive credit expansion. To thwart this abuse, they came up with the idea of an *independent treasury* in which the federal government would no longer deposit its tax receipts in any part of the banking system but simply hold its revenues in vaults throughout the country, and pay its bills in specie through *sub-treasury* offices. The largest sub-treasury was established in Wall Street's Federal Hall, where George Washington had been sworn in as President. The controversial idea for an independent treasury originated at the tail-end of Jackson's presidency, was implemented by his treasury department, and given Congressional sanction in the 1839 Independent Treasury Act during the term of his successor, Martin Van Buren. It bore the imprint of James Hamilton's consistent advocacy of a narrow federal banking policy. Even though the Act was quickly repealed when the Whigs won the 1840 presidential election, the damage done to the confidence in American financial markets was sufficient to cause a withdrawal of British capital, a deeper financial crisis, and delay economic recovery.[39] *The Times* of London, reacting to the way in which domestic politics produced poor financial policy, wrote: 'The people of the United States may be fully persuaded that there is a certain class of securities to which no abundance of money, however great, can give value, and that in this class their own securities stand pre-eminent.'[40]

While the specie circular and independent treasury policies curbed inflationary abuses in the banking system, they also created severe deflation and depression as money and credit were sucked from the financial system into idle reserves that were locked up in iron vaults. Building on the medical metaphor, this is how Hone described Wall Street on 11 May 1837 in the midst of the most serious financial panic The Street had witnessed in 45 years: 'A dead calm has succeeded the stormy weather ... All is still as death. No business is transacted ... The fever is broken, but the patient lies in a sort of syncope, exhausted by the violence of the disease and the severity of the remedies.'[41] The closing of the Philadelphia National Bank

6. The Sub-Treasury
A new element in the language of financial politics of the 1830s came from the cartoonist's satirical pen and ink. This commentary on the Sub-Treasury likened it to an 'office-holder's elysium,' with sacks of money dropped into the Sub-Treasury at the top by Main Street depositors falling through a false bottom into the hands of the 'office holders.' Holding the key, the official on left says 'Specie for the office-holders, but these [referring to the 'Treasury Notes' in his grasp] are good enough for "cobblers and Tinkers"!' (Published in 1838 by H.R. Robinson, Library of Congress, Prints and Photographs Division.)

in February, 1836 and Biddle's death eight years later at the age of 58 ended a chapter in American finance but did not end the controversy.

On Charles Dickens' first trip to the United States in March 1842, he wrote from Philadelphia:

Looking out of my chamber-window, before going to bed, I saw, on the opposite side of the way, a handsome building of white marble, which had a mournful ghost-like aspect, dreary to behold. I attributed this to the sombre influence of the night, and on rising in the morning looked out again, expecting to see its steps and portico thronged with groups of people passing in and out. The door was still tight shut, however; the same cold cheerless air prevailed. ... I hastened to inquire its name and purpose and then my surprise vanished. It was the Tomb of many fortunes; the Great Catacomb of investment; the memorable United States Bank.[42]

The ghost-like impression that Chestnut Street's Bank left with Dickens in 1842 is different from the one he would have formed had he visited

Wall Street's new home for securities trading: the Merchants' Exchange Building, which opened in that same year and replaced the one destroyed by fire in 1835. Chestnut Street's tomb had given way to The Street's incubator for new financial fortunes.

With the demise of its Chestnut Street rival, financial power eventually moved to a Wall Street that was largely unencumbered by the political locus of the nation on Pennsylvania Avenue. Jackson's successful assault on the Second National Bank left financial authority in the hands of private institutions on The Street, a consequence not intended by him or his followers on Main Street. It took 75 years of relentless conflict among the three streets before the public became represented once again in banking policy in the United States.

4   The New Metropolis

It was one of those random, but not unusual, pre-Christmas windy and frigid evenings when on 16 December 1835 a great fire consumed virtually all of Wall Street and its environs. Not much was left standing of Wall Street's first built environment when the fire finally exhausted all of the fuel from the wooden structures of the early republic. The inferno became so intense that it engulfed the marble of what its builders thought was the impregnable Merchants' Exchange. At 4 a.m. the Tontine Coffee House succumbed. Inadequate pressure contributed to water's freezing in the fire hoses; and the wind splashed the fire everywhere. Aaron Burr's corruption of the city's first effort to establish an adequate water system was thus exposed with its consequent neglect of the public's safety.[1] Water from the East River was limited because it had partially frozen. When the fire ended, 674 buildings had burned down and almost every structure from Wall Street south had some damage. Twenty-three of New York's 26 fire insurance companies subsequently went bankrupt. The optimism and energy of Wall Street was not destroyed, however. Business resumed and the exchange restarted operations four days after the fire. A year after the fire, 500 new structures were under construction or completed, and a new and better Wall Street rose like the phoenix from the ashes.[2]

Wall Street emerged from the destruction of lower Manhattan's 1835 fire as visibly and confidently as it emerged from Jackson's destruction of the nation's financial structure. As hotels and shops moved north along Broadway, and residences spread east and west from Broadway to the two river boundaries, Wall Street was the underwriter of and speculator in every new venture that engaged the imagination of the city. Superstitious when it came to finance, Wall Streeters apparently saw no omen in the Great Fire of 1835. There was no premonition of a financial system about to become rudderless two years hence, or of an imminent financial crisis. Instead, they constructed a physical space grander than the one destroyed and created new institutions to cope with a post-National Bank financial environment.

After the 1835 fire the New York Stock and Exchange Board (NYS&EB) lived a nomadic existence until it moved into the most imposing of the new Wall Street edifices: a rebuilt Merchants' Exchange that opened in 1842 on the site of the previous Exchange. Built at a cost of $1.8 million, the Exchange took up an entire city block between Wall Street and Exchange Place, Hanover and William Streets.[3] Designed by Isaiah Rogers in the ubiquitous Greek neo-classical style, the Exchange's twelve massive ionic columns facing Wall Street, each weighing 45 tons, were cut from a single piece of stone, floated south from a quarry in Quincy, Massachusetts on specially constructed rafts, from where they were moved from the docks by 40 teams of oxen.[4] In the grand rotunda of the new Merchants' Exchange, 3,000 dealers in merchandise of all sorts could mill about. The NYS&EB met there from 1842 until 1854 in the 80-foot-high Board Room that was 138 feet in length and 112 feet wide and conceived by Rogers as a grand financial emporium with innovative lighting, heating and ventilation, along with massive steel basement vaults for stocks, bonds and documents.[5]

This exercise in architectural grandeur was highly leveraged. In the year the new Merchants' Exchange opened its doors, British bankers had to advance capital to service the debt on its defaulted building loans.[6] Philip Hone, former Mayor of New York, a wealthy merchant and patron of the arts, has left this contemporaneous account of what a 'stranger' would encounter during a walk along Wall Street at the time of the opening of the new Merchants' Exchange:

> eight or ten banks, each a palace for the worship of mammon; and the new Exchange, with a portico of granite columns such as Sir Christopher Wren had no notion of ... an edifice the cost of which sunk all the money of myself and other fools who subscribed for it, besides contracting a debt of which nothing will ever be paid out of the income.[7]

Led by Rogers and Richard Upjohn, the architect of the new Trinity Church, Wall Street began to assert a harmony in its architectural form, cognizant of axial relationships in the siting of its buildings. Never again would one architect – Isaiah Rogers – be given the commission for five major buildings that were erected in a single year (1839): United States Bank, Manhattan Bank, Merchants' Bank, City Bank, and Union Bank.[8] Spilling over from Wall Street, the new construction – on the carpet of a post-fire warren of meandering narrow streets and tiny lanes that were left over from the original Dutch colony – posed a challenge for a new commercial enclave whose size and complexity dwarfed its original street designers.

Formality, decorum and ritual marked the conduct of the twice-daily auction of stocks and bonds at the NYS&EB, in contrast to the hurly-burly of dealings outside of the exchange. The members met from 10:30 a.m.

until noon for the first auction and at 2:45 p.m. for the second. Fines were levied on any member who failed to conform to the dress code or otherwise behaved in an indecorous manner. Membership was more clubby and closed than ever. Three black balls were still all that was needed to deny membership to an applicant, and few made it past this minority veto.

7. Wall Street as Sacred Site
A re-built Wall Street after the 1835 fire as shown in this 1847 painting, demonstrating the coordinated architectural renderings of Isaiah Rogers. With this imagery Wall Street began to create itself as a 'sacred site' in the American psyche, reifying its mundane money activities into an illusion and metaphor that aligns it with the religious symbolism of Trinity Church (center), which towers over and anchors Wall Street. (By Augustus Kollner (painter) and lithograph by Isidore Laurent Deroy, Library of Congress, Prints and Photographs Division.)

In an overdrawn metaphor that reflects The Street's clumsy efforts to align itself with the common working man on the one hand and a Wall Street under construction on the other, a financial writer and broker described how he and his colleagues 'converged into the central mine, echoing with the hoarse cries of the workmen in stocks, as they wielded the monetary pickaxe and spade ... prepatory to some explosion which was to shake the rooted pillars of finance.'[9] NYS&EB members, 'adorned with high stocks, swallow-tail coats, and tall chimney-pot hats,' arrived each day to take their seats in a room where:

At one end ... was the rostrum, at which the president stood, gavel in hand, to call the stocks, while the industrious secretary, at his side – old Bernard Hart – scribbled a record of the transactions. Two parallel rows of massive columns ran lengthwise through the hall, while in the nave stood a long table, forming three sides of a hollow square, at which most of the members had their seats.[10]

In contrast to the starched routine of the NYS&EB, a more raucous scene could be observed outside on the streets and from time to time in new exchanges that sprouted up, then withered and died. Many of the stock issues traded outside of the NYS&EB were not fly-by-night operations but those associated with major new industries ignored by the official exchange: petroleum, railroads and mining. Specialized exchanges were set up to trade in the securities of these industries, such as the Mining Board at 57 William Street (1857), the Gold Exchange (1864) and the Petroleum Board (1877).[11] Some of these were general-purpose exchanges that traded in securities the NYS&EB did not want to touch because they were new, untested or simply outside the settled routine of the Board. One such effort was the New Board of Stock Brokers of the 1830s that did not survive the 1837 financial crisis. Another more ingenious group, according to Wall Street lore, rented rooms next to the NYS&EB, drilled listening-holes in the wall, and charged a fee of $100 for the opportunity to listen to the Exchange's auctions.[12] This pattern of a major central exchange – with closed membership and a conservative skepticism about new industries – in tension with the outsider-upstart remains central to an understanding of The Street, from the 1830s through the present contest between the New York Stock Exchange and such challengers as NASDAQ.

The most colorful contestant for importance on Wall Street started in the 1830s and 1840s and reached its zenith of power after the Civil War when it took on the securities of the great new industries in America that the NYS&EB shunned. This became the *curb market*, so named because its dealings took place on the sidewalks in the smaller streets off Wall Street. So long as the curbers did not threaten the exclusive purview of the NYS&EB by trading in the securities sold at its auctions, they were allowed to operate. In fact, the curbers were encouraged, because they provided a place for the Board's members to deal in securities not listed at the NYS&EB's auctions. If, however, the curbers encroached on the Board's territory, they were swiftly dispatched by a blacklisting which denied them access to trading with any members of the NYS&EB.

Smug NYS&EB members described the curbstone broker as 'the scullion in the brokerage kitchen, feasting on remnants and odds and ends, ... obliged to serve his time before he can be admitted to the banquets and privileges of the parlor.'[13] Many of the curbers represented ambitious immigrant groups, especially German Jews or Irish Catholics who were systematically denied admission to the NYS&EB club. The same contemporary broker remarked that 'a very strong prejudice for a long time existed against Jews [who] were almost always promptly black-balled, notwithstanding some of them ... Nathan Seixas and Bernard Hart, had been prominent in forming the organization, and [Hart] had acted as Secretary down to 1840.'[14] By the end of the century and the start of the next, many of the great Wall Street names had begun their careers on the curb.

The curb was creative in its methods and developed techniques that were eventually adopted by the NYS&EB. *Continuous trading*, for example, was started on the curb. Instead of the NYS&EB's twice-daily auction, the constant buying and selling of securities on the curb provided for ever-changing prices, kept the market more liquid and led to a significantly higher turnover on the curb than at the NYS&EB auctions. Individuals who specialized in particular companies or industries stood at one place all day on the curb. From this was born the *trading post* and the *specialist* that characterizes the stock exchange since the twentieth century.[15]

From time to time the curb brokers decided they had enough of foul weather and rented rooms for trading. The NYS&EB, however, saw this as a breach of the unwritten agreement that only it could trade indoors. Persistent battles inside and outside the courts after the Civil War led to the novel legal and economic concept that in a free-market and *laissez-faire* financial universe only one institution had the right to trade securities indoors.[16]

THE STOCKBROKERING PROFESSION AND WALL STREET INNOVATIONS

The 1830s produced the first group of full-time stockbrokers: individuals whose only business was the buying and selling of securities. Heretofore, the securities business had been but one of several lines of merchandise handled by a broker. In the 1830s and 1840s the most famous practitioner was Jacob Little, who elevated the practice of the short sale and the long buy to a new height. Going short meant that Little contracted to sell securities he did not possess at some future date – 30 or 60 days hence – at a specified price. He was betting the price would be lower in the market when he had to fulfill the contract, because then he would buy securities at a price lower than he had contracted to sell. So if Little agreed to sell at 50 and the market price was 45 when he had to make good on his contract, he would turn a nice profit by buying at 45 and selling at 50.

All was not hunch, clever analysis of market trends or luck, however. Little orchestrated the movement of stock prices by cornering the market on certain securities, or spreading false rumors, or using others to aid him in moving the market where he wanted it to go. For every short seller there had to be a long buyer – someone who agreed to buy at the specified price in the future and was banking on the price of the stock going up. If the price in the market had risen to 55, then the long buyer won, not the short seller. The buyer would purchase the securities from the short seller when the contract came due at 50, then turn around and sell the securities in the market for 55. The short seller, meanwhile, lost when he had to buy at 55 and sell at 50.

Tall, hunched forward and carelessly dressed with a faraway look in his eyes, Little's distracted air did not prevent him from attending to every detail in his business. He always delivered his own securities, 'hurrying through the streets,' wrote a contemporary broker of Little's, 'diving into basements and delivering his stocks like an errand boy' to assure himself they would not be lost or delivered to the wrong person.[17] Little made and lost at least three fortunes until the 1857 Panic wiped him out for good, sentencing him to that life of relative financial deprivation so many others on Wall Street would endure. His most famous fortune was made in the mid-1830s when he cornered the market on the Morris Canal & Banking Co. by going long on futures contracts, driving the price up from $10 a share to $185 and forcing short sellers to fulfill their contracts and sell him shares below the market price.[18]

His fall after the 1857 Panic from which he never recovered left him, noted a broker who knew Little, with 'his face bearing the marks of the fierce struggles of his life.' Little ended his career associating with many of the less successful new breed of full-time stock-player, described as 'non-descripts ... who hang around the Exchange ... men who have seen better days ... ghosts of the market ... [who] never "put up" a penny, and yet they are perpetually asking the prices of stocks which they never buy or sell.' Little, writes this broker-colleague, 'haunted the Board Room like a spectre where he had once reigned as King, offering small lots of five shares of the same stock, the whole capital whereof he had once controlled.'[19]

The demise of the Second National Bank placed Wall Street and its bankers at the center of American finance. Because of size, safety and security – and because they paid interest on other banks' deposits with them – New York banks became the repository of choice for deposits from banks around the country. Where previously Biddle's bank on Chestnut Street fulfilled this function, Wall Street's banks now collected deposits from banks in other cities, from rural areas and from The Street itself. These became known as *bankers' balances*.

Dealers in stocks and bonds used these bankers' balances to lubricate and nurture their businesses. Unlike London, Paris or Amsterdam, Wall Street's securities markets from the beginning had settled accounts on a daily basis. The others settled over a fortnight or a month. This meant that Wall Street brokers had to have a source of readily available, short-term credit to tide them over a daily shortfall. New York banks provided such credits, dubbed *call loans*. They were given this name because banks had the authority to call them in at their discretion. In effect, brokers were buying and selling securities for which they did not have cash on hand; 'buying on *margin*,' it would later be called.

The combination of bankers' balances, call loans and credit purchases shaped the unique character of Wall Street's securities markets. This combination also tethered everyone together like a team of mountaineers scaling the face of a mountain. One break in the chain and everyone suffered – the small town rural bank as well as the money center banks in New York. Many interruptions in smooth financial operations were the result of the normal seasonal rhythms of agriculture that dominated the American economy. Credit requirements of farmers in the fall were the reason so many financial crises happened in that season. The famous British political economist, William Stanley Jevons, wrote about this in his 'The Autumnal Pressure in the Money Market' (1866). The financial historian, Margaret G. Myers, notes that the 'need of farmers for cash to pay off their farm hands and meet their other obligations at the end of summer created a tremendous demand for currency in the interior and a withdrawal of funds from New York.'[20] Rural banks withdrew deposits from the Wall Street money-center banks to support their agricultural depositors' demands for credit in the fall. The Street's money-center banks had to honor these withdrawals and, when pushed, would call in their loans from Wall Street brokers whose only recourse was to liquidate some of their holdings bought on margin whenever they could not meet the call loans out of ordinary turnover. A domino effect was thus created, vacuuming money out of Wall Street.

Through this complex mechanism, farmers on Main Street became more than bit players in Wall Street's drama. If the predictable scenario of seasonal transactions intersected with some other negative and unforeseen economic event – such as the effects of Jackson's bank policy in 1837 – a chain reaction was set off that led to a financial and economic implosion. The financial crisis of 1837, and eight more that followed through the Great Crash of 1929, derived from this pyramiding of credit. Reflecting on the 1837 Panic, George Templeton Strong evoked the house of cards analogy:

> Commerce and speculation here have been spreading of late like a card house, story after story and ramification after ramification till the building towered up to the sky and people rolled their eyes in amazement, but at last one corner gave way and every card that dropped brought down a dozen with it.[21]

THE TELEGRAPH

Alongside these Wall Street institutional innovations of the 1830s was the invention of the telegraph, which reshaped the technology of financial markets. Prior to the telegraph, the most rapid transmission of information was by private semaphoric service between Wall Street and Chestnut Street. Individuals were stationed on the tallest hills and buildings every six to eight miles between New York and Philadelphia. Using flags and telescopes, prices could be transmitted in 30 minutes across more than 100 miles.[22]

Samuel F.B. Morse, the telegraph's inventor, was an excellent portrait painter who turned his imagination to technology when he could not succeed as an artist. His most important commission was awarded to him by the city of New York, a full length portrait of the Marquis de Lafayette who in his advanced years made a triumphal 16-month trip to the United States in 1824. He preferred, however, the genre of history painting. His first effort, *The Old House of Representatives, 1822–23*, was largely ignored by the public during its tour to Boston and New York.[23] To hone his metier, he made a second extended stay abroad, in Paris (1829). His first was to London between 1811 and 1815 where he perfected his portraiture style, borrowing heavily from the British idiom. In Paris he practiced the craft of history painting, entering that city's great temple of art, the Louvre, as an experienced and accomplished painter and draftsman.

He had in mind a monumental painting that combined history and art. This revealed Morse the dreamer who in this painterly role tried to elevate American taste by reproducing the paintings of 38 old masters in one montage – da Vinci, Raphael, Titian, Rubens, Van Dyck, Caravaggio – which he called the *Gallery of the Louvre*.[24] In this picture, Morse stands in the center of the Salon Carré looking over the work of a student while in the left corner background his friend and American novelist, James Fenimore Cooper, chats with his wife and daughter. Morse selected paintings from the Louvre he valued rather than those actually hanging in the Salon Carré at that time. He selected those masterpieces he thought Americans needed to see, a 'totality of the history of western art, beginning with the classical sculpture of *Diana*,' one art historian muses, moving the viewer through more than three dozen other works, mostly paintings. In this he failed. While 'he intended his version of the Salon Carré to be an educational vehicle that would refine taste and spark cultural awareness in America,' according to a catalogue interpretation of his painting, 'the lack of public attention that the exhibition of this work received in the United States caused in Morse a lasting sense of disillusionment.' Toward the latter part of his life, and after he had invented the telegraph, he wrote to Cooper that 'painting has been a smiling mistress to many, but she has been a cruel jilt to me. I did not abandon her, she abandoned me.'[25]

Today Morse's reputation as an early American painter is growing and perhaps, as the telegraph gives way to a new form of electronic communication, he may be remembered as much for his work with canvas and brush as with dots and dashes. In the year 2000 the last American navy operator of the Morse code retired, thus ending the use of this great invention. His portrait of *The Marquis de Lafayette* hangs frequently in New York's City Council Chamber and his *Gallery of the Louvre* has an honored central place in the Musée Américain, located next to Claude Monet's house and garden in Giverny, France.[26] Underwritten by such grand Wall Street names as John Pintard, artists and writers like Morse and Cooper found a patronage that allowed them to devote their full attention to these crafts, not the infrequent stabs at cultural production to which their predecessors had been confined in the early republic.

Morse invented the telegraph in 1832, a few years after his return from painting in Paris, but could not interest investors in building a demonstration of its usefulness until 1842, when he constructed a line between Governor's Island and the Battery, adjoining Wall Street in lower Manhattan. Two years later he constructed the first overland telegraph line between Baltimore and Washington, and in the same year the Magnetic Telegraph Co. built a line between New York and Philadelphia. From the beginning Morse envisioned Wall Street as the principal user of the telegraph. When he could not raise capital in 1832, he set up an office on Wall Street and charged an admission fee of 25 cents for a demonstration of its potential to Wall Street investors.[27]

8. The Semaphore Alphabet

Charles Parker, a mute, invented what he called the 'Brachial Alphabet,' which he described as an 'original method of communicating thoughts, when distance precludes the possibility of using the voice, and which may be made available ... to the range of telescope.' (Library of Congress, Prints and Photographs Division.)

By the mid-1850s there were over 50 telegraph companies operating – Western Union was started in 1856 – and by the end of that decade Wall Street was connected by telegraph to every major city's financial district. Around the same time it became common for newspapers in big cities and small towns to report on Wall Street and list share prices.[28] On 16 August 1858 the first transatlantic telegraph transmission occurred between London and Washington, but a month later the cable snapped and was not restored permanently to full service until 1866.[29]

Morse did not affect American artistic taste to anything like the extent that his telegraph revolutionized communication and, specifically, American financial markets in two ways. First, it bound far-flung communities into a central securities market. Second, it compressed the time required to complete a transaction and extended the geographic space over which the transaction occurred. This was useful during normal times. But the combination of the telegraph and the tethering together of Main Street and Wall Street through call loans and bankers' balances made matters worse during financial panics.[30]

THE CLASH OF CLASSES

In the two decades between the financial panics of 1837 and 1857, Wall Street carved out a new role as a financial enabler for New York's first urban-planning experiments. The city moved northward along a street grid designed for traffic flows that simply overwhelmed each new transportation system dreamed up to cope with the unending traffic congestion. This plan had first been presented in 1811 to coincide with the Erie Canal which expanded the city's commerce beyond its previous borders. It bore a resemblance to that preference for a geometric ordering so cherished by the republicanism of the day – 'beauty, order, and convenience,' proclaimed the planning commissioners. As if to confront Pierre L'Enfant's circles and diagonals that informed Washington's urban form, New York's conveniently permitted a use of space that maximized square lots for real-estate development, easily identifiable by class and value through the plan's numbering system. Twelve avenues, each 100 feet wide paralleled the north–south trajectory of its river borders. Transecting at right angles every 200 feet were 56-foot wide streets that cut east–west across the avenues. At half-mile intervals these streets were widened to 100 feet.[31] North–south avenues were given names, the east–west cross streets, consecutive numbers.

This plan's execution gave New York its distinctive urban core and perfectly framed a later, vertical, rectangular skyscraper architectural form that became its signature in the twentieth century in order to maximize value within narrow rectangular lots. As with so many plans, however, the absence of diagonals made traffic more contentious, since to move anywhere other than directly north and south or east and west required moving at right angles. The real estate speculative requirement to make every square inch saleable foreclosed the option of service alleys that would have allayed the frustrating congestion caused by loading and unloading of merchandise, collecting trash and other normal functions of life in a big city. 'In Manhattan – a city of capital, not a capital city – considerations of efficiency and economy came first,' historians of New York have concluded with a decided tone of resignation.[32]

Beyond the north–south confines of the two river boundaries, the city's population expanded eastward and westward into suburbs that were supposed to capture the best of the urban and the rural rhythms of life. 'From the pleasure gardens to the blooming new gentry preserves,' effuse two historians of New York, 'from Vanderbilt's mansion to the rising village of Harlem, from one side of the harbor to the other, the sound of hammers and saws was everywhere as the rail and realty boom shifted into hyperdrive.'[33] To provide open green space in the midst of the crowded grey city, Central Park was conceived. As the city's splendor blossomed, however, so did its underside of the poor, of disease and urban squalor. A public-school movement was just one of the reform impulses that tried to cope with the obverse of New York's phenomenal commercial growth and personal prosperity.

Wall Street in the 1840s began to look closer to its environs and to take a keen interest in all these developments in the new metropolis. It became involved in the planning for the neighborhoods contiguous to its narrow streets, played an important role in the financing of the city's development, and was a focus of opposition from New York's working class that saw this wealthy elite encroaching on its culture and on its neighborhoods. A clash of classes and cultures symbolized the maturation of New York's urbanism in the middle of the nineteenth century.

A majority of the city's half-million residents in 1850 had come from elsewhere, either from outside the country – over 150,000 came from Germany in the one decade of the 1830s – or other parts of the United States. The suburbs added another 150,000 people to the metropolitan area, and a decade later the metropolitan area of New York became the first to exceed 1 million inhabitants. Over 100 daily and weekly newspapers – 78 million copies a year – and 54 monthlies with a half-million readership made New York the media capital of the nation.[34]

New York was a city of contrasting extremes: splendid opulence and forbidding shabbiness. Philip Hone left this entry in his diary on 29 January 1847:

Our good city of New York has already arrived at the state of society to be found in the large cities of Europe, overburdened with population, and where the two extremes of costly luxury in living ... are presented in daily and hourly contrast with squalid misery and hopeless destitution.[35]

In 1845 the top 1 per cent of wealth-holders in New York owned 40 per cent of all the wealth.[36] The poor in New York lived in wretched conditions, described in 1854 by the diarist George Templeton Strong in this way:

malarious aromata rampage invisible through every street, and in the second-rate regions of the city ... atmospheric poison and pungent factor and gaseous filth cry aloud and spare not, and the wayfaring man inhales at every breath a pair of lungs full of vaporized decomposing gutter mud and rottenness.[37]

Poor public health and the lack of civic cleanliness produced cholera epidemics that killed as many as 1 in 27 New Yorkers in 1855.[38] The energy from individualism, which produced the wealth that built the metropolis, was the same ideology that short-changed civic responsibility and public amenities.

An unlikely event, laden with symbolism, focused this tension. The two cities met in a bloody encounter at the 1849 Astor Place Riot over the content and style of theatrical performances. Such clashes, between an indigenous popular theater of 'low culture' and an elite 'high culture' imported from England, had led to earlier riots in 1831 at the Park Theatre and in 1834 at the Bowery Theatre. The 1849 skirmish was the bloodiest, however. The high culture of the elite had crept steadily northward until it bordered on the popular culture centered around Vauxhall Gardens, which Horace Greeley's New York *Tribune* characterized as a 'cheap rendezvous for infamy.'[39] One of the Gardens' favorites was the popular American actor, Edwin Forrest, who brought the political and the cultural together in a theater of democracy in which, as one critic put it, his characters are 'great roaring boys that cry like fat babies, and puff and blow like sledge men.'[40]

He took an intense dislike to the famous English actor, William Macready, during an 1845–6 tour in England where Macready was alleged to have incited British audiences to hiss and boo Forrest during his performances. When Macready came to New York in 1849 to appear in *Macbeth* at the Astor Place Opera House, Forrest was coincidentally appearing in the same role downtown at the Broadway Theatre. Cheek-by-jowl with Vauxhall Gardens was the new Astor Place Opera House, designed by the architect of a new Wall Street, Isaiah Rogers. The Wall Street tycoon, John Jacob Astor, had conceived of Astor Place as one of the first property development schemes to integrate luxury housing with high culture. His name, and the money that built it, spoke to a New York of wealth that was seeking cultural respectability of the sort only European and British theatrical manners could supply.

Led by a tabloid journalist, Ned Buntline (a pseudonym for Edward Z.C. Judson), the Vauxhallians were incited to give Macready a 'New York welcome' to avenge Forrest's reception in England. On 7 May 1849 Macready was greeted by more than just hisses and boos; rotten eggs, potatoes, pennies and chairs forced him off the stage. A published appeal in the newspaper by what Hone calls the 'highly respectable citizens' of the city persuaded Macready to return to the stage on 10 May, protected by a phalanx of 200 policemen who were supported by 300 standby militiamen. In the riot that ensued 22 people were killed, scores more injured and over 100 were arrested. Buntline was sentenced to a year in jail for his part in instigating the riot. Using the clothing of another actor in the play to disguise himself, Macready was smuggled out of New York in a carriage up to New Rochelle, then onto a train to Boston, from whence he sailed to England.[41]

Such lapses in decorum were not unusual in the 1840s and were not confined to the lower sorts. Hone tells of an incident between two top officials of the Manhattan Bank in 1840 in which a manager of the bank, Jonathan Thompson, had brought a charge of mismanagement against the bank's cashier, Robert White. On 18 March White and his brother, 'meeting ... Thompson in Wall Street, near the bank, ... attacked him with a club from behind, knocked him down, and bruised and wounded him considerably.'[42]

New Yorkers, who awoke in 1849 to read about the Astor Place Riot, were at the midpoint of a two-decade redesign of their city. The select among them had visited Europe or Great Britain and found in Paris, London and Vienna cities that were trying to cope with their growth and complexity by employing new forms of urban design. The more-than-doubling of New

9. Edwin Forrest as Macbeth
The popular American actor, Edwin Forrest, as Macbeth from Act IV, Scene 1.
(Library of Congress, Prints and Photographs Division.)

York's population between 1840 and 1860 was both a problem and an opportunity for Wall Street. It could plan the city's growth as it reached out to absorb new space, but the tensions caused by clashes between classes remained unattended and became inflamed by the city's relentless expansion into previously working-class districts.

PLANNING FOR THE NEW METROPOLIS

Expansion equated with planning for the new metropolis. Transportation was at the core of New York's initial attempt at urban design. The older, lower tip of Manhattan around Wall Street was in perpetual gridlock in the 1840s as merchandise was moved from the docks after being offloaded or carried by cart and dray to the docks to be loaded. Passengers remained stuck in horse-drawn coaches as they competed for the limited space on narrow streets, while merchandise that could reach its destination contributed to the congestion as it was unloaded in one of the two available traffic lanes. Public transport was in the form of horse-drawn omnibuses owned privately under city license. Some 22 companies were operating 683 omnibuses and carrying 100,000 passengers a day by 1853.[43]

As the city expanded northwards trees were cut down, hills leveled and a grid street pattern was imposed on what was once a varied and, at some places, rugged terrain. The new metropolis's planning challenged Manhattan's very name, which comes from the Algonquin, meaning 'hilly island.'[44] Straightening out nature was done to produce straight streets in order to speed up the horse-drawn traffic that could move with more comfort and speed on thoroughfares with easy grades.

Relief from the congestion was envisioned by combining horse-drawn omnibuses with the fixed-rail system coming into use with the railroads. The New York and Harlem Railroad had been financed by Wall Street interests in the 1830s to carry horse-drawn vehicles on rails, thus speeding up the journey and lowering costs because of the reduced horse power needed to move people over fixed rail. The fear of reduced property values on the streets used by the Harlem prompted petition drives by other Wall Street interests to try to stop its construction. Hone was one of those opponents because, as he wrote in 1833, it 'will be attended with inconvenience and danger, and affect most unfavorably the value of property in the streets through which it is to be carried ... .'[45] Once again a 'wall' was erected to separate Wall Street from outside incursions. This time it was the New York and Harlem that for nearly two decades was unable to penetrate the invisible border with a Wall Street consumed by the protection of its property values.

The Harlem Railroad originated north of Wall Street, starting at City Hall, up Broadway and Fourth Avenue to such northern residential communities as Yorktown. The profitability of this transport method encouraged others to seek licenses for construction of a line south of City Hall to Wall Street. To prevent this competition, the Harlem wanted to extend its line to Wall Street. Politics, payoffs and opposition from the existing omnibus operators – who were barred from running their vehicles on streets with fixed track – delayed implementation of this transport scheme to connect the Wall Street district to City Hall until 1851.

By 1857, 23 million passengers were paying a nickel a ride over the city's 23 miles of track.[46] London copied New York's system, and for the first time urban design was exported across the Atlantic from the United States. The lines laid for the surface rail system in New York established the general contours of the city's transport system until the subway trans-formed it at the turn of the century.[47]

Transportation was only the first infrastructure project addressed by the city. Its perpetual water-quality problems went back to the feud between Aaron Burr and Alexander Hamilton.[48] On 14 October 1842 the massive Croton Water System was completed at a cost of some $12 million. From the Egyptian-inspired architecture of the Croton Reservoir in Westchester County, 40 miles of aqueduct carried some 15 million gallons of water a day, through 180 miles of pipe, ending at what is today the New York Public Library.[49] It did not entirely end the cholera that continued to plague the city, however, but certainly contributed to the public health of the residents of New York and established the foundation for ridding the city of water-borne diseases.

Emboldened by the success of the Croton water project, New York visionaries moved to apply the same grand conception to the need for green space in the city. The result was the idea for Central Park, which remained a concept until the City Council established the Central Park Commission in 1857 and made it free from political meddling.[50] Under the brilliant direction of Frederick Law Olmsted and Calvert Vaux, Central Park became the standard for green respite from the grey tones of American cities.[51] The motivation for Central Park, however, was more than a public display of New York's urban maturity and a healthful antidote to the confined spaces of the older city. Property speculation was at the heart of the interests of wealthy New Yorkers, as well. Prominent Wall Street names such as Frederick and Rufus Prime were involved, and James Beekman, from an old Wall Street family, led the fight in the New York Senate.[52]

The oft-maligned, corrupt politics of city government under the control of Tammany Hall, thus, in two decades presided over the opening of the nation's largest water and sewerage system, redesigned the street and transport systems, created the institutional foundation for Central Park and built many smaller parks, rebuilt docks and markets, established a pro-fessional police force and expanded prison facilities, created a public school system, and opened up a debate on how to provide public social services for the city's underserved.

New York's second city of poverty and disease began to engage enough of New York's first city of wealth and comfort so that for the first time impulses for urban reform appeared. Erastus Benedict's and George Henry Evans's promotion of the suburbs was designed as much for an urban middle class that lived poorly in the city as it was for the transplanted country squire. Joseph McKeen, the County Superintendent of Education, spearheaded the public school movement to assimilate immigrant children so that 'we, as a nation, may stand a united and homogeneous people,' as well as to provide opportunities for the indigenous poor that 'would put an end to many unnatural and oppressive inequalities, in which some are raised to thrones of virtue, and others degraded to slavery without crime.'[53] Motives for social reform were mixed, however. Some joined because of fear of street crime. In 1857 George Templeton Strong commented on how so many of his friends were 'investing in revolvers and [they] carry them about at night, and if I expected to have to do a great deal of late street-walking off Broadway, I think I should make the like provision.'[54]

Women were prominent in the new social reform movements. Of the 14 benevolent societies organized by women, some were exclusively charitable but others were political and promoted women's rights in education and employment for the some 25,000 women who worked in manufacturing by 1860. Dr. Elizabeth Blackwell established a Dispensary for Poor Women and Children in New York in 1854. Women's temperance organizations were responding to the widespread availability of liquor in drinking houses that grew in number from nearly 4,000 in 1849 to close to 6,000 by 1852. Anne Lynch Botta, who taught English for a half-century at the Brooklyn Female Academy, hosted a weekly intellectual salon in her uptown home, serving 'the citizens of the kingdom of Mind instead of the kingdom of Mammon.'[55]

The New York city that served Mammon no doubt invited this comparison. From one perspective its new hotels and commercial estab-lishments inspired awe. From another angle of vision, with the poor behind a scrim shading the outlines of the great edifices going up on Broadway, one saw a different city. Among New York's 45 hotels was the Astor House with a new system of climate control, described in the hotel's 1853 promotional material as being 'heated in winter by warm air from below; and in the summer, jets of cold air will be blown into the room, moistened by the perpetual play of Croton fountains; and at all seasons the ventilation from the roof will keep the atmosphere fresh and pure.'[56]

New York clothiers copied London and Paris fashions, which the *Tribune* called a 'revolution in the price of fashionable clothing.' To sell the merchandise, emporia were built on Broadway that used grandeur to compete with each other. The largest was Alexander Stewart's Italian Renaissance, palazzo-like structure at 280 Broadway, which had two acres of floor space over its five floors, covered by a domed skylight, its 15 large glass windows supported by cast iron columns, sheathed in a pure white Tuckahoe marble, employing 300 people when it opened in 1846 to this description:

> The main entrance opens into a rotunda of oblong shape, extending the whole width of the building, and lighted by a dome seventy feet in circumference. The ceilings and sidewalls are painted in fresco, each panel representing some emblem of commerce.[57]

In a new form of merchandise display, Stewart placed the products on gleaming mahogany counters marked with a fixed price for the customer to pick up and buy from different 'departments,' leading to the characterization of these emporia as 'department stores.'[58]

EVANGELICALS CONFRONT MAMMON

Amidst this contrast between opulence and indigence, the peculiarly American evangelical movement acquired a new energy, which it used to replenish the city's soul that had gotten lost in its infatuation with commerce. Wall Street's Trinity Church, which had been razed in 1839 because of structural decay and rebuilt on the same site in 1849, typified the contradiction between wealth and piety. The tallest structure in the city until the late 1860s, the new Trinity was designed by Richard Upjohn, an émigré from England in 1829, and described by an architectural historian as the 'beginning of the mature Gothic Revival in the United States [with] furnishings and decorative details average by European standards, but remarkable for a country that was then an artistic backwater.'[59] The new Trinity found it difficult, however, to provide spiritual guidance for a prosperous membership that sought a rationalization for wealth but not a religious message that elevated its sights.

To fill the twin vacuums between wealth and faith, opulence and poverty, Charles Finney brought an evangelical message to the city to address the theological relationship between church and commerce. He had begun his mission in upstate New York among the workers on the Erie Canal and the surrounding communities, whose lives were disrupted by the incursion of the commercial market system into a settled way of mainly self-sufficient agricultural pursuits. In 1832 he converted the abandoned Chatham Street Theatre into the Second Free Presbyterian Church in the Chatham Street neighborhood near Wall Street, where he tried to work out the relationship between Christian virtue and commercial gain by using the 'power of the Church to regulate the commerce of the world.' With a seating capacity of 2,500 worshipers, he appealed to the growing middle class of white collar employees, craftsmen who were becoming employers, and a new group of manual workers – all caught between desire for opulence and fear of indigence. 'Only make it your invariable principle to do right and do business upon principle,' he preached, 'and you can control the market.'[60] For printed materials to accompany Finney's and other evangelicals' ministries, the American Tract Society, that had its origins in 1825, recruited over 1,000 distributors delivering 481,000 copies of the Bible and 6 million shorter tracts. To propagate more evangelicals, Finney initiated the New York Theological Seminary, which opened its doors in 1839, later renamed the Union Theological Seminary, one of the great centers of theological scholarship in the twentieth century.[61]

Another influential evangelical, Henry W. Bellows, Minister of Broadway's Church of the Divine Unity, spoke directly to the middle class – approximately 30 per cent of the quarter-million employed in New York in 1855 – about the connections among material progress, clean living and religion's teachings:

> The whole tendency of rude, ill-furnished, indigent homes, is to make or perpetuate within them rude, graceless, and reckless inhabitants. The increase of comfort, beauty, convenience, and grace in the homes of Christendom is directly productive of the order, self-respect, dignity, and decency which are first conditions of moral sensibility and spiritual life.[62]

Arthur and Lewis Tappan were the evangelicals who combined commerce and Christianity more effectively than any others. They founded the influential daily newspaper, the *Journal of Commerce*, and the first credit-rating agency that subsequently became Dun and Bradstreet. It was called the Mercantile Agency, and character – Christian character, to be specific – figured prominently in their credit assessments. From their credit-rating records words appear such as 'intemperate habits,' 'likes to drink too much,' 'leads a sporting life,' 'has been pretty wild but has recently married and will probably be more steady now.'[63] With the establishment of the American Bible and Tract Societies in New York, they and other evangelicals added another national center to the city's growing list.

The Tappans along with famous names in journalism and letters – Horace Greeley and William Lloyd Garrison – awoke at 5 a.m. to have a cold bath, 'followed by a breakfast of fruit, wheat pudding, tepid gruel, and cold water or milk,' along with a special fiber cracker invented by Sylvester Graham (the Graham cracker), who lectured on the relationship between diet and disease, healthy habits and the virtuous life. In what has become a Wall Street ritual of episodic health fads, the Tappans and other Wall Streeters finished their early morning regimen, went to work on The Street and returned for a 'midday vegetarian meal accompanied by wheat-meal bread and cold filtered rainwater, then returned again in the evening for exercise and a cold-water wash.' The regimen did not shelter either Graham or Tappan from the realities of Wall Street life, however. Graham experienced a nervous breakdown during the Panic of 1837 and lived out his life as a semi-invalid. No reservoir of devout belief protected Arthur Tappan from going bankrupt on 1 May 1837.[64]

The Tappans were no hypocrites when it came to applying their creed of religious responsibility to the condition of the poor. They were leaders in the Abolitionist movement, for example. Using the same technique of a massive distribution of printed material they had invented for their evangelical campaign, the Tappans printed over 1 million anti-slavery tracts in 1835 for the American Anti-Slavery Society. For their efforts, hooligans attacked and ravaged their Rose Street home, forcing the family to flee to Harlem.[65]

The evangelicals could claim prophecy when in 1857 a severe Panic overwhelmed Wall Street. The proximate cause was the collapse on 24 August of the Ohio Life and Trust Company, an Ohio-based company that financed western land sales but was overwhelmingly Wall Street owned. The problems with this bank in a remote state, however, revealed how Wall Street had become the pivot of a financial system, bound together through bankers' balances and call loans, with its news transmitted by telegraph to a Main Street audience that was reading about Wall Street in hometown newspapers. By 13 October nearly every bank in the country had to suspend payments of specie to depositors. A Wall Street broker and on-site observer wrote about the destruction of 'confidence everywhere' brought about by 'such an alarming shrinkage, attended by the suspension of specie payments and the sensationalization of the telegraph and the daily press.'[66]

Main Street and Wall Street were now part of the same financial edifice. Pennsylvania Avenue's withdrawal from banking supervision and financial policy 20 years earlier, after the collapse of the Second National Bank in 1837, turned a crisis into full-scale panic in 1857. 'The entire country was in stocks,' commented an eyewitness-broker. 'The farmer, the country lawyer, jobbers ... the whole foreign trade, were more or less holders of shares, bonds, county, city, or state paper.' He pointed out that these shares were used as collateral to expand bank loans to borrowers who 'based their business movements upon the belief that this property could always be converted into coin.'[67]

In the midst of the financial panic, Wall Street witnessed something it had never seen before: a spontaneous evangelical revival in the heart of Mammon. Characterized as 'one of the most unusual revivals in the history of religious awakening in America,' it started spontaneously in the heart of the financial district of New York, in an upper room in the old North Dakota Church on Fulton Street.[68] Less than a year later 20 daily prayer meetings were being conducted in lower Manhattan. The diarist George Templeton Strong added a secular reason to the revivalists' appeal when he talked about how citizens had surrendered trust 'in the solvency of our merchant princes.'[69]

Wall Street's soul-searching was brief, however. The Panic was over by the end of 1858. The Street returned to business as usual. This brief flirtation with an ethical query into the life of Mammon, nevertheless, left a marker on The Street's national imagery that has never disappeared. A permanent quandary became hard-wired onto America's psyche and attitudes toward Wall Street. Infatuated with the seductive allure of riches, Americans at the same time were troubled by the absence of soul that was another side of this new coin of the realm. Their following temporarily swelled during the Panic of 1857, the Evangelicals became part of a broader sentiment that was troubled by the country's drift toward what later came to be called 'the Age of the Robber Baron.'

5   Wall Street and the Civil War

The recovery from the 1857 Panic anticipated by Wall Street offered it a respite from the woes of that financial crisis, only to be confronted with far more serious events that would threaten the nation itself as a unified country. The political choice for The Street between union and secession was not apparent. Abraham Lincoln had received little support on Wall Street during the 1860 presidential campaign, 62 per cent having voted for other candidates.[1] His election aroused fears that the southern states would repudiate their northern debts and disturb the important banking and commercial relations between southern cotton producers and Manhattan, thereby damaging an essential segment of The Street's financial operations. These apprehensions were fanned by southern editorial opinion that began to call for a suspension of debt repayment and by laws introduced in several southern legislatures to postpone debt payments. As the sectional divisions between North and South widened and war became a possibility, Wall Street was torn between its loyalty to country and to commerce.

In the run-up to the Civil War, public opinion in New York was divided with many important media and financial potentates in favor of a splitting of the nation. Their motives varied. Some wanted to force the slavery issue on the South by declaring it unconstitutional, thereby forcing the slave states either to abide by the constitution or leave the Union. Others sought a peaceful separation as best for the North and its future prospects, wanting simply to be rid of a nagging political issue that would not go away no matter how clever the compromises brokered by politicians from the two sections. Horace Greeley, editor of the nation's largest newspaper, the New York *Tribune*, with a circulation of 300,000 and a readership estimated at 1 million, led the media effort to forge opinion in favor of a peaceful separation during the period between Lincoln's election and the start of the Civil War, a position from which he retreated once the war started. Although decidedly anti-slavery, Greeley wrote 'Let the act of secession be the echo of a popular fiat,' and his editorial viewpoint was seconded by the *New York Times*, the *Journal of Commerce* and a half dozen other newspapers in New York.[2]

The city's mercurial mayor, Fernando Wood, supported not only southern secession in the tense interval between winter 1860 and spring

1861 but secession for the city of New York as well. His proposal for an independent city-state arrangement for New York was backed by such prominent Wall Streeters as Gazaway Bugg Lamar, a native Georgian but longtime New York resident who had established the Bank of the Republic at Wall and Broadway in 1851, later tried to supply guns to the South, returned to Georgia in May of 1861, and became a financial adviser to Jefferson Davis's Confederate government.

Mayor Wood's projected new nation of 'Tri-Insula' took in Manhattan, Staten Island and Long Island. 'Why should not New York City,' he reasoned, 'instead of supporting by her contribution in revenues, two thirds of the expenses of the United States, become ... independent ... why may not New York disrupt the bonds which bind her to a corrupt and venal master,' referring to the government on Pennsylvania Avenue in the capital.[3]

A DIVIDED WALL STREET

Fernando Wood was the first in the lineage of larger-than-life New York mayors whose personality, style, vision and charisma projected him onto a larger national stage. First elected in 1854 on a reform platform for the Democratic Party, he came to power with the enthusiastic support of working-class New York, especially the growing importance of Irish voters in the districts surrounding lower Manhattan's Wall Street. His efforts at reform in the 1850s coupled with an ambitious public building plan became a prototype for other cities' similar projects and reflected the pressures of large new immigrant populations in the major urban centers whose size began to overtake the capacity of their older infrastructures. The 1857 Panic, which shook New York and sharpened class divisions, compelled Wood to stand by his distraught working-class supporters but cost him what elite backing he had. The event that signaled this was a 5,000-strong march under the chant of 'We Want Work' on the citadel of Wall Street power and its most imposing symbol, the Merchants' Exchange.[4] The ensuing damage to Wood's coalition of financial and working-class constituencies cost him the election in 1857, only for him to be re-elected two years later in 1859.

Wood's conclusion that New York would be better off as an independent city-state, separate from the United States, reflects the confluence of several forces. First, New York's political leadership had been unable to persuade the Republicans in Washington of the city's interest in compromising with the South. A bipartisan 30-member delegation of Democrats and Republicans from New York, armed with a petition signed by 40,000, traveled by train for Washington in January 1861 to meet with Republican members of Congress to plead for a change in policy that would not lead to the South's secession. This extraordinary effort followed on Wood's proposal to the Common Council that 'New York be, and from henceforth forever hereafter shall be and remain, a free city of itself,' thereby in the interpretation of a recent history of New York freeing the city 'from the meddling and plundering of upstate Puritans and ... federal-dictated tariffs.'[5] The petition was unsuccessful and soon thereafter the Republicans introduced into Congress the restrictive Morrill tariff that enraged the South and embittered Wall Street. Next, seasoned by his experience of defeat after the Panic of 1857, Wood feared the commercial consequences of a North–South escalated conflict – namely, the defection (from him) for a second time of Wall Street's financial community. Finally, Wood could afford to stake out a position that was not unreservedly pro-Union, because his political constituency did not include New York's powerful abolitionists in the city's media and social organizations who were solidly in the Republican camp. The division of opinion was punctuated by a petition organized on 18 January 1861, signed by 40,000 under the rubric of the 'Peace Society,' headed by Samuel F.B. Morse, that opposed any war between the North and the South.[6] All this came to a head in New York's first face-to-face meeting with the newly elected Lincoln in 1861.

On his way to Washington for the inaugural, Lincoln stopped in New York where his reception was polite but chilly. At a meeting with the Common Council, Mayor Wood said to Lincoln, 'We fear that if the Union dies, the present supremacy of New York may perish with it,' in an appeal to Lincoln to back down from his strong anti-slavery posture. To which Lincoln replied, in defiance of this pressure, that he would never consciously assent to the 'destruction of this Union, in which not only the great city of New York, but the whole country has acquired greatness.'[7] As Lincoln left New York on the final leg of his journey to Washington for the March 1861 inauguration, Wall Streeters were genuinely perplexed about whether to accept a two-nation resolution to the endless regional friction that deadlocked the country, or throw their lot in with Lincoln in favor of a United States even at the cost of war, with emphasis on that key word, 'united.'

The enthusiastic response of ordinary New Yorkers to the 2 April 1861 firing on Fort Sumter resolved Wall Street's dilemma. New York responded with such an immediate display of pro-Union sentiment that any latent southern sympathies or support for a negotiated secession were drowned in the swell of patriotic enthusiasm. Flags and bunting appeared sponta-neously on buildings and in shop windows. Whether The Street joined in because of genuine belief or because it did not want to be seen as out of step with the city's popular sentiment cannot be conclusively determined. What is known is that the New York Stock and Exchange Board (NYS&EB) raised the flag over its rostrum and on 17 April 1861 passed this resolution:

> We, the members of the New York Stock Exchange, impressed with a deep sense of the duty, which should animate every heart, of sustaining the Government of the United States in the support of the Constitution and laws, desire, in this period of public exigency, to give encourage-ment to the Government by pledging our fidelity to the Union, and our resolute determination to stand by it under all circumstances ...[8]

This was followed a month later with a resolution that 'forbade its members under pain of expulsion, to deal in securities of any seceding state, issued subsequent to its rebellion.'

The mayor, like any good politician without very strong principles, changed his position and became an eager war supporter, at least for public consumption. George Templeton Strong, the Wall Street lawyer and diarist, was not taken in, however. On 15 April 1861 he recorded this note about Fernando Wood: 'The cunning scoundrel sees which way the cat is jumping and puts himself right on the record in a vague general way, giving the least possible offence to his allies of the Southern Democracy.'[9]

The South had been counting on support from New York, which was a center for such Copperheads – northerners with southern sympathies – as the esteemed Wall Street lawyer and founder of the Century Club, Giulian Verplank, who never abandoned his pro-southern and pro-secession positions. From the South came this defiant message, from the Richmond *Dispatch* which warned that, 'New York will be remembered with special hatred by the South for all time,' reflecting its sense of betrayal by New York's and Wall Street's unanticipated display of pro-Union sentiment.[10]

Wall Street's fears that debts would be abrogated and financial links severed were realized after its loyalties became unambiguous. One southern debtor wrote to his northern creditor: 'I cannot return the goods, as you demand, for they are already sold and the money invested in muskets to shoot you-Yankees.' And another wrote: 'I shall pay, of course, every farthing I owe you, in cash, but not till I pay it in the currency of the Southern Confederacy.'[11] Not all southern debtors behaved this way; some southern bankers and merchants faced their own conflicting loyalties to country and commerce with the same juggling act practiced by their northern counterparts. Remittances from New Orleans, for example – the South's preeminent mercantile city – continued to flow northward for some time after the start of the Civil War.[12] Speaking for many populists with disdain for both northern and southern *haut financier* ambivalence, Zachariah Taylor of Michigan noted wryly, 'from the days of Carthage ... the great mercantile centres have been peaceable – ever ready to buy immunity but not to fight for it.'[13]

In the spring of 1861 few on The Street or elsewhere in the Union imagined there would be a long war. One decisive battle and the superior northern forces would triumph, they thought. The vexing problem of secession would then be done with, though no one in the North knew what would come next. The mood in New York among the merchants on Broadway and the brokers on Wall Street, however, was cheerful. The war brought enough new economic activity to compensate for the losses from the drop in southern business. Reflecting New York's buoyant spirit of patriotism and anticipated profit, a fledgling department store magnate took out a newspaper ad that read:

Tremendous Excitement: The Irrepressible Conflict: ... R.H. Macy relies upon ENORMOUS REDUCTION from the usual prices as the GENTLE PERSUADER which will ... carry peace and happiness to EVERY HEARTH-STONE, and LIFT THE CLOUD OF GLOOM which has hung like a pall over the EMPIRE CITY.[14]

Uniforms needed for soldiering as the war dragged on benefited New York's textile industry. Brooks Brothers received orders for 12,000 uniforms at the outset of the war in 1861 and A.T. Stewart's annual receipts from war business amounted to $2 million during the course of the war.[15]

Euphoria turned to shock as a stunned Wall Street, along with the rest of the Union, read with disbelief about a defeat and humiliation of the Union army at the first Battle of Manassas (Bull Run) on 21 July 1861. A sober realism set in about the war as well as uncertainty about its leader, the self-taught mid-western lawyer, Abraham Lincoln, who was often found wanting and never quite persuaded Wall Street that he had the style or capacity to govern. After a meeting with Lincoln about the Sanitary Commission – which George Templeton Strong, Frederick Law Olmsted and others had formed to care for the health of soldiers – Strong wrote:

He is lank and hard-featured, among the ugliest white men I have seen. Decidedly plebeian. ... He seems to me clear-headed and sound-hearted, though his laugh is the laugh of a yahoo, with a wrinkling of the nose that suggests affinity with the tapir and other pachyderms; and his grammar is weak.

Three years later, after another meeting when Strong had changed his position somewhat on Lincoln and become an ardent anti-slavery campaigner, he credited Lincoln with a 'sagacious policy' that forged a fragile consensus on the issue but could not resist saying in the same diary note that 'I do wish [he] told fewer dirty stories.'[16]

Cycles of Union and Confederate alignments in New York coincided with the cycle of fortunes of the two sides in the war. The nadir of Union fortunes occurred in the summer of 1863 with General Robert E. Lee's deepest incursion into the North. In the six months leading up to this, violent class abrasions shook Wall Street and the city. On 1 January 1863 Lincoln issued his Emancipation Proclamation which freed all slaves in the southern secessionist states. It was greeted with euphoria among New York's abolitionists and with alarm among nascent Copperheads, many of them found among Wall Street's habitués who feared what this would mean for a post-war return to business as usual. The coincidence of the Emancipation Proclamation and Lee's steady advance up the Shenandoah Valley – his defeat of Union forces at Winchester, Virginia and his symbolically and militarily important crossing of the Potomac River which separated North and South – brought the repressed conflict in New York to the surface.

The immediate spark that kindled class conflict was the draft and the ensuing riots that took place between 13 and 16 July 1863 which stretched from Wall Street all the way up Broadway to 50th street. Most grating to the lower stratum of New York's Irish and other laborers was the provision of the draft that allowed individuals to purchase a substitute for $300. Among those of draft eligible age who bought their exemption from the war were such financial personages as Jay Cooke (the Union's chief war financier), James Fisk (whom we will meet in the next chapter), John D. Rockefeller, Andrew Carnegie and the most illustrious of all, J. Pierpont Morgan, for whom the $300 was a fraction of his profits earned from underwriting an arms deal that backfired on the purchasers (or even of his 1863 cigar bill).[17] The greatest incident of civil disorder in the nation's history, the draft riots led to confirmed deaths of only 119, though at the time as many as 1,000 were presumed killed. Scores more were injured:

178 soldiers and 128 civilians. Six thousand troops were diverted from the war with the Confederates and brought into the city to quell the riots. Brooks Brothers was sacked and the swell of rioters would have marched a few blocks south to Wall Street had not The Street been the most fortified in the city, with guns passed out to employees, tanks of sulfuric acid readied, cannon put into position, and a gunboat stationed at the end of Wall Street.[18]

Targeted for the protestors' fury was the majestic sub-treasury building at Wall and Nassau Streets, its Greek Parthenon-inspired, 32-foot-high porticos, each five-and-a-half feet in diameter, standing there as if a fortress arrayed against the populist passions of the less fortunate who were targeted to fight in a war whose casualties were mounting by the day. The rioters, however, trained their anger as much on New York's black population whom they saw as the beneficiaries of emancipation – even though this was not overtly the case – and the proximate cause of their

10. Civil War Draft Riots

'Rioters Sacking Brownstone Houses' is the title on this 25 July 1863 image of New York's working-class whites retaliating against the city's wealthy who avoided the Civil War draft by purchasing their exemption. Note the mulatto-looking woman on lower left, apparently fleeing, who prominently is the lone individual not part of the tumultuous riot scene. (From the *New York Illustrated News*, 26 July 1863, Library of Congress, Prints and Photographs Division.)

being drafted. This moved Benjamin Strong to lament the 'unspeakable infamy of nigger persecution,' as he saw them as the most 'peaceable, sober, and inoffensive of our poor, and the outrages they have suffered during this last week are less excusable ... than ... the Jew-Hunting of the Middle Ages.' In despair he sarcastically concluded: 'This is a nice town to call itself a centre of civilization.'[19]

The proximate source of the confrontation was twofold. The draft was imposed on the poor because the rich were permitted to purchase an exemption. Second, the Emancipation Proclamation exposed the dual loyalties of the city's, and especially Wall Street's elites. On 3 June 1863 Fernando Wood joined the opponents of the draft by presiding over a massive Peace Convention at Cooper Union, where James Gordon Bennett's New York *Herald* proclaimed the war a rich man's battle that would lead to large displacement of southern blacks to the North, thereby playing both on the fears of New York's working class and aligning the Democrats with emerging populist political tendencies in the city. The events of 1863 split Wall Street's elites as well. On 6 February 1863 the eminent Wall Street financier, August Belmont (Rothschild's New York representative), and Samuel F.B. Morse, among others, launched the Society for the Diffusion of Political Knowledge at a dinner in the posh Delmonico restaurant just off Wall Street, which produced tracts opposing the war and emancipation, many of which found a friendly outlet in the New York *World*. To counter such Copperhead sentiment, leaders of the Sanitary Commission, Frederick Law Olmsted and George Templeton Strong, labeled the Belmont–Morse crowd as 'vulgar parvenus' in order to assuage potentially wavering Europeans that the war was not 'waged by the rabble of the North, or by politicians, but that the intelligent, cultured, gentlemanly caste sustain it.'[20]

All this points to a grid of divisions as between Copperheads and supporters of the war among the city's financial community, and between them as a class and the middle and lower classes, who did not want to be exposed to a draft to which only they were subject, particularly at a time when the North's fighting ability seemed most uncertain.

COUNTRY VERSUS PROFITS

Faced with the reality of a longer war, the Lincoln administration was forced to confront the problem of the war's financing in a country that had never sorted out its post-Jackson confusion over national banking policy. There was essentially no system for national government debt financing or issuance of national currency in 1861. Banking and currency had become exclusively a state prerogative after the demise of the Second National Bank. The absence of a unified national banking system in 1861 afforded the Treasury limited access to the Union's financial resources that were needed to prosecute the war. Paper currency was the province of state banks whose bank notes, backed by deposits, circulated so long as soundness and security could be sustained. The Federal government was strapped by the Independent Treasury Act, which had severed the Treasury from the private banking system by requiring it to sequester tax receipts in sub-treasury vaults until withdrawals were authorized to pay government bills.[21] To address these deficiencies, the union government, led by Treasury Secretary, Salmon B. Chase, constructed a set of ambitious statutes adopted by the U.S. Congress between 1861 and 1865, with consequences for the nation's financial architecture that extended beyond the war's end.

Wall Street – the Union's great potential financial arsenal – was, however, a reluctant participant in Chase's war-financing measures. It had long favored a new national bank but was troubled by the large debt accompanying war-financing. The Street's ambivalence about the war project itself was, therefore, punctuated by its long-standing aversion to national debt. Combining its reservations about the war and its aversion to national debt, a diffident Wall Street confronted this financial challenge with an absence of its usual assurance and determination, and with none of the clear focus and commitment to a concentrated objective that it had shown, say, for the Erie Canal. This was one factor that removed The Street from the pivot of wartime financing. Another was its own greed.

Apprehensions about Wall Street's fidelity on Pennsylvania Avenue were fueled by revelations of profiteering on The Street at the expense of the Union treasury and the army's fighting capability. A prominent example involved the Morgan banking house. J. Pierpont Morgan, 25-year-old son of Junius Spencer Morgan, headed the New York office for his father's London-based operations. In one of the more egregious instances of profiteering at the expense of fighting efficiency, he provided a $20,000 loan to arms broker Simon Stevens to buy 5,000 obsolete carbines for $11.50 each from another arms dealer, Arthur M. Eastman. Eastman had previously bought them from the government for $3.50. Stevens, the beneficiary of Morgan's loan, turned around and sold them back to the government – to Major General John C. Fremont, commander of Union forces in Missouri – for $22 each. This pyramiding of a profit chain was magnified by Stevens's claim that he had repaired the rifles. This was false. Many of the carbines failed to fire or blew up in a soldier's hands when triggered. In another example, the clothing that Brooks Brothers and others made was often 'shoddy,' using remnants of seconds, shards that were glued together and fell apart in the rain or boots whose 'soles, made of pine chips pasted over with thin leather, dropped off after a half-hour's hike.'[22]

As the war progressed, the public grew suspicious, as well, of the inside information Wall Streeters acquired about developments on the military front and how that information was used by The Street to profit on currency, stock and bond movements. A Wall Street investor in securities at that time described how the 'earliest information could be obtained from the front, not only from the Union, but from the Rebel army ... often before it was known to the Government [by] giving those at the front who gathered and transmitted the information a certain interest in stocks.'[23] J.P. Morgan, for example, installed the first private telegraph wire in his office toward the end of the war and received information directly from Grant's telegraph operator.[24]

WARTIME FINANCIAL MEASURES

Initiated by the brilliant Treasury Secretary, Salmon B. Chase, three acts of Congress produced not only wartime financing that yielded a strategic advantage for the Union but also set the foundations for a post-Civil War new American economy: the Legal Tender Act (1862), National Banking Act (1863–4), and the Tax on State Bank Notes (1865). This triad of new financial laws enabled the national government to finance the war by the creation of a national currency and the elimination of state bank notes, the establishment of a national banking system, and the coupling of Treasury financing with the private banking system. Chase's efforts, which bound the Union together financially and established national financial machinery for the next half-century, prepared the nation for its expansive industrialization in the post-Civil War period.

Chase was an imposing presence in the management of war finances – a large, handsome man described as ceremonious in his dealings with other people and imperturbable in his negotiations with potential creditors.[25] In the summer of 1861 his immediate problem was raising some money for the start-up of the war. Rejecting taxation for political reasons, the administration decided to borrow $250 million by selling bonds.

Chase sought the advice from Wall Street's financial markets about the best way to raise this money. George T. Lyman, manager of the New York Clearing House for Wall Street banks, wrote to him on 21 June 1861 with a blueprint he largely followed. Lyman advised Chase not to borrow from foreign governments and instead to borrow broadly from individual Americans, whom Lyman claimed were prepared to support the Union. 'Let ... the government debt be distributed among them in small amounts,' he urged, 'they will show the world that a government dependent upon the people may be as strong and as rich in resources as it is free.'[26] The ever-present, loquacious James Hamilton, who apparently never abandoned his role as unsolicited financial adviser to the Treasury, weighed in with a 4,000-word memo to Chase on 19 November 1862, which he ended with a p.s. that read: 'If I can ever be of service, you can command me without hesitation.' Chase politely responded in 60 words, noting that he would 'benefit much by your knowledge and judgment,' but pleaded for relief from Hamilton's request for a meeting by appealing to the urgency of the business of financing the Union's war: 'It would do me good to have you here to talk and advise with me, but I cannot hope for that advantage now, and would not trespass on your kindness by asking for it.'[27]

On 17 July 1861 President Lincoln signed Congressional legislation authorizing the Treasury to borrow $250 million on what became the first tranche on several authorizations. To permit the Treasury to re-circulate these funds through the private banking system, the Independent Treasury Act was suspended by Congress in early August. Chase, however, bypassed Wall Street when he had to market the bonds because of continuing Copperhead sentiment on The Street, high commissions demanded by brokers and bankers, and the less-than-enthusiastic reception Chase had received during his initial negotiations with Wall Street representatives.

He turned, instead, to a relatively young and unknown Philadelphia banker, Jay Cooke, who had only recently opened his own banking firm. With his brother Henry Cooke working out of Washington, this team created the first mass sale of war bonds. They sold bonds in small denominations everywhere: in churches, on the battlefield, in factories and offices. Together with Chase they came up with the idea of pricing the 1861 bonds at 'seven-thirty' – a slogan that clearly identified the 'product.' This referred to the bonds' interest rate of 7.30 per cent in denominations running as low as $50. The interest rate of 7.30 per cent conveniently came to earnings of two cents a day over a year on a $100 bond. Moreover, interest was payable in gold specie and higher than rates paid on major benchmark railroad bonds that were running between 5 and 6 per cent at the time.[28]

This effort foreshadowed the mass marketing and brand identification that was to become a trademark American commercial invention later in the century. By using advertising and brand identification and by circumventing the middleman – the broker – the Cookes established a marketing template later used to sell branded biscuits, or soap, or breakfast cereal directly to a consumer who asked for a particular brand instead of buying from the generic barrels in which these products were displayed in the typical American general store.[29] Following Lyman's advice as executed by the Cookes, this method of direct sales departed from the convention of selling initially to brokers who then re-sold the securities or held them. This system focused on marketing and the brokering role became more one of distributor than intermediary. Wall Street, of course, was not pleased with the circumvention of their brokering role, felt threatened by the Cookes's innovation and fought back.

THE COOKES OF PHILADELPHIA

Jay Cooke's long-flowing, silken, and graying trademark beard emphasized his tall angular frame. He was both a financial journalist and a banker, starting at the age of 19 with a daily column called 'Money Markets' in the Philadelphia *Daily Chronicle*. Acquainted with the potential of journalism as a medium of persuasion, Cooke launched his marketing campaign on 5 September 1861 with a lavish press effort that included advertising (in German as well as English), editorials, newspaper articles and broadsides, one of which said: 'The United States Government, to which we owe our prosperity as a nation ... calls on each individual to rally to its support – *not* with donations or gifts ... BUT WITH SUBSCRIPTIONS TO HER LOANS.'[30] His was the most extensive public relations campaign organized to market financial products in the nation's history. He hired a publicist, Sam Wilkeson, an editor of Horace Greeley's New York *Tribune*, and the advertising firm of Shattuck, Peaslee and Co.[31] On 2 November 1861, he proudly announced at a press conference that 1,000 out of 1,500 employees in the transportation department of the Philadelphia and Reading Railroad had subscribed to the war bonds, using another innovative marketing device of Cooke's: weekly payroll deductions in which the convenience of buying bonds was made all the more appealing by having payment for them directly deducted from payroll checks.[32] This device cleverly locked in the bond sale and did not have to rely on individuals remembering or wanting to pay each time a portion was due. For the individual it was a small, regular deduction from take-home pay that was not as painful as more and larger periodic payments would have been.

    The success of Chase's and Cooke's initial war-financing effort was not matched on the battlefield, however. By the close of 1861 the Union's battlefield failures forced the Lincoln administration to raise and pay for a larger army and buy the arms, uniforms and medicine associated with a broader and longer war. The absence of a national currency and Treasury's reliance on state bank notes had limited the Union government's ability to control the rate of expansion of the money supply and, therefore, restricted its borrowing capacity. The only way round this was to create a national currency.

Congress adopted Chase's legislative proposal to establish a national currency by passing the Legal Tender Act on 25 February 1862. It provided for the issuance of $150 million in a new national currency that came to be called 'greenbacks.' They were authorized as legal tender for all transactions with two exceptions, both payable in gold: interest on federal debt – including interest accruing from Cooke's bond sales – and import duties. The greenbacks, however, were not redeemable in gold. With this law the Union government no longer paid its bills in gold but in greenbacks that it and Congress created by fiat. This initial February 1862 authorization was the first of four installments on a new national money supply that a year later stood at nearly $450 million.[33]

No fiat money system works without the confidence and support of its users. The test of its effectiveness lies first in whether it is accepted by the public and second, in this period, the price of its competitor: gold. This was understood at the time as evidenced by this contemporaneous statement from a Wall Street broker: 'The government must pledge its credit to the people, to raise money to sustain [the] army. The money must be in the form of *promises to pay*, for hard currency was not to be had, the faith of the government must be pledged upon the face of it, and it must have the chief attribute of gold, viz: the power of extinguishing debts ... legal tender.'[34]

As currency accepted by the populace, the Union's greenbacks fared reasonably well. National paper currency was accepted throughout the Union. The government found suppliers willing to accept them in payment for war *matériel* and services. The price of gold, however, which was traded against greenbacks, was not stable. It fluctuated with the Union's fortune on the battlefield. The Treasury's Chase used Cooke to perform the stabilizing functions of a central bank because President Jackson had removed this capacity from Pennsylvania Avenue several decades earlier. Cooke intervened in the gold markets in an effort to stabilize its price against greenbacks. Speculative attacks against greenbacks from Wall Street were singularly cited as evidence of The Street's competing interests by supporters of Cooke's surrogate central bank functions. 'The mere mention of his name,' noted an observer, 'terrorized gold hoarders [and] disloyal speculators ... on government bonds in Wall Street.'[35] Such efforts could not overcome market realities, however. On the eve of the battle of Gettysburg in summer 1863, for example, as General Robert E. Lee launched his invasion of the North and succeeded with his deepest penetration, a greenback dollar fell to its lowest level: the equivalent of 35 cents in gold.[36]

The circulation of greenbacks through the financial system demonstrated the usefulness of a national currency for financing national government projects. The Union government first paid for its personnel, services, soldiers and products in paper currency and then this money entered the banking system. Individuals used some of the currency to buy Chase's and Cooke's war bonds, thereby creating a revolving door through which currency circulated. With the ability to calibrate the growth of the supply of money, the Treasury had a larger financial reservoir from which it could draw borrowed funds.

The 1862 Legal Tender Act was accompanied by another authorization for bond sales, this time dubbed '5-20s' to refer to their maturity of 20 years and redeemable after five years. Owing to Wall Street's qualified support for the flotation and Cooke's favored position with the Treasury, he was made sole subscription agent for the sale. Fresh from his success with the 7-30s, Cooke expanded and perfected his operation. He took out ads in newspapers around the country in both English and German, repeating his earlier successful ad campaign. Postmasters were importuned to put a circular in postal boxes; Edward Sackett in Chicago obliged by placing Cooke's material in 4,000 letter boxes. At the peak of activity, he employed 2,500 sales agents to roam the Union. Clergy were asked to advise their parishioners to subscribe. Offices remained open at night to accommodate those who were employed during the day. Not one to pass up any human interest angle on the marketing of the bonds, Cooke circulated this testimonial from an Irish woman who asked to see Cooke as she was disposing of her life's savings of $1,200 to buy bonds: 'All that I am worth I acquired here. I had not a cent when I came to this country. ... I take this much [in bonds] for Old Abe and the country.'[37] Never before had financial products been mass marketed this way in the United States or any other country.

Cooke employed traveling agents to sell bonds to soldiers in the field, used show cards, postcards, pamphlets and broadsides, kept offices open at night to reach factory employees, farmers and small tradesmen. County offices were paid a fee to allow Cooke access to taxpayer rolls for direct solicitation. From an army sergeant in the field a letter to Cooke explained that a 'number of men in the Company to which I belong ... have requested me to write to you in relation to subscriptions to the new ... U.S. loan.' He asked Cooke whether it would be possible for him to hold purchases from the soldiers in an account until the war was over, or if they were killed, to pass them on to a designated beneficiary. 'By so doing,' he continued, 'you will confer a great favor upon some poor soldiers ... who would lay by a few dollars instead of gambling it away as they have done.' Cooke wrote back that he would be 'happy to undertake the safe keeping.'[38] He even had his agents follow Union troops on their forays into southern towns to sell war bonds to the defeated citizens of the Confederacy. One journalist wrote that 'Mr. Cooke expects the way to Richmond to be opened shortly and he is ready to offer the inhabitants who remain a better investment for their money than Confederate bonds.'[39]

By the end of 1863, Cooke estimated that he had more than a half-million individual purchasers, and in a letter to Chase described them as 'of all classes – high and low, rich and poor, white and black ... and of all nations and tongues, trades, occupations, and professions.'[40] His agents sent back reports to him about crop conditions, public attitudes on the war and other information he used to refine his marketing strategy. This yielded the first national compilation – a crude survey – of the nation's views and attitudes. Never one to pass up press coverage, he invited journalists from small newspapers outside Philadelphia to visit his flagship store in that city. In the rural newspaper, *American*, from the city of Media, Pennsylvania he received this typical report:

> At nine o'clock ... the people were as thick as bees in a molasses hogshead. They had come to gather honey as well as deposit sweets in Uncle Sam's honeycomb. Bonds! Bonds! Bonds! ... All day long that line of citizen soldiery ... marched up single file to do the nation service.[41]

Cooke sold a half-billion dollars of bonds in total and established the feasibility of mass marketing of securities for Wall Street to imitate after the war.

WALL STREET FIGHTS BACK

Wall Streeters, left behind by Cooke's mass-marketing innovations, were quick to ridicule the public buyers of Cooke's bonds on the Main Streets of the Union. 'Country players,' they were labeled, cheerful but untutored in Cooke's 'guile,' they had a belief that was 'child-like and sublime,' says the Wall Street player and writer, William Fowler. 'They make money at the start,' he solemnly warns, 'but in the end they almost invariably lose.'[42] In novels, around this time, Main Street's bond buyers were depicted differently, depending on whether seen through the narrative voice of The Street's broker or Main Street's investor. Through Wall Street's prism, Main Street investors are described as country bumpkins, 'uncomfortably stuffed into a business suit with starched shirt, high collar, and cravat.'[43] Through Main Street's angle of vision, frequently the 'country bumpkin' is depicted as more clever than the Wall Street sharpy.

In one such treatment the 'country bumpkin' turns the tables and outsmarts Wall Street, a nod to a popular audience for penny novels. In *The Man from the West*, the Wall Street firm of Flam & Whipple await Henry Armitage from Galveston, Texas whose father has died. He carries with him a letter of credit for $121,000 from Texas's Clark & Weaver who managed Armitage's father's accounts. Much of the accumulated wealth in the Armitage family derived from Cooke's Civil War bonds in the story. The scene is set for Armitage's arrival. 'Messrs. Flam & Whipple present an appearance of affluent leisure,' to the Main Street visitor, 'that would seem to indicate that business, to be profitable, does not need to be conducted with strenuous exertion, and that wrestling with finance does not imply the sweat of labor or the strain of knotted muscle.' A code known only to Armitage and Flam & Whipple, 'From Chaparral to Wall Street,' is offered by the Texan, and he requests a $20,000 advance on the letter of credit to set up his residence in New York, with which Flam & Whipple comply with great flourish: 'Certainly. The funds in deposit with us are now at your disposal.' No sooner does he leave than another Armitage appears reciting the same code, also possessing what appears to be the same authenticated letter of credit. And there the story takes off.[44]

This literary treatment appeals to a popular reading audience that wants to know more about Wall Street – the novel is replete with abundant financial subplots – while at the same time letting it be known that not all cleverness and misdirection is monopolized by The Street. Main Street's two Mr. Armitages have plenty of guile too.

By circumventing Wall Street brokers, Cooke's direct sales to bond buyers such as Armitage was a threat to their livelihood. The Street countered with the sort of attacks on both Cooke and his Main Street customers that continues their earlier efforts to couple themselves with the common man on Main Street. Obviously opportunistic, it also revealed a Wall Street ambivalence toward Main Street that wanted Main Street's business but was not averse to elitist ridicule when the role of broker/

middleman was challenged by Cooke's model of mass marketing and direct purchase of a branded financial product, innovations Wall Street appropriated after the Civil War with its accustomed gusto.

With success, therefore, came attacks on Cooke both from the North and the South. From the South came this jibe from the Richmond, Virginia *Examiner* that called Cooke an 'eccentric financier [trying] to sustain [an] explosive and inflated paper system. ... Nothing more than an immense money job, it enriched the commercial centres of the North and by artificial stimulation preserved such cities as New York from decay.' Setting aside this hyperbole, the newspaper realized that these 'efforts of the Yankees ... has [sic] so far been marked by great ingenuity, resolution and success' and the war itself would turn on the North's greater financial resources. 'Whether they will succeed in conquering the South,' wrote the *Examiner*, 'depends in a great degree upon their continued success in upholding this paper system.'[45]

Wall Street realized it had made a mistake and squandered a lucrative opportunity when its bankers and brokers had demanded high fees to compensate for what they thought would be a difficult product to sell. In an effort to correct their mistake, newspaper commentary such as this from the New York *World* sought to discredit Cooke: 'What may be the motive of Messrs. Jay Cooke and Company in ostentatiously parading the name of their house in connection with a "great national loan",' the editors asked, and accused Cooke of exacting higher commissions than New York bankers would have charged – precisely the opposite of what had actually happened. They concluded their May 1863 editorial with the warning that these high commissions 'will be a matter for inquiry at another time.'[46] Responding some years later in his memoir, Cooke reflected on how 'New York, whilst containing many patriotic citizens ... was undeniably the centre and very hotbed of Southern sentiment and scheming ... a great place of rendevous of the secret emissaries of the South and disloyal politicians,' all adding up, he thought, to the 'centre of speculation in gold.'[47]

Once Wall Street understood what it had lost by approaching Chase initially with high commissions and a business-as-usual strategy for marketing the Treasury's war bonds, it regrouped and embarked on its own war with Cooke. The Street never took Chase's idea seriously in the beginning – even though he had been advised by The Street's own George T. Lyman – in coupling war financing with expanding the popular support for the Civil War by engaging the citizenry directly through 'ownership' in the Union's war. Eventually attacks from Wall Street worried Chase, however, and he began to distance himself a little from Jay and Henry

Cooke. Cooke's repeated use of reports from his agents were now dismissed as sentimental testimonials and not as persuasive as they once were. This 18 April 1865 account, therefore, did not have the influence on Chase it once had: 'Farmers who live in a little cabin,' reports Cooke's agent from Vermont, Illinois – a Mr. Tug – 'wear their home-spun clothes and ride to church and town in their two-horse wagons without springs [and] have in many instances several thousand dollars loaned to the government.'[48]

UNIFYING THE NATION'S FINANCES

Two additional Treasury-sponsored Congressional actions specifically supported The Street's interests as against the Cookes' and completed the centralization of Union financial policy: the National Bank Act (1863–4) and the tax on state bank notes (1865). The National Bank Act was a concession to Wall Street by Chase, who was under pressure from The Street to jettison Cooke. The 1863 statute, as amended a year later, enshrined in law the practice of using Wall Street banks as depositories for other banks around the country. It granted exclusive rights to Wall Street banks to offer interest on these bankers' balances, thereby confirming The Street's role as the nation's money center. This reinforced the immediate post-Jackson organic development of Wall Street banks as the core money center for the country that arose when Pennsylvania Avenue defaulted on its functions as central bank and regulatory entity.[49]

The National Bank Act provided for nationally chartered banks for the first time in the nation's history. Unlike earlier national bank laws of 1792 and 1817, which established one national bank, this measure provided for an unlimited number of federally chartered national banks so long as the applicants met chartering criteria. To weaken further the power of state banks, the Congress in 1865 imposed a 10 per cent federal tax on the value of new state bank notes that were issued. This effectively erased the hodgepodge of state bank notes and left the federal greenbacks standing alone as the nation's currency.

The National Bank Act went beyond a simple chartering mechanism: its requirements for chartering expanded Union influence and policy. First, to obtain a federal charter applicants had to assent to hold public securities – state and federal bonds – as assets against liabilities. To qualify initially for a charter, the applicant was required to purchase federal bonds and deposit them as collateral with the Treasury. This conveniently created a market for Treasury bonds. To this was added a provision that these newly chartered national banks could not engage in mortgage lending, a measure that was designed to remove this area of speculative banking that had led to earlier financial crises. This had the effect of increasing the quantity of public bonds in these banks' portfolios at the expense of land mortgages. It brought Wall Street back into the game by centering new financing on the more traditional brokering role and sidestepping to some extent Cooke's mass marketing and direct sale methodology.

Secondly, the legislation codified and strengthened the system of bankers' balances that had been evolving throughout the century. A hierarchy of banks was established, beginning with small rural banks, then ascending to larger city banks, and finally to the apex of the pyramid: Wall Street banks. In each strata banks were assigned reserve requirements, idle funds that had to be sequestered against deposits. These reserves could be deposited in the next higher segment. The large metropolitan banks – called reserve city banks – were required to hold 25 per cent in reserve; half of this amount could be deposited in New York and earn interest. The capacity of New York banks to pay interest on reserves was an exclusive grant of authority to them, not permissible by any other bank in the chain of reserve deposits and, consequently, made them the equivalent of a money-center banking system, a grant of immense financial power and influence. The effect of this arrangement was to make Wall Street the money center for the Union, consolidate financial policy on Pennsylvania Avenue and link more closely Main Street to Wall Street.[50] It confirmed the reality that Wall Street was, in fact, the Union's money center.

By the end of the war there were some 700 new nationally chartered banks; many were converted state banks. State bank notes disappeared virtually overnight after the 1865 tax. The combined effects in the financial system of all the Chase-inspired laws was not unlike the war's meaning for the nation. From references to *these* United States before the war, the country typically called itself *the* United States after the war and subtly altered the inflection to suggest unity by conventionally placing emphasis on 'united' instead of 'these.' Scattered state bank-driven financial policies before 1861 largely vanished and were replaced by a unified national financial policy. Other path-breaking reform measures passed in 1863 by the wartime 37th Congress were to have far-reaching impacts and are now considered some of the most creative legislative enactments in the nation's history: the Morrill land grand act that created the system of state universities; the Homestead Act that spread land ownership across income classes and fostered the development of the west and the country's interior; and finally the National Bankruptcy Act that facilitated national industrial development by eliminating the diversity of state bankruptcy laws and rendering uniform, and therefore predictable, bankruptcy procedures wherever the default occurred.[51]

Wall Street – notwithstanding its ambivalence toward the War – benefited handsomely from the consolidation of government financial policy. It effectively became the nation's central bank after the 1863 National Bank Act granted it unique access to other banks' reserves. Until the Federal Reserve was established just prior to World War I, Wall Street could dictate financial terms to the nation as it set interest rates and controlled liquidity. The financial power and influence of both Pennsylvania Avenue and Wall Street were elevated in the aftermath of a war that centralized the formation of economic policy on Pennsylvania Avenue and its execution on a Wall Street that was fed through the banking system by Main Street depositors. The resilience of Wall Street was once again revealed. At the outset an outsider to the Cookes of Philadelphia in war financing, it emerged from this marginality after the firing on Fort Sumter in 1861 stronger than ever as the fulcrum of a newly unified United States financial edifice.

This experience of Wall Street during the Civil War revealed another of its traits that has sustained it: its ability to adapt to changing circumstances and its willingness to abandon temporary ideological positions in pursuit of a larger interest in financial hegemony. Beset by internal divisions and a reluctant supporter of secession and the Union, challenged by Philadelphia once again – this time by the Cookes – it nevertheless exited from the war ready to consolidate its grasp on the nation's finances in the great era of industrialization that marked the last quarter of the century. The Street survived a challenge to its financial supremacy, largely of its own making, as it would others down to the present, owing to its malleability and pragmatic pursuit of a single objective: to prevail over adversaries contesting its site as the financial center of the country.

6   Wars, Other than Civil

The Civil War was not the only war to occupy Wall Street in the ante- and post-bellum periods. New commodities such as gold and railroads reached a sufficient stage of maturity and their share values became battlefields. The tactics employed by one side or the other – corners, stock watering, buying political favor – bore a similarity to the evolution of tactical moves on the real fields of battle in Gettysburg, Petersburg and Vicksburg in that each developed a new strategic sophistication after one skirmish or another. Stocks and bonds on The Street were the spoils of battle around which speculative bubbles grew and burst, engulfing the high and the mighty: war hero and President, Ulysses S. Grant, that quintessential Knickerbocker – Manhattanites who descended from original Dutch settlers of New Amsterdam – 'Commodore' Cornelius Vanderbilt, and a duo of two outsiders, the carny-raised, country deacon, Daniel Drew and the Gilbert and Sullivan character who held two fictitious military honors, 'Admiral' and 'Colonel' Jim Fisk. All of these performers in this drama effectively employed both raw power and misdirection in pursuit of their objectives. No one was more adroit at the straightforward application of power than the popular Commodore Vanderbilt whose name created the illusion of great lineage but belied his illiteracy and impoverished origins on his father's Staten Island farm.[1] His adversary was the equally crafty, Daniel Drew – the Deacon – whose *métier* was misdirection.

Daniel Drew, master builder of the antebellum Erie Railroad and still its treasurer was an old man when the Civil War ended. Raised on a hard-scrabble, Putnam County New York farm, he grew up with the young republic and sought out the entrepreneurial opportunities at its margins. Drew left home at 13 to work with a circus, enlisted in the War of 1812, then drove cattle to market in Manhattan from upstate New York farms, and in 1834 began to operate steamships from the New York harbor, as did his future and perennial rival, Commodore Vanderbilt.[2] Subsequently drawn to Wall Street, where a shrewd young man without formal education or important family background might make money as a broker, he found it useful to maintain his rural mannerisms and attire that was studiously old and tattered, evoking more a disheveled look than that of an overdressed Wall Street dandy. An active Methodist, founder of the

Drew Theological Seminary in Madison, New Jersey – which later became Drew University – he affected a bland, good-natured humility that caused him to be mistaken for a country deacon and disarmed his Wall Street competitors until, that is, they experienced his ruthlessness in business.[3] An 1870 characterization of Drew by James Medberry, who wrote about the individuals that shaped Wall Street in this period, emphasizes the apparent contradiction between religiosity and speculation. Drew, he said, 'singularly lacking in popularity ... never hesitates to sacrifice his friends ... if the necessities of speculation require it. ... The foible is more salient on account of the genuine piety of the man ... [because] all who have heard him speak at Methodist Conferences are struck by the fine religious fervor and earnestness of his demeanor.'[4]

Half carny, half evangelical and fully devoted to acquiring one of America's new fortunes, the lanky, pinch-faced and untidy Drew was well-equipped to do battle with one of America's established fortunes in the person of the handsome and still physically powerful Cornelius Vanderbilt. As Drew's rival for dominance in steamships, 'The Commodore,' as he was known, had made his money and taken his honorary title from merchant steamships. He turned his attention to railways when the 1849 discovery of gold in California made a connecting rail line across Nicaragua necessary to link the Atlantic and Pacific for his steamships. During the Civil War Vanderbilt acquired a controlling position in the city's Harlem and Hudson Railroad and began to assemble feeder lines into Manhattan from upstate New York. These short lines, north of Manhattan to Albany and west to Lake Erie, generally followed a route alongside the Erie Canal and, when connected, formed Vanderbilt's New York Central Railroad, connecting Manhattan to Buffalo.

A line that connected the port of New York to the lucrative shipping lanes from the mid-west was the great prize that rivaled the route of commerce on the highly profitable Erie Canal with the Mississippi River as its spine and feeder canals off it at a terminus. This allowed the collections of smaller shipments into larger freight cars on rail lines that could achieve greater economies of scale and speed than the Erie's flatboat canal barges. Vanderbilt's New York Central challenged the previous monopoly that the earlier Erie Railroad had constructed a decade earlier in pursuit of the same bounty.

At the end of the Civil War the Erie Railroad was the nation's largest. Started in 1833, by 1842 the Erie completed a route that ran from the Great Lakes south, then east across the southern counties of New York that border Pennsylvania and into a Jersey City terminus across the Hudson

River from Manhattan. By 1868 its 773 miles of broad-gauge track used 371 locomotives, and the railroad employed some 15,000 people to carry 2 million passengers and more than 3 million tons of freight each year.[5] With broad-gauge tracks set six feet apart that were built uniformly for the rail line, the Erie enjoyed a competitive advantage, because it could accommodate larger freight cars than the narrower gauge New York Central that had been cobbled together from eleven small separately built and owned railroad companies.[6] While Drew, the Erie's treasurer, knew little about the actual construction and management of a railroad, his financial instincts elevated him to a position that placed him in charge of a central part of the nation's new industrial power. Now in his advanced years, he found that, just as for the nation itself, there was to be no rest, no time for self-congratulation after the Civil War.

The two aging protagonists, Drew and Vanderbilt, each with their own railroad and competing for the same freight and passenger traffic, could not have been more different in demeanor. According to William Fowler, the 1870s Wall Street writer and speculator, Vanderbilt 'graduated as a commodore of the commercial marine, a rank to which he was raised by the spontaneous voices of his countrymen, and a title as worthily earned as if won upon the gun-deck.' He is always presented as an 'imposing figure ... tall and broad-shouldered ... handsome face and florid complexion. All his life he carried himself erect,' continues Fowler and his 'immense physical strength stayed with him long into old age' when he confronted his ultimate adversary, the melodramatically drawn heavy, Daniel Drew, who had an 'odd, grotesque face, with an air of self-communion, brooding over it, and a pinched look, from the corrugated forehead, down the rectangular jaw. ... All the lines of his bewhiskered cadaverous face and long, lanky body were downward lines.'[7] In one of the first histories of Wall Street (1905), the author claims Drew and Vanderbilt were 'master makers of Wall Street history ... Drawn together by a common desire for gain and mutual recognition of brains ... alike in their capacity for management and finance, and for their disregard, when expedient, of every consideration but the single object in sight.'[8]

RAILROAD WARS

Wall Street's fracas for control of the new industrial nation centered on its most visible symbol, the railroad. As early as 1850, 38 railroad securities were regularly traded on Wall Street, accounting for half of all securities by the middle of that decade. This remarkable transforming invention freed travel on land from the constraint of either human or horse power for the first time in history and removed the movement of freight from the sole province of water-based forms of transportation. It increased the speed of movement on land from a maximum of about 10 miles per hour to 20–30 miles per hour and, since it no longer depended on an animal for mobility, allowed that speed to be generally maintained over longer stretches of geography with fewer stops for regeneration.[9] More than simply a means of transport, railroads excited the imagination not only of financial dreamers but also of poets, such as Ralph Waldo Emerson who saw them as a 'work of art which agitates and drives mad the whole people; as music, sculpture, and picture have done on their great days respectively.'[10]

An initial feint and parry took place during the Civil War when Vanderbilt acquired approval from New York's Common Council to extend the Harlem and Hudson Rail Line to the edge of Wall Street. This lucrative prize had been tied up in a multitude of false starts. While fixed-rail trains began to crisscross upper Manhattan, they stopped short of lower Manhattan's warren of old and narrow streets, still serviced only by horse-drawn conveyances, because of the fear of explosions from steam engines in the densely populated tinder box that was lower Manhattan. The Harlem and Hudson was one such line that was poised to venture into this territory from its terminus and depot at Twenty-Sixth Street and Fourth Avenue. In what became the first of several clashes with Vanderbilt, Drew sought to profit from Vanderbilt's contract by simultaneously driving down the price of Harlem and Hudson share values while executing short sale contracts on the stock exchange. One of Drew's moves was to connect Erie to New York's questionable politics, by appointing William M. ('Boss') Tweed and Peter B. Sweeny to Erie's Board of Directors. The Tammany Democratic party political machine, controlled by Sweeny and Tweed, would ensure Erie's clear sailing in the Manhattan courts and Common Council, Drew thought, and immunize Erie from a counterattack by Vanderbilt.

The Council's approval of Vanderbilt's extension in 1863 increased the road's stock value, but behind the scene Drew was preparing a classic short position in which he agreed to sell Harlem shares in the future in antici-pation of a fall in Harlem's share values. In this financial transaction, Drew, the short seller, contracted to sell Harlem and Hudson stock he did not actually own at a specified price in the future. If the market price at the time he had to fulfill this contract was lower than his contract price, he stood to make a profit. For example, if the actual market price at the time of contract expiration was five dollars below the contract price, Drew simply entered the market, bought at the lower price, and sold at the agreed-upon higher price. For every short seller there is a long buyer who bets on the price being higher at contract expiration. If the price increased, the long buyer could purchase from Drew below current market value, turn around, and sell it at the market value above the purchase price. Drew would then lose if he had to buy dear and sell cheap. Vanderbilt was the long buyer to Drew's short position, accumulating Harlem stock by agreeing to pay a specified price at future delivery of the stock. With Council approval of his petition, Vanderbilt stood to profit handsomely if the price of Harlem shares increased. Any outsider would also anticipate a rise in Harlem's share values because of the exlusive grant to Vanderbilt of a highly profitable rail line in lower Manhattan. Added to all this were the impeccable credentials of the wealthy and powerful 'Commodore.' Consequently, there was no lack of long buyers to the highly leveraged short sales that Drew was putting together, but neither Vanderbilt nor the fellow travelers in this speculative venture reckoned with the cunning of the less-than-cultured Daniel Drew.

To ensure the success of this counterintuitive short gamble, Drew purchased votes in the Common Council by opening brokered short accounts for enough of the Council members to orchestrate an annulling of their previous approval of Vanderbilt's application. The subsequent fall in Harlem's stock price, after the Council's reversal of its previous approval for the Harlem's extension, appeared to signal a victory for Drew and his co-conspirators on the Council. Drew and the Council's short sellers stood to profit as the price fell below the future contract price and Vanderbilt, the principal long buyer, would lose as would his fellow long-buy investors. Not easily defeated, however, Vanderbilt used his vast wealth to buy up all of Harlem's stock and execute a complete corner in which he could dictate the price that the short sellers were required to pay to purchase the stock in order to fulfill their sales contracts. Trapped, unable to escape Vanderbilt's corner and standing to lose $1.7 million, Drew was forced to negotiate a $1 million settlement with Vanderbilt in which he paid him this amount in return for Vanderbilt's canceling his long contracts with Drew.[11]

Round one for Vanderbilt, as these two financial combatants mirrored the fortunes of those two great Civil War generals, Robert E. Lee and U.S. Grant, with Lee winning the initial battles of that war only to succumb later to Grant. Vanderbilt's Knickerbocker stature and profile in Manhattan, with a name that conjured images of a Dutch lineage from New Amsterdam – not to mention his war chest of wealth from shipping – enabled him to corner the market for Harlem and Hudson securities, leaving the defeated and disreputable Daniel Drew in tatters, the con man who took his style from the carnival huckster. This lesson was not to be lost on Drew, and the next time these two met in battle he had designed a new tactic to thwart Vanderbilt's use of wealth to execute a complete corner and defeat him.

ROUND TWO

As with many new ventures into profitable territory that require a large reservoir of capital to build the foundation for some economic activity, railroads rapidly became overbuilt with too much capacity for the commerce that was available to travel over them. Part of this conundrum derives from the very nature of the undertaking. With such large amounts of front-loaded capital expenditures, investors want to see a return. Typically, such returns do not materialize immediately, and it is only after very long periods of time that the aggregate rewards justify the investment. This is especially true of transportation ventures, from the first long-distance sailing ships to the most recent Channel Tunnel connecting Great Britain to the continent of Europe. They have in common an imbalance between long-term rewards for relatively large initial capital investments and short-term impatience of investors who want to see a quick return on their outlay.

Added to this is the character of new products such as railroads. Once they had achieved their maturity after the Civil War as a commodity to which capital was drawn, the railroads exposed an imperfection in the market's ability to value properly a large, fixed-cost venture for a new product whose long-term profitability had not yet established an experiential history. When a new product emerges and attracts vast investor interest, there is a tendency to overbuild and overinvest because its profitability throughout an extended period has by definition not yet been authenticated. The first investment tranche is, typically, lucrative, but further down the queue subsequent investments become less so. Markets do not have a clear path to arrive at the 'true' value of such new items until a shake-out period settles them into a form of stasis in which overshooting and undershooting have run their course. This usually means a period in which a speculative bubble attracts not only those on Wall Street to speculation but small investors on Main Street as well. The burst of the bubble yields an undervaluation for a time until some equilibrium is established that more closely aligns with the value of this commodity's stock value. Such endemic patterns with new inventions and new commodities are as old as the Tulip mania of the seventeenth century and as recent as the dot.com bubble at the turn of the twentieth.[12]

One way to work out the problem of overbuilding and excess capacity is through collusion, and this was Vanderbilt's ploy. In 1867 he tried to construct a market-sharing and price-fixing arrangement among the three great eastern railroads – the Erie, New York Central, and Pennsylvania – the latter a competitor for the same business that traversed the Appalachians directly east from the Ohio River to the port of Philadelphia. Pennsylvania Railroad agreed to Vanderbilt's scheme, but he was rebuffed by the Erie Board, led by his old foe and principal Erie shareholder, Daniel Drew. In retaliation Vanderbilt mounted a bid to purchase a controlling position in Erie, a tactical move reminiscent of his successful earlier ploy against his once-again enraged rival. For a second time Drew was pitted against Vanderbilt, but this time he acquired two younger associates in his corner, Jay Gould (31) and James Fisk (32), who were every bit as clever and ruthless as Drew. Both were members of the Erie Board. Like Drew, they were more interested in the financial opportunities Erie offered through stock manipulation than in running a railroad. In fairness to Vanderbilt, on the other hand, he was a latecomer to financial battles, less tutored in the art of stock manipulation than his adversaries, and more interested in railroad management – albeit with a decided predilection toward monopoly pricing practices. His strength derived more from wealth and prestige in contrast to his adversaries' street fighting tactics.

The Erie presented an immense financial challenge even to someone of such vast wealth as Vanderbilt. Its 250,000 outstanding shares had a market value of $17.5 million when Vanderbilt began buying Erie securities on 2 March 1868.[13] He reckoned he needed around $10 million of Erie securities to attain a controlling interest, appoint a new Board, and get on with his scheme to regulate price and market share with the Pennsylvania Railroad. He failed, however, to anticipate Drew's counterattack that stretched the limits of even Vanderbilt's efforts to do what he had done with the Harlem and Hudson: simply buy enough of what he wanted to control.

Drawing on the lessons of the Harlem and Hudson humiliation, Drew counterattacked by authorizing the Erie Board to issue additional shares of stock, thereby making it more expensive for Vanderbilt to buy a controlling position in the Erie. He did this under an obscure New York state statute Drew himself had earlier crafted that permitted a railroad company to issue new stock in exchange for the purchase or lease of another railroad. To oblige the law, Drew bought the worthless Buffalo, Bradford & Pittsburgh Railroad solely for the purpose of 'watering' Erie's stock, a tactic that originates here, and compensated himself and his allies against Vanderbilt with a goodly portion of the new shares in the inflated Erie stock portfolio. The Erie directors issued $2 million in bonds which were bought for $250,000.[14] This had two effects. First, Vanderbilt had to buy more shares to gain his controlling interest. Second, Vanderbilt's buying profited Drew and his allies who were in control of the Erie. Because of Vanderbilt's purchases, share value in Erie initially rose in the market, more than compensating for the increased supply of Erie securities as outside speculators on Wall and Main Streets joined in the advancing values of Erie's shares. But this could only be sustained for a short time until the market valuations once again caught up with what were truer values in an industry of excess capacity and excessive supply of securities in the Erie Railroad. Here is a contestable market as old as securities issued by joint stock companies: a race between objective values and psychologically driven speculations. In this instance it was Drew who was in control of the moves. He was in a better position to engineer the decline in share values, because he held the steering levers through stock watering and a controlling position in the stock's market value.

Wall Street lore attributes this scheme of stock watering to Drew's experience at a younger age as a cattle drover. He would bring the cattle to Manhattan, stay at the Bull's Head Tavern cattle yards at Twenty-Fourth Street and Third Avenue, and feed his stock enormous quantities of salt. On the next day just before sale, he took his cattle to water where they proceeded to fatten themselves on the fluid just prior to sale. The plump cattle's stock, inflated by the water, went up in value but fell just as quickly after the water coursed through the animal's body. Now with Erie stock, Drew was doing the same to Vanderbilt. He issued another 100,000 shares of Erie stock that represented 40 per cent of the total Erie stock outstanding at the time of Vanderbilt's takeover bid.[15]

Vanderbilt countered Drew's stratagem with a new steering mechanism, the judicial system, by seeking an injunction against Drew's issuance of new Erie stock from Judge George C. Barnard in Manhattan. His title of 'Supreme Court' judge was a peculiarity of New York's legal system in which 33 separate Supreme Court judges, sitting in a like number of different jurisdictions, each had equal status in equity action, could issue writs overturning those of others and rule on matters outside their jurisdiction. Even the title was misleading, because the Supreme Court was at the lower end of the judiciary, not the highest in the state. This prototypical court official of the nineteenth century profited personally from the rhythms of Wall Street's markets, offering himself for sale to both sides of the street at prices influenced by market valuations of the cases before him. At his death, after a career in which he served the political interests of the Democratic party political machine's Tammany Hall, Vanderbilt and later Gould and Fisk, Judge Barnard was found to possess that staple of New York corruption: a tin box containing nearly a million dollars in cash and securities.[16]

Barnard's injunction was ignored by the Erie group, which quickly proceeded to have Barnard's writ nullified in the Supreme Court of Judge Ransom Balcom in Cortland, New York. It was a poorly kept secret at that time that judges took payments for their rulings. The British *Fraser's Magazine* commented that in 'New York there is a custom among litigants … of retaining a judge as well as a lawyer.'[17] And retain lawyers and judges they did: Erie's bills were reported to be $150,000 in its legal contest with Vanderbilt, touted by the contemporary Fowler as a 'carnival for the legal fraternity.'[18]

Barnard forced the issue with Vanderbilt's encouragement by issuing an arrest order for contempt against Drew, Gould and Fisk. Although his injunction had been countermanded in Cortland by Balcom, the police were under Barnard's control in Manhattan and moved against the Erie group. The Erie party learned of their impending arrest while dining at Delmonico's, contemplating the specialties of a favorite French brasserie of the Wall Street crowd, perhaps while dining à la française on *Perdrix roti avec Truffles* and *Pommes de terre a la Lyonnaise*.[19] They executed their pre-arranged escape plan and slipped across the river to Jersey City. There they established themselves at the Hotel Taylor close to the Erie's depot. To guard against abduction into Barnard's jurisdiction, they fortified their position with Jersey City police, Erie railway police, three 12-pound cannon and a flotilla of four naval vessels under the command of 'Admiral' Fisk.[20] This titanic struggle was not about running trains or building an industrial structure. It was about stock manipulation, financial stratagem and a test of wills. Wall Street's financial culture had always been drawn to such theatrical flourishes, but now the stakes were higher.

The battlefront shifted next from the courts to the New York and New Jersey state legislatures. In New Jersey, the state legislature was importuned to make Erie a New Jersey corporation so that Erie and its directors would be removed from the reach of New York law. This completed – perhaps too quickly by the New Jersey legislature, because as the New York *Herald* reported the legislators 'are in despair at finding that by the hasty passage of the bill … they have unconsciously deprived themselves of … a promising and profitable contest … [to be] waged in Albany' – the Erie group then had their friends in the New York legislature introduce a bill which legitimated *ex post* everything the Board had done and forbad the consolidation of Erie and the New York Central on anti-monopoly grounds.[21] The ever-cynical New York *Herald* reported that this bill 'comes as a godsend to the hungry legislators and lobbymen, who have had up to this time such a beggarly session that their board bills and whiskey bills are all in arrears.'[22] As the buyers of votes converged on the state capital with suitcases full of money, the price of votes began to look more like the stock exchange where demand and supply determines the price, in this case the price of a vote.

Vanderbilt defeated the bill in New York's lower house on 27 March 1868. From his exile in New Jersey Drew's compatriot, James Gould, traveled to Albany knowing full well that arrest awaited him unless he could purchase his freedom. He sought approval of the bill in the New York Senate, thus countering its defeat in the legislature's lower house. Gould paid an exorbitant half-million-dollar bail set by Judge Barnard and installed himself one floor below the Vanderbilt team, in Parlor 57 of the Delavan House in Albany. There he brashly displayed his suitcase full of cash as legislators passed through his suite where the liquor was as available as the cash.[23] The Senate passed the Erie bill as some Senators saw their wealth increase by as much as $20,000.[24] The financial maneuvers were at a stalemate, with one legislative branch – the lower house – voting for Vanderbilt and the other, the Senate, for Erie, each having blocked the other's feints and parries.

The deadlock was broken by the two elderly combatants, Vanderbilt and Drew, now in their seventies, each drawn from a different social stock but equally fatigued by their interminable financial wars. Restless in his Jersey City exile, Drew began to make secret visits to Manhattan where he was observed by private detectives hired by Gould and Fisk – his erstwhile but now suspicious allies – meeting with Vanderbilt. All three saw in Drew a character flaw. Fowler writing in 1870 said that Vanderbilt knew Drew had no 'backbone and would be inclined to compromise;' Gould and Fisk understood the 'workings of his timid and vacillating nature.'[25] The two old rivals came up with an agreement to end the Erie war, which by this time produced a stalemate of litigious claims, counter-claims, legal judgements, injunctions, writs, escalating legals costs as well as costs of buying legislative support, all enveloped in a stalemated legislative thrust involving two state legislatures. The deal provided that Erie pay Vanderbilt $4.75 million for his 100,000 Erie shares. In return, Drew would drop all claims against Erie; he would resign from the Erie Board and pay Erie $540,000 to settle all claims against him that arose from his stock-watering scheme; and Judge Barnard would settle all the legal injunctions against Erie Directors at ten dollars each.[26]

Gould and Fisk were furious about the deal, but Drew controlled the Erie Board. Other parties found their value diminished. In the state legislature, Charles Francis Adams wrote shortly afterward, 'a rumor ran through Albany as of some great public disaster, spreading panic and terror,' because, as the New York *Herald* reported, 'prices came down ... Those who had been demanding $5,000 were now willing to take anything not less than $100' for a vote that was now no longer needed.[27] The market had broken on legislative votes as it had broken on Erie share values on Wall Street. Like so many outside players on Wall Street, many of New York's legislators had failed to time their moves and so missed the market's turning point. Those who sold their votes at the right moment profited from the estimated $700,000 doled out by Vanderbilt and Gould.[28]

To those who sustained a vision of the republic as virtuous and decorous, the antics of everyone associated with the Erie war were offensive. No one reflected the general repugnance better than Charles Francis Adams, Jr. who left an impressive account of the episode in his seminal early writings that spanned 1868 and 1869. Adams lamented:

no portion of our system was left untested, and no portion showed itself to be sound. The stock exchange revealed itself as a haunt of gamblers and a den of thieves. The halls of legislation were transformed into a mart in which the price of votes was higgled over, and laws, made to order, were bought or sold.[29]

For Daniel Drew, it was his last hurrah. Unable to overcome the financial losses from his Erie defeat, he filed for bankruptcy on 14 March 1876 and died five years later. From a fortune worth $13 million, Drew was left with a gold watch and chain, a sealskin coat, other clothing valued at $100, a rare bible valued at $530, outstanding asset claims against others of nearly $700,000, against liabilities of over $1 million.[30] Loaded with debt from the aftermath of the stock-watering scheme and subsequent engagement with Vanderbilt, Erie paid a stock dividend in 1873 but did not pay another until 1942.[31] The more financially solid Vanderbilt died on 4 January 1877 at age 83, six years after completing his monumental Grand Central Station and leaving a fortune of $100 million and the country's greatest railroad empire up to that time to his family heirs. Upholding the tradition of peculiar behavior by wealthy Wall Streeters in their advanced age,

Vanderbilt became enamored with spiritualists who helped him communicate with the dead Fisk and Drew, both having pre-deceased Vanderbilt.[32]

THE GOLD WAR

With Vanderbilt and Drew removed from financial interests in the Erie, effective control reverted to Jay Gould and Jim Fisk. One year after the Erie war and armed with Erie's arsenal of capital, Gould set out on the most ambitious financial scheme that Wall Street had yet witnessed: a corner of the gold market. Fisk was a sometimes ally in this project when it suited Gould. To make it work Gould's audacious plan had to reach as high as the White House itself and to the North's Civil War military hero, now President U.S. Grant.

Ulysses S. Grant was elected President in 1868 as a hard-money candidate who advocated paying off the Civil War debt of more than 2 billion dollars in war bonds. He promised to redeem for gold the $450 million of greenbacks outstanding as quickly as possible, in order to return to the gold standard in which specie would replace fiat currency.[33] In 1869, when Gould began accumulating gold for his corner, the gold stock in the country was worth around $100 million, of which 80 per cent was held in government vaults and 20 per cent circulated in the economy. True to his campaign pledge, President Grant had his Treasury Secretary, George S. Boutwell, buy up paper currency by selling about 1 million dollars of gold a week in the early months of his administration. With this policy emanating from the Treasury building on Pennsylvania Avenue, Gould had little chance for a successful gold corner on Wall Street without the complicity of Grant and Boutwell, because the large gold sales increased the supply of this commodity and should, therefore, lower its price, making gold an unattractive investment. Gould, however, did not see it this way.

Fisk and Gould were a study in contrast, the one theatrical and impulsive, the other meticulous and studious. Fisk was described by a contemporary as 'large and portly of person, boisterous and boastful of manner, loud voiced, red-faced and jovial ... reddish-yellow hair parted just west of center, to flare at the temples into curls ... generous moustache ... waxed at the end to dangerous keenness.'[34] He joined Van Amberg's Mammoth Circus and Menagerie at the age of 15, became a traveling salesman for his father in New England where he painted their five wagons with circus themes, then was a jobber for Boston's Jordan, Marsh & Company. During the Civil War Fisk became wealthy by buying contraband cotton from the South and selling it to Jordan, Marsh, which used the smuggled cotton to make blue army uniforms under contract to the Union government.[35]

Resembling a circus barker teasing a crowd to pay to see what's behind the tent, Fisk's auburn hair, large waxed moustache, fancy suits, and cherry-sized diamond in his shirt were deliberately designed to attract a throng of gullible customers. Inheritor of Drew's legacy of the country bumpkin fooling the sophisticates, Fisk lacked but one attribute of Drew: an evangelical zeal. George Templeton Strong, while repulsed by Fisk's flamboyance, was nevertheless aware of a 'certain magnetism of geniality that attracted to him people who were not particular about the decency of their associates.'[36]

The more calculating and less theatrical Gould was described as 'slight of stature, quiet, cool, adroit, and uninfluenced by passion.' Drawn from the same rural stock as his compatriots Fisk and Drew – the son of a poor farmer from Delaware County in New York – Gould was, however, very different in temperament. Adjectives used to describe him are 'slight, consumptive, dark, secretive, and scheming,' rather than 'flamboyant' and 'theatrical' in the case of Fisk, or 'messianic' in reference to Drew.[37] Gould's initial career as surveyor and cartographer, long an excellent entrée into the American landscape, introduced him to railroads and then to Wall Street, where he applied his surveyor's ability to discern the lay of the land and his map maker's command of detail to engineer financial gambles that at their peak left him in sole control of the Erie, about half the railroad mileage in the southwest, New York's elevated railway, and the Western Union Telegraph Company.[38] Unlike Drew, Gould died a wealthy man on 2 December 1892 with an estate appraised at $72 million.[39]

After emerging as the power in Erie, Gould indulged Fisk's theatricality by agreeing to purchase the recently built and elaborate Pike's Opera House at Twenty-Third Street and Eighth Avenue, a white marble edifice festooned on the outside with fancy cornices and garish statues and on the inside with a bronze bust of Shakespeare. Dubbed 'Castle Erie' by the press, part of this property was used for Erie offices, which contained a seven-story safe, accessible on each floor and built at a cost of $60,000. To visit Fisk's office on the second floor, a visitor 'entered through carved oak doors that led into an anteroom protected by a bronze gate guarded by ushers.'[40] The overall effect on the contemporary observer, Meade Minnigerode, was:

The most fantastic offices ever occupied by a business corporation – a splendor of marble, and black walnut inlaid with gold, and silver name plates, and crimson hangings, and painted ceilings, and wash stands decorated with nymphs and cupids.[41]

Fisk became the impresario of the House's theatrical performances that were held on a 70-by-80-foot stage for an audience of up to 2,600, with six proscenia and 27 dress-circle boxes. Fisk built a private apartment in the adjoining Erie property with a private walkway to his personal box in the theater and installed his mistress, Josie Mansfield, in a nearby townhouse. Fisk merged the theater of financial markets with entertainment performance into a seamless duality:

> though the rules governing credit in the market ... may have differed in detail from the conventions governing credibility in ... theatrical booths, ... in either instance the customer's will to believe was ... a conditional act, a matter less of faith than of suspended disbelief.[42]

To George Templeton Strong, diarist of older New York manners, Fisk was 'illiterate, vulgar, unprincipled, profligate, always making himself conspicuously ridiculous by some piece of flagrant ostentation.' He described Fisk's New Year's Day calls on acquaintances 'in a gorgeous chariot ... with four smart footmen in flamboyant liveries. When he stopped ... his marmelukes descended, unrolled a carpet, laid it from the carriage steps to the door, and stood on either side in attitude of military service, while their August master passed by.' Fisk kept 15 horses and employed five stablemen to tend to six coaches, two clarences (one lined with gold cloth) and a barouche.[43]

To round out his trappings of majesty, Fisk awarded himself the twin titles of Admiral of his Narragansett Steamship Company fleet of elegantly appointed passenger steamships – that plied the coast from Long Island Sound to Massachusetts, Connecticut and Rhode Island – and Colonel of New York's Ninth Regiment. To display his dual commission, he had designed gaudy Gilbert and Sullivan uniforms and recruited the famous British cornetist, Jules Levy, at an annual salary of $10,000, to anchor the Ninth Regimental Band.[44]

Gould's earlier speculations in gold persuaded him that he could corner the market, drive the price up and sell at a profit. Vanderbilt's use of this tactic in the Harlem corner taught Gould that he could force the short-sellers – who were betting on a price decline – to buy at the price Gould set. With the government dumping gold on the market, logic would dictate that its price was due for a tumble. Gould, however, decided to buy long contracts, wagering on a rise in gold's price. There was no lack of short sellers because of Grant's pledge to strengthen the paper dollar by selling gold from the Treasury, thereby increasing the supply of gold on the market and driving down its price. If the market price of gold increased above Gould's long-contract price, however, those short sellers with future contracts would be forced to buy at the higher market price and sell to Gould at his lower long price. Gould could then sell his gold at the higher market price. Gould would pocket the profits arising from the difference between the higher market price and his contract obligations. All this was counterintuitive, the psychological feint required of all market corners, much like the magician's use of misdirection to dazzle and impress an audience. How was Gould going to inflate the price of a commodity whose supply was increasing faster than ordinary demand? The answer was found in a tactical maneuver known only to Gould that was designed to rapidly inflate the price. For this he needed two ingredients: first, a 'theory' as to why the future price of gold would increase to boost demand and, second, a compliant collaborator on the selling end who would sharply curtail new supply from coming into the market.

To inflate demand, Gould justified his financial maneuver with a crude theory based on how a high price of gold would yield American farmers more greenbacks for their export sales when they converted gold specie into paper money. Export farm sales were paid in gold. If the exchange value of greenbacks for gold was high, farmers would receive more of them when they converted their gold into greenbacks. This was a crude arbitrage arrangement even for its time. Gould dressed up this very dubious economic reasoning by dubbing it the 'crop theory' and peddled it as wise public policy, importuning everyone he could reach to support a strong gold-price regime on behalf of Main Street's farmers, whom he enlisted in his cause – not the first nor the last time a Wall Street player justified his financial maneuver on behalf of Main Street's personal interests. Its rationale, however, was nothing more than a case for inflation and the illusion that the same gold converted into more dollars would really mean higher income for Main Street farmers after generalized inflation had coursed through the economy. Such a money illusion was, nevertheless, convincing.

Gould began his purchases of gold contracts in the late summer of 1869. As a second element in his strategy, he needed to find access to the Treasury in order to time the decline in gold sales, thereby reducing supply as he was inflating demand for gold through his purchases and the silent partners he engaged. To gain access to President Grant and the Treasury for this aspect of his campaign, he used Abel Rathbone Corbin, a Wall Street dabbler who had married Grant's sister, Virginia (Jennie) Paine Grant. Gould and Corbin had first met at Saratoga, New York – a favorite summer retreat for Wall Streeters – a few years before the gold corner. Gould's scheme could only work if at a minimum the Treasury remained neutral and did not increase sales from its vast stock of gold which would have the effect of driving the price down before Gould took his profits. Preferably, the maximum Gould move would involve the Treasury reducing gold sales. Corbin became the instrument Gould needed to accomplish this.

Gould sold Corbin on his crop theory and opened a $2.5 million gold account for him in his firm. Unknown to Jennie Corbin, a third was placed in her name.[45] Gould and Fisk first met Grant through Corbin in mid-June of 1869. Fisk entertained the President on 15 June in his opera box and the next day hosted him on the *Providence*, the pride of his Narragansett steamship line, on a pre-arranged trip from New York to Boston. News accounts had the somberly-dressed President greeted by 'Admiral' Fisk in a 'blue uniform, with a broad gilt cap-band, three silver stars on his coat sleeve, lavender gloves, and a diamond breast-pin.'[46] Entertaining Grant in splendor on the appropriately named *Providence* and amid this atmosphere, Gould introduced the President to his crop theory of gold prices.

Gould and Corbin next used their access to the President to obtain the appointment of a potential ally, General Daniel Butterfield, the Assistant U.S. Treasurer for New York whose father was a friend of Corbin's. This was a critical position, because any gold sales ordered from Washington were executed in New York. At the critical moment it would become important to control gold sales in the city, possibly delaying execution of an order emanating from the Treasury on Pennsylvania Avenue in Washington. The compliant 38-year-old Butterfield was the son of American Express founder, John Butterfield, and in 1872 became president of the company, notwithstanding his acknowledged complicity in the gold corner.[47] Gould opened a gold account for Butterfield that reached $1.5 million, and Butterfield kept Corbin informed of any unusual gold sales ordered from Washington.[48] All the planning elements were now aligned for a classic corner in which purchasers drive up the price by artificially creating a demand for a commodity whose price should be going in the other direction because of increased supply. Those observing this move who are outside the inner circle typically join in the surging market, only to be ambushed when the time comes and the cornerers reverse gears and sell.

Subsequent to the meeting with Grant, Gould persuaded the *New York Times* to carry a Corbin-authored article about the crop theory, which concluded that 'until the crops are moved [the President] will not send gold into the market and sell it for currency to lock up in Treasury vaults.'[49] This had the effect of cornering Treasury Secretary Boutwell. If he denied the story, panic could ensue as speculators rushed to sell gold. If he confirmed the story, Gould succeeded in his ploy. He subsequently did what public officials always do when their options have been eliminated: neither confirm nor deny the President's position on gold sales. Gold sales from the Treasury, however, fell from $6 million in May and a peak of $8 million in June, 1869 to $2 million in each of the next two months.[50] Gould and Corbin correctly interpreted this as a victory in their effort to impose the 'crop theory' on public policy.

September 1869 was the month Gould's gold corner came to a conclusion. The cabal was propelled into action earlier than they had wanted, however, when Corbin learned that Grant had issued orders to Boutwell to sell an additional 4–6 million dollars of gold in September. To calm a nervous Fisk, Gould told him, 'This matter is all fixed up ... Corbin had got Butterfield all right, and Corbin has got Grant fixed all right.'[51] However, Gould did not tell Fisk about this new piece of information from Corbin, namely Grant's decision to increase gold sales.

To execute the denouement in their corner strategy, Gould had Corbin arrange for Grant's removal from the capital by orchestrating a visit in the middle of September by the President to his wife's cousin in Washington, Pennsylvania – a town that was 30 miles from Pittsburgh, without direct telegraph connection and reachable only by horse. Grant left behind instructions to Boutwell that said: 'a desperate struggle is now taking place [on Wall Street], and each party want the government to help them out. ... I think ... I would move without any change, until the present struggle is over,' signifying a status quo that would redound to the benefit of the cornerers.[52] This order was unknown, however, to Abel Corbin who could not stand the pressure and panicked. He overplayed his hand and telegraphed to Grant that something rotten was afoot in the Treasury's posture on gold sales even though there was no available evidence for his nervousness.

Now Gould and Corbin were in a theater familiar to the military tactician, Grant, who began to see them as opponents on a field of battle. This was a terrain familiar to Grant while the maneuvering over esoteric issues such as the crop theory was not. Corbin wrote a letter to Grant, with Gould's blessing, and hired a messenger, William A. Chapin, to take the letter personally to Grant in Washington, Pennsylvania. The letter reiterated Gould's crop theory and implored Grant to restrain Boutwell from selling additional gold. Grant became suspicious upon receiving the letter and, paradoxically, it was the nervousness of the very schemers who had arranged his isolation that persuaded him to cut short his period of being incommunicado. Fed by Corbin's jitters, Gould's approval of the letter to Grant aroused the very suspicions he had assiduously avoided previously. It was his single mistake in an otherwise bold and flawless campaign.

Grant had his wife, Jennie, write to Jennie advising her husband to remove himself from any contacts with Gould and Fisk: 'Tell Mr. Corbin that the President is very much disturbed by your speculations and you must close them as quickly as you can.'[53] The letter arrived on 22 September, and the now-panicked Abel Corbin showed it to Gould, who admonished him to show the letter to no one else. With $100 million tied up in long gold contracts, Gould wanted no one – not even Fisk – to know what had to be done: sell gold immediately and burn those among the ten to fifteen thousand speculators who had gambled with him on rising gold prices. On 21 September Grant left his cousin's house first by carriage and reached the capital on Gould's Erie Railroad on Wednesday night, 22 September. The next day Gould sold a considerable amount of gold through camouflaged brokers – much of it to Fisk who still thought the play was to buy gold. By late Thursday 23 September Grant decided to have Boutwell sell $4 million from the Treasury the next day and break the gold corner. In New York Butterfield received the order at noon on what has become known as Black Friday, 24 September 1869.[54]

Gold was traded in 1869 in an exchange called the Gold Room whose appointments were worthy of the metal bought and sold there. Unlike its 1862 origins in the dreary basement room of the Coal Hole at 23 William Street, the Gold Room's traders crowded around a circular iron railing in the center of a 30-foot trading floor, which enclosed a large bronze fountain that was fittingly stocked with gold fish. Its nearly 500 members watched the gold ticker that was run by the 22-year-old Thomas Alva Edison.[55]

The gold price broke on the morning of Friday, 24 September and fell from $160 to $135. It was accompanied by a potential riot of vengeful buyers of gold who were outside the corner and had not profited as had Gould who had inside information and knew precisely when to reverse modes from buyer to seller. Even before Butterfield received his sell order and had time to execute it, Gould's heavy selling the day before and that morning was enough to set off alarm bells and convince the Gold Room that the Treasury had finally decided to sell gold. The National Guard was called out to maintain order on the streets outside the exchange but could not prevent the angry crowd from surging down the street toward Gould's office. Experienced with strategic retreats, Gould and Fisk sneaked out the back door of the Gold Room and made their way safely to Gould's office where they pondered their next moves.[56] There were few left except to tally up the gains and losses, wait out the fury of the mob outside that chanted for Gould's head, and stay put until the gold price settled again.

THE AFTERMATH

The scandal was widely reported in investigative newspaper stories. A grand jury was convened to look into possible criminal activity but found none because, however unethical, the activities of Gould at that time violated no laws. A Congressional hearing investigated the role of government officials, including the President. Gould portrayed himself as the innocent victim of Washington's policy inconsistencies, as a speculator engaged in legitimate activity, and as a seer whose crop theory would enliven the American economy for the benefit of Main Street's farmers. He failed to mention that he earned a profit of between $10 and $12 million on his gold speculation, even after he had to sell a considerable amount at a loss after Black Friday.[57]

The erstwhile insider but never full confidant of Gould, Jim Fisk continued to capture the fancy of a New York public ever hungry for news of his exploits. On one occasion he actually saw 'combat' action in his military capacity as Colonel of the Ninth Regiment. At a 9 July 1871 march of Irish Protestant Orangemen to celebrate their 1690 victory over Catholics, the parade ended up reenacting the battle. Fisk had willingly taken on the military duty of maintaining order, as he had done on other occasions, not expecting combat action. Dressed in his white summer uniform, sword on hip, he led his troops in a peacekeeping formation down Eighth Avenue.[58] When the skirmish began he and his men scrambled. Never one to pass up an opportunity to embellish the story, Fisk told a reporter:

I was set upon by the mob with stones and brickbats and pitched in the gutter. When I got up, my coat was all torn off and I found I was wounded. I limped into a house ... I got there a big overcoat and hat, blackened my moustache and otherwise disguised myself, and hobbled over a fence into the street.[59]

Forty-seven deaths among the Irish factions resulted, including two from the Ninth Regiment, along with 83 wounded.

Six months later Jim Fisk was murdered by Edward S. Stokes, a business rival and the new favorite of Fisk's by now former mistress, Josie Mansfield. Fisk and Stokes not only had a mutual interest in Josie Mansfield. Both had financial interests in the Brooklyn Refining Company. As revenge for the theft of Josie, Fisk used his influence with New York's judicial system to convert their dispute over financial mismanagement into Stokes's arrest on charges of embezzlement. Upon release, Stokes counterclaimed against Fisk in a civil suit in which Josie Mansfield testified for Stokes.[60] Into this snowstorm of suits, counter-suits, writs and affidavits appeared once again the ubiquitous Judge George C. Barnard of Erie fame who was allied with the Tammany political machine and, therefore, with Fisk as well. On 6 January 1872 Barnard informed Stokes that a grand jury had indicted him for blackmail. Upon hearing this news, Stokes went to the Grand Central Hotel and shot Fisk. Fisk's body was taken to his beloved Opera House and received a military funeral clothed in the $5,000 dress uniform he had used for his duties as Colonel of the Ninth Regiment.

In life Fisk had cultivated the image of a man of the people, giving money away freely to the poor and the lame, organizing relief for victims of the 1871 Chicago fire and fashioning himself as a self-made millionaire who had never forgotten his humble beginnings and was always a man of the common people. In death 25,000 people paraded behind his coffin, singing 'He Never Went Back on the Poor.' Josie Mansfield, the woman who aroused the passions of Fisk and Stokes and the proximate source of their dispute, went to Paris and, with intervals in the U.S., died there at the age of 83 in 1931. The only note of her death was by a *New York Times* reporter who wrote about her sparsely attended funeral of three mourners in the rain at the Cimetière de Montparnesse in Paris.[61] Stokes was tried three times for murder but was only convicted of manslaughter and served just four months in prison. Judge George C. Barnard, the object of so much attention from Drew, Vanderbilt and Fisk, was impeached in late 1872 and removed from the New York judiciary.[62]

After completing a second term as president, Ulysses Grant joined a Wall Street brokerage partnership with a firm headed by Ferdinand Ward. One investor in the firm was his sister, Jennie Corbin. Ward traded on Grant's name to obtain clients, but his poor investment decisions ran up debts of some $15 million. One day in 1884 he disappeared, leaving Grant with a bankrupt Wall Street brokerage house and a half-million-dollar personal loss. Strapped for income and in failing health, Grant retired to a cabin in the Adirondack mountains where he worked on his memoirs with a $20,000 advance furnished by his publisher-patron, Mark Twain.

Completed one week before his death in July 1885, the memoir received critical acclaim and achieved sales of a half-million copies.[63]

If there had ever been any doubts about the importance of Pennsylvania Avenue for Wall Street, the Civil War and the financial wars after it should have laid them to rest. The two thoroughfares became inextricably intertwined, while the outsiders on the nation's many Main Streets were used when convenient – as during Cooke's mass sale of war bonds – and misused when convenient, as with Gould's crop theory. Writing in 1870, the Wall Street observer, James Medberry, in typical language of the period testified to the 'sparks of electricity that fly up from the marshes of the Mississippi Valley, from the golden desolation of Nevada, from factory hamlets in Connecticut, from the pastoral seclusions of Vermont bearing emergent orders to sell Hudson short,' referencing the first Drew–Vanderbilt engagement, in 'villages whose names are scarcely known beyond the boundary of their counties,' each one of which, he writes, have their 'rustic Fisks and Vanderbilts.'[64] Main Street's small investors relearned a lesson during the Erie wars and Gould's attempted gold corner which they had forgotten from Duer's 1792 scheme. If you try to play in the major financial league without the requisite financial resources and privileged information, the chances are you will lose. It is a tale that subsequent generations on Main Street continued to forget – or ignore at their peril. Broken hearts and bank accounts inevitably followed on the illusory dream of riches hidden behind this circus's sideshow, hawked by those old circus roustabouts, Drew and Fisk.

Gold and railroads were the tissue that would bind the nation together into one national economy, with national industries operating in national markets and a process of capital accumulation that stretched from ocean to ocean and from the borders of Canada to Mexico. Another quarter century would intervene, but the framing of financial conflict over the spoils of this bounty was set immediately after the Civil War just as the war itself settled the political question of whether the American part of the continent would be one or two nations. The gold war was revelatory of the importance of the country's first experience with a national currency. The Erie and New York Central conflict was a dry run for battles surrounding the reach of rail systems across the entire continent that would throw forth a new form of economic organization, the trust, and a new breed of Wall Street operator who became pejoratively known as 'robber barons,' suggesting a lordly rule of capital, but achieved not by monarchial grant but by theft.

Lost was an older republican sensibility, echoed by the Adams's lament that 'a business community which tolerates successful fraud or which honors wealth more than honesty ... merely incite[s] others to surpass them by yet bolder outrages and more corrupt combinations.'[65]

Perhaps more suited to the post-Civil War national mood was the deliberately cynical theatrical satire, *Wall Street in Paradise*, a minor musical in which Gimmaksnider is 'A Wall Street operator who ... finds his way to Olympus, and wishes to teach Jew-Peter the "ropes".' It commences with this lyric: 'Well, I guess I'm in a regular fix; the bubbles burst, and I am worth just nix. I sold out one thousand Eries for a flyer – Thought they'd go down – but they have gone up higher,' and continues later with a refrain, 'But I got tired of speculation, having picked clean the bone; I resolved to try a change of air, and leave for parts unknown; So I mounted my aerial car higher than my greatest hopes; And here I am Jew-Peter. Shall I teach you the ropes?'[66]

7 Trustee Over the Nation's Economy

In the last quarter of the nineteenth century Wall Street asserted its trusteeship over America's economy by acting as guardian of the nation's wealth, planner for its economy, and repairer when things broke down – in contrast to a somnolent Pennsylvania Avenue that continued to ignore the growing complexity of the country's finances. To accomplish this, Wall Street bankers created a new institution – the *financial trust* – demanding compensation for financial protection just as feudal lords had exacted tribute in return for their military protection. The great investment banking names of J.P. Morgan and Jacob Schiff personified what has been called 'the Baronial Age' in which private bankers battled for control over industrial property as medieval Barons had over land.[1] At the same time a prairie populism and nascent urban trade union movement began to challenge this great concentration of economic power on behalf of a Main Street whose appeals to Pennsylvania Avenue's political charges would have to await several more decades before they were seriously considered. Nevertheless, the ideology of opposition takes on its twentieth-century form at this juncture, amidst the creation of an economy that became truly national with financial markets reaching north to south from border to border, east to west from ocean to ocean, and a commercial economy likewise connected by transcontinental railroads.

The field of contention for the new financial baronage was a national financial market that was prepared by a far-reaching restructuring of the country's financial system during the Civil War and sewn together after the Civil War by the telegraph, stock ticker and telephone. Cementing the physical integration of a continental economy were railroads, which linked the Atlantic and the Pacific oceans. Rail track breached the Mississippi, then pushed over the Rocky Mountains to meet track approaching from the Pacific Ocean along a new transcontinental transportation grid, building a consolidated national economy that offered Wall Street opportunities it had not known before.

A national economy begot a national financial system with instruments of credit flowing seamlessly from ocean to ocean. Encouraged by a compliant Pennsylvania Avenue and an infatuated Main Street, Wall Street became the organizer of this unification of America's capital and financial markets. Its Stock Exchange was the fulcrum on which the consolidation of the nation's financial markets was balanced. Atop this pinnacle of financial administration was a new Wall Street agent, the private investment banker, who altered the hierarchy of power on The Street. Promoter of the concept of Wall Street as trustee over the country's wealth, he nudged aside the broker who had ruled The Street from its origins and became the most significant force on Wall Street in the last two decades of the century.

The most powerful of the new breed of investment banker was J.P. Morgan, who built a grand edifice in 1873 on the corner of Wall and Broad Street. Six stories high, it was one of the first in New York with an elevator and drew electricity from Thomas Alva Edison's generating station on nearby Pearl Street. Subsequently Edison established his Edison Electric Illuminating Co. in 1878, backed by Morgan financing, and in that same year he was employed by Morgan to fashion the first illumination by electricity of a private residence for his home at 219 Madison Avenue.[2] Morgan's symbolically and strategically placed office building faced both the Sub-Treasury building on Nassau Street and the Stock Exchange on Wall Street – metaphors for the public and private economic spheres that Morgan would come to dominate – just as his concentration in both railroad securities and government bonds straddled Wall Street and Pennsylvania Avenue.[3]

The private investment banker was not new on Wall Street; Nathaniel Prime had played a central role in canal-financing after the War of 1812.[4] Now, however, he was transcendent. The American investment banker descends from the British *merchant* banker, so-called because he had started typically as a purveyor of merchandise for which lines of credit were advanced. The transition from primarily a seller of merchandise to financial underwriter of commerce and investment is what distinguished a merchant banker.[5] Either alone or in syndication with other houses, the investment banker operated as an underwriter, who purchased new stock and bond issuances of companies for which a management fee was charged, and then sold the new securities in financial markets. The banker's word was enough to assure investors that companies were healthy. Such assurances filled a void created by the absence of any government supervisory structure that regulated prospectuses on new security issues. As an example of how skimpy stock prospectuses were, the New York Central's proclaimed 'the credit and status of the company are so well known that it is scarcely necessary to make any public statement.'[6]

Financial enterprises came to be known by their banker's name or banking house, so-called because invariably the investment banking firm was a family affair. Their origins in Great Britain and Europe were associated with the financing of international trade requiring the acceptance of letters of credit in remote places solely on the basis of the name attached. The letter had to inspire sufficient faith to enable the transaction to be completed with an exchange of signed paper for merchandise, followed only later by the actual transfer of money – hence the significance of a family name associated with the great houses of finance that made these distant transactions a trusted family affair. The investment banker's discretion and foreign contacts also gave him unusual access to government leaders, who frequently used them to conduct back-channel diplomacy. The distinction between the public and private became blurred between government and investment banker as it did between financier and overseer of industry.[7]

The essence of capital formation in the hands of an investment banker is the conversion of short-term money from a multitude of investors into long-term industrial investments. It requires selling short-term investors on the worthiness of the industrial project while assuring them of its value. Value, however, is an elusive target and this is where faith and confidence in the investment house is critical. Character and reputation is everything, and these attributes are trumpeted even in architecture and interior office design.

An investment bank's office arrangement and architecture conveyed that it had a different purpose from that of the commercial bank. As a wholesale banker serving governments, industrial magnates and the new rich, the investment banking house presented no teller windows to the visitor and offered no checking services. An early-twentieth-century pamphlet gushes over the

air of omniscience as if nothing unexpected could ever happen. Doors do not slam, men walk softly upon rugs, voices are never lifted in feverish excitement over profit and loss ... one gets the feeling of space from the manners of the person in uniform who attends to the noiseless opening and closing of the main portal.[8]

Upon entering the bank, one could discern the order of importance of its personnel by their desk placement; junior partners were sited toward the front and along a railing, which separated them from senior partners who sat on an elevated platform several steps above. Along the windows were the desks of the most important members of the banking house. This deployment of spatial dispersion contrasted with the cubicle-like configuration of desks in a broker's office, whose occupants operated on more limited margins, at a more frenetic pace and in more limited space.[9]

J.P. MORGAN

J.P. Morgan, the reigning monarch of Wall Street in the last quarter of the nineteenth century, took his cues from his father, Junius, and fashioned himself after the traditional London merchant banker. In the mode of a Victorian gentleman banker, he valued trust, honor and self-regulation effectively to calibrate a complex economic engine.[10] J. Pierpont (J.P.) Morgan was the son of Junius Morgan who had moved to London in 1854 to work in the merchant bank founded by George Peabody of the famous Massachusetts banking family. J.P. became the U.S. representative for Peabody and then in 1861 formed J.P. Morgan and Company. He merged with the Philadelphia firm of Drexel in 1871 and formed Morgan, Drexel, and Company.

Wearing the stiffest of winged collars and highly starched shirts, J.P. Morgan presided over his financial empire from a large roll-top desk in his strategically placed Wall Street headquarters. The fear he was able to instill with his stentorian voice disguised an insecurity that was heightened by a lifelong affliction with *acne rosacea* – derived from *rhinophyma*, a condition that produces an overabundance of growth of sebaceous tissue – which especially affected his nose and, over the years, produced what has been described as a cauliflower texture that was always carefully air-brushed out of photographs.[11] He lived in the Murray Hill section of Manhattan, with disdain for the nouveaux riches who built copies of continental European chateaux on upper Fifth Avenue. Morgan's home, built in 1882 at 219 Madison Avenue, exuded the privacy and discretion of the London merchant banking world. He loved to sit at his massive wooden desk in the middle of a mahogany-paneled library amid his splendid collection of rare books, illustrated manuscripts and objects of the decorative arts. Like so many of his predecessors on Wall Street, when not ruling over a financial world largely of his own creation, Morgan dabbled in the occult during his frequent consultations with the astrologer, Evangeline Adams.[12] Railroads, gold, oil and steel – the core of the new American industrial economy – were his preferred sectors and British wealth his important source of capital. His first daring moves were in railroads between the late 1860s and the Panic of 1873.

11. J.P. Morgan and Colleagues
J.P. Morgan, the sire of the great House of Morgan, in a candid photograph that shows his disfigured nose in the center with Wall Street colleagues in the year of his rescue of the U.S. financial system. (c1907, Library of Congress, Prints and Photographs Division.)

The country had ignored Cornelius Vanderbilt's warning that 'building railroads from nowhere to nowhere at public expense is not a legitimate undertaking.'[13] Railroad mileage had doubled between 1865 and 1873; the excess capacity led to price wars and preferential rates given to the new concentrations of corporate power: Andrew Carnegie in steel and John D. Rockefeller in oil, both Morgan clients. As a counterweight to the monarchical style of investment bankers – preferential granting of freight rates and the concentration of financial power – populists on the Main Streets of America satirized Wall Street's role in railroad development with political cartoons that depicted an anti-democratic appropriation of economic power by a clique of economic royalists, whose allegiances were defined more by foreign capital than by the interests of Americans. This led to populist campaigns for intercession by Pennsylvania Avenue. A political fault line was emerging that would dominate American politics into the twentieth century.

The country's introduction to the impending Morgan era came during a battle between Jay Cooke, the ingenious seller of Civil War bonds, and Morgan over the Northern Pacific Railroad, one of two competing thrusts toward the west. Chartered in 1864 with government subsidies and generous grants of land, the Northern Pacific represented Cooke's dream of the 'valley route,' through the cleavages in mountains carved out by the Red, Yellowstone and Columbia rivers.[14] Cooke tried to replicate his Civil War-inspired, mass-marketing techniques by selling $100 million of Northern Pacific bonds with advertising brochures that showed fruit-tree farms dotting either side of his railroad cars, as passengers traveled through a Great Plains landscape. For his European customers in Germany and France, who knew little of this terrain and topography, he offered to guide these investors through this financial wilderness by describing the Northern Pacific hub in Duluth, Minnesota as the 'Zenith of the Unsalted Seas.'[15]

The familiar railroad bust after a boom happened in 1873. Once again we observe a new commodity whose stock values become inflated when there is no settled value established by the market, leading to the classic financial bubble and its inevitable puncture. With such high fixed-entry costs, railroads could not yield a return sufficient to cover start-up borrowing costs until the roads were finished and established a market, typically a long period of time when the carrier was earning little or nothing in profits. This disjuncture caused by the long construction cycle, high fixed costs of construction and short-term borrowing opportunities produces a typical chasm between the demands of short-term investors and the exigencies of the longer-term character of railroad start-up.

Cooke's Northern Pacific gambit succumbed to the financial panic in 1873, and for the first time forced the Wall Street Stock Exchange to close its doors for ten days in September. The proximate cause was a scandal involving Credit Mobilier – the financier and builder of the rival Union Pacific Railroad – and an overextension of credit to the competing railroad lines that were approaching the Pacific Ocean. British and European investors, who stood to lose some $600 million, appealed to Morgan to do something that would limit their losses and restore the wealth of those who had invested in the American railroads.

Morgan decided on a bold new strategy in the face of the failure of cartel-like price- and market-sharing agreements. He decided to reorganize the nation's railroads and place them directly under his control, thereby circumventing the petty feuds, as he saw them, among competing railroad owners. The instrument of his control was the *trust*, in which stockholders converted their direct ownership position in a company through the securities they owned into trust certificates issued by Morgan. By so doing they gave up their right of control, while retaining a right to earnings from ownership of a trust certificate. The individual holder of a trust certificate was one removed from voting influence, which was ceded to the trustee, Morgan. The trustees were elected by the holders of trust certificates, given complete authority and control over the corporation, and acted as executors on behalf of the owners of the trust certificates. The transfer of an ordinary security into a trust certificate that separated earnings from control was attractive in the nineteenth century, because liability was more limited. The trust was reputed to have been designed by the first of the new breed of Wall Street lawyer: Samuel C.T. Dodd.[16] Investors owned a railroad security only indirectly with this investment vehicle – for example, where direct ownership was exercised by the trust controlled by Morgan with others' capital. By the end of the century Morgan directly controlled the Erie, Chesapeake and Ohio, Philadelphia and Reading, Santa Fe, Northern Pacific, Great Northern, New York Central, Lehigh Valley, Jersey Central and the Southern Railway – one-sixth of railroad mileage (33,000 miles) with revenues approximating to half of the U.S. government's tax receipts.[17]

In the hands of J.P. Morgan, the trust form of organization, however, was more than simply an instrument for order and control in large oligopolistic industries that were prone to overcapacity, price wars and financial chicanery. It was an ideology: the *Gentleman Bankers Code*. Because the investment banker underwrote and sold bonds to recurring customers, he assumed a duty under the code to intervene directly in the affairs of the companies whose bonds he underwrote when those companies found themselves in difficulty. *Dictum meum pactum*, my word is my bond, was the investment banker's credo, and he used it to acquire his customers' trust. By way of contrast, the Wall Street broker's was *caveat emptor*: buyer beware. In return for settling disputes among contentious railroad owners, Morgan exacted tribute not only in the form of money, but in power and control as well. He demanded, and invariably was granted, a position as director of the railroad. Using this as a wedge, he inevitably came to control them totally.

This muddied the distinction between banker, financier and overseer. It led to what came to be called 'relationship banking,' in which a particular company was tied to its banker through the trust that was controlled by the investment banker. Morgan, consequently, set himself apart from earlier Wall Street sovereigns, such as Drew, Fisk, Gould and Cooke. A 'moral crusade' is the way a biographer interprets Morgan's mission: he 'saw himself as a proxy for honorable European and American investors, a tool of transcendent purpose representing the sound men on Wall Street.'[18] Morgan and the other Wall Street investment bankers asserted claims as trustees over the nation's emerging industrial wealth, planning an economy more effectively, as they saw it, than could any other institution – certainly preferable to Pennsylvania Avenue administration. Their very names were trumpeted as objects of faith that should, according to the Bankers' Code, invoke the same confidence as their forbears' names had in international commerce.

JACOB SCHIFF AND EDWARD HARRIMAN

Morgan's battle with Cooke in 1873 over the Northern Pacific was a dress rehearsal for yet another war over railroads, this time the attempt by Edward Harriman to assume control of both transcontinental lines. As the century was drawing to a close, Morgan had by this time acquired control over Cooke's Northern Pacific and built nearly a complete east–west network across the northern tier of the country, anchored in the east by the New York Central – the Vanderbilt line, bought by Morgan from Vanderbilt's son and heir in 1879 – and in the west by the Northern Pacific. His rival was Edward Harriman who took control over the southern route of the Union Pacific in 1895 from Morgan when Morgan decided to abandon the bankrupt Union Pacific and concentrate his attention on the Northern Pacific. Harriman began to cobble together a southern transcontinental line, from the Union Pacific across the southwest to connecting southern roads he owned.[19] To make the Union Pacific work for him when it had failed others, Harriman's strategy was to neutralize the principal competition from the Northern Pacific by simply taking control of it from Morgan.

Harriman's banker was the German-born Jacob Schiff, of the investment banking house Kuhn, Loeb & Co., a formidable opponent of Morgan's and second in importance on The Street. Schiff was the first in the line of great Jewish investment bankers on Wall Street. They ascended to prominence during the Civil War, when the ambivalence of the City of London toward the Union created an opening on Wall Street for Jewish bankers to grow by gaining a larger market share of financial activity with the Treasury by activating their close ties to German and French banking houses. They became wealthy and powerful during the Civil War, while the Morgans, with their Siamese twin-like connections to the City of London and the City's ambivalence toward the Union, lost some influence. Like British merchant banking houses, Kuhn, Loeb started out as dry-goods merchants:

Cincinnati clothiers. Other Jewish banking houses had similar origins: Lehman Brothers, Alabama cotton brokers; Goldman, Pennsylvania clothing store owner; Lazard, New Orleans dry-goods.[20]

While ethnically different, Schiff and Morgan were quite culturally similar. Jacob Schiff was not unlike J.P. Morgan in his imperiousness; when he traveled it was normally with more than one private Pullman car. Schiff's strict and domineering views on how his only son should be raised were similar to those of Junius Morgan's in his treatment of his only son, J. Pierpont. Schiff's son, Morti, was required to write his father every day when they were apart; once Jacob scolded him, 'I notice you always write every morning. I would prefer that you write late in the afternoon, because you could assure me that you've been a good boy and no trouble to your mother.'[21]

With the support of John D. Rockefeller and his banker, National City Bank, Harriman and Schiff decided to mount a takeover assault on Morgan's Northern Pacific by secretly buying some $78 million in Northern Pacific securities.[22] The magnitude of their raid would not be matched until the takeover battles of the 1980s. This was done to block Morgan's efforts to splice his eastern and western roads together, to complete the Northern Pacific, which he was trying to accomplish by taking over the Chicago, Burlington, and Quincy.[23] The frenzy of activity in the various securities, resulting from Morgan's and Harriman's takeover efforts, produced the expected rollercoaster on The Street: first the shares went wildly up in value, only to crash. The Harriman raid failed, because Morgan was too powerful and too motivated to lose. From his Paris office in the midst of the conflict, Morgan was defiant and contemptuous of both his critics and his rivals: 'I owe the public nothing. I feel bound in honor when I reorganize a property and am morally responsible to protect it, and I generally do protect it.'[24] The dreams of both Morgan and Harriman to create not only a transcontinental railroad monopoly but also to extend this with steamship lines across the Pacific to Asia (Harriman) and an Atlantic monopoly (Morgan) were now checkmated.

When Harriman's takeover strategy failed, the *status quo ante* prevailed: Harriman controlled the Union Pacific line and Morgan the Northern Pacific route. The battle among these titans was nothing new for them or Wall Street. What changed, however, was Main Street's perception of the great trust builders. Confidence in their Bankers' Code and their assertion of guardianship was shaken and never would they have the respect they had before the Northern Pacific raid was executed. Morgan's biographer puts it this way:

He was too large for the flimsy regulatory structures that encased him; he had outgrown his age. ... the Northern Pacific corner reinforced the view that the public was being held hostage by the stock manipulations of a few Wall Street moguls.[25]

This was the first outcome of the continental railroad contest. The second was the emergence of clear fault lines among Wall Street's investment banking houses: between Jewish and Protestant houses on the one hand and continental European versus British interests on the other. While associations between the City of London and Morgan remained in place, new alliances were defined between Jewish investment banks on The Street with Paris and Frankfurt.

DE FACTO CENTRAL BANKER

As Morgan vied with Harriman over the Northern Pacific, he was also thrust into the role of the nation's de facto central banker, stabilizing the dollar vis-à-vis gold for a grateful President Grover Cleveland. The gold problem surfaced between 1894 and 1895 when, following on a second major American financial crisis in 20 years, European investors began to redeem their dollars for gold. This led to such an outflow of gold that U.S. reserves fell below the psychological $100 million floor on gold holding, which was considered essential for management of the country's finances.

President Grover Cleveland was a friend of Morgan's; in fact, J.P.'s only Democratic vote was cast for Cleveland who had worked in a Wall Street law firm for Morgan's father-in-law, Charles Tracy, in offices next to Morgan's building.[26] By 24 January 1895 gold reserves had fallen to $68 million. This prompted a meeting a week later among Morgan, August Belmont (Rothschild's New York representative) and Assistant Treasury Secretary, William E. Curtis.

Morgan came up with a scheme in which he issued bonds that were purchased for gold by the U.S. Treasury and by the Rothschilds. Morgan pledged to hold the gold he acquired for his bonds and stabilize its price, thereby acting as a 'private' central bank. His name and guardianship were sufficient to arrest the gold outflow when the name, faith and credit of the U.S. government were not. A void created by Andrew Jackson's veto of the Second Bank of the United States enabled Wall Street's Morgan to assume the functions that in Great Britain and Europe were public activities performed by central banks. This turned out to be a dry run for an even more precarious gold crisis in 1907 when Morgan essentially took over the operations of the Treasury and acted as trustee for the nation's finances writ large. In these undertakings Morgan was merely extending the model of the trust he had perfected in the private sphere to the public sector, fulfilling the ideological concept of acting as warden over public and private assets so they would not be susceptible to the erratic whims of the purely competitive market inhabited by a *mélange* of rascals. His management of the assets embraced a neo-republican philosophy with wider responsibilities placed on individual capitalists such as only he and a few others understood and accepted. Morgan's great frustration was that Main Street never understood this.

The Wall Street–Pennsylvania Avenue alliance, represented by Morgan and Cleveland, was now firmer than ever before. Main Street opposition saw this Wall Street potentate – dressed impeccably in blacks and grays, tall top hat and gold watch chain stretched across his ample paunch – as a monetary monarch hostile to the country's pastoral image and its Jeffersonian republican origins.[27] Populists vilified the 1895 meeting as a Wall Street–Pennsylvania Avenue conspiracy in league with foreign capital, at the expense of American small-town interests.[28] The Jacksonian clash between Main and Wall Streets remained unresolved.

The surge of the investment banker to prominence threatened to leave traditional Wall Street behind. It put pressure on The Street's habitués – brokers and officials of the Stock Exchange – either to modernize and adapt or to atrophy. When the New York Stock and Exchange Board (NYS&EB) condensed its name to the New York Stock Exchange (NYSE) in 1863, it also decided to erect its own building and cease renting space on Wall Street.[29] It purchased a site at 10–12 Broad Street, just south of Wall, and hired as the architect John Kellum who departed from the reassuring solidity and balance of neo-classical Greek architecture for financial structures. He designed a building in the Italianate palazzo style, evoking a sixteenth-century Florentine palace and an architecture that reflected the national trend toward display of wealth in the Gilded Age. On the second floor of this four-story building was NYSE's imposing Member's Board Room where its members congregated, 75 feet long by 53 feet wide with walls draped in heavy green damask to lessen the noise from brokers on the floor below.[30]

First introduced in the grandiose A.T. Stewart department store in 1846, the palazzo style, in its adaptation to financial institutions, reflected a flaunting of wealth that was characteristic of the Renaissance merchant prince. This architectural form was a statement by a new Wall Street elite that displayed its material achievement and departed from the idealism associated with the Greek temples of the post-Federalist period.[31] It also aligned itself with the new investment banker aristocracy in its competition for financial hegemony on The Street. The pride of a contemporary broker comes through in this sentimental description of the new building:

> a stately marble facade, free from any of the shams and flauntings of the 'American' style of architecture ... with spacious halls furnished ... with all the fitting appointments of an imperial business.[32]

NYSE'S TRANSFORMATION

The cautious pace of the NYSE's operations brought forth a formidable rival in the Open Board of Brokers, which had its origins around 1863 in the curb markets outside the exchange. The official exchange did not trade securities in odd lots and charged high commissions. The exclusion of odd lot trading – selling securities in less than blocks of 100 shares – meant that the small investor had no place on formal Wall Street. Because of its conservatism and resistance to change, the NYSE was reluctant to list new companies, and it missed out on the dynamic new industries that were shaping the post-Civil War American economy.[33] This is a recurring story line. In the second half of the twentieth century NASDAQ was to emerge to challenge a staid NYSE and e-trading to do the same to NASDAQ at the end of that century.

It was still very difficult to attain membership in NYSE's closed guild. In 1861, for example, 29 applications were submitted and 22 were black-balled.[34] The Secretary passed around a box and each member signaled approval by selecting a white marble ball or disapproval by a black ball – more precisely the black ones were squares. In 1865, only eleven black balls out of a total membership that exceeded 500 were needed to exclude an application.[35]

In an effort to shake up its image, adapt to the competition and incorporate new members, the NYSE changed the way one became a member in 1868. It provided for a fixed number of 'seats' that would be sold on a market, subject to a purchaser's approval by the exchange's membership committee, instead of a vote of the entire membership in which a very small minority could defeat an application. The selling of seats on the exchange converted the authority to trade securities from a privilege granted by a guild-like organization to a property right exchanged on a market. The price of a seat on the exchange traded for around $4,000 in the early 1870s, went up to $34,000 before the Panic of 1873, fell to $15,250 in the 1893 depression year, and sold for $80,000 by 1901.[36] Even with these changes, however, the NYSE could not keep pace with its rivals, particularly the expanding *curb market.*

Informal and operating without written rules, the curb market appeared as 'obstreperous [and] burly' to James Medberry, a broker on The Street at that time. 'This odd confabulation,' he said, 'whose roof was the sky, whose offices were in their pockets, whose aspirations were boundless,' did not fit the decorum preferred by Medberry and his colleagues.[37] If the curb disturbed Medberry and his associates, they were even more distressed by another securities trading activity below the curb in the hierarchy: the *bucket shop.* These took their name from the City of London's down-and-outs who would go from tavern to tavern with their own buckets, asking for the remnants from the proprietors' kegs. In lower Manhattan, near Wall Street, the bucket shops were housed in shabby offices that were leased on lower Broadway and the Bowery by brokers who dealt in the least reputable securities, the remnants from the more established securities markets.[38] A hierarchy of status and standards among these markets – NYSE, the curb and the bucket shops – would be repeated in the twentieth century, albeit with different names and identification.

The curb market's historian contrasts NYSE members, who lived on Park Avenue or fancy parts of Westchester and 'might take off early to witness a polo match on Long Island and drink champagne afterwards at a North Shore club,' with curbers who might enjoy a weekend picnic near their New Jersey or Brooklyn Heights neighborhoods. Among the curbers, personas were fashioned that were different from the pursuit of a new financial royalty associated with the great Wall Street barons. There was 'Gowanus Pete,' a dog-meat dealer when not speculating on the curb, 'shoestring Bill' who would commit himself to a municipal hospital after his periodic losses.[39] While Protestants dominated the official exchange, the unofficial curb market was populated by many Jews and Irish Catholics blackballed from the NYSE. A contemporary observer described the crowd on the pavement on Broad Street outside the Exchange building as a group with 'less decorum, – cigar-smoke mingling freely with the shouting, – queer habiliments, queer faces, the Jew physiognomy predominating over the Gentile ... whose aspirations were boundless, and whose lives were in incessant romance.'[40] At the curb the receipt of an order would be passed by a hand signal to a recording clerk who was perched above the street on the window ledge of an office leased by the curbside broker. To identify the transmission from curb to window ledge, the curbside broker wore garish clothing in order to stand out from the crowd: brightly colored hats, scarves, anything that would enable his clerk to see him distinctly. *The Times* of London was bemused by this 'web of human life ... woven in colors so glaring and diversified as to strike with painful effect upon eyes accustomed to the more subdued tints and graduated shades of European existence.'[41] The clerks would stand precariously on the outer window ledges or with one foot inside the office and the other outside on the ledge in good weather. Often the number of brokers and customers overran the narrow curbs, spilled out into the streets and immobilized traffic. There were, consequently, persistent conflicts between the curb market and the police who had to be compensated for their forbearance.[42] The sheer volume of activity transformed The Street from a restricted community to an industry operating around the clock. Thousands of lower-paid workers were employed to clean and run the buildings, provide the food, clear transactions overnight, transport the transactions from those selling to those buying with an army of runners, pad shovers who recorded the transactions and took them to brokers and their assistants who were engaged in the actual buying and selling of securities.

By 1864, as the pace of activity grew on the curb and the situation became excessively chaotic, it was in everyone's interest that it move inside. When some of the curbers formed the Open Board of Brokers in 1864 and settled in at 16–18 Broad Street, they formalized their brokerage practices and adopted rules for many of their innovations: admitting the public to its trading room, continuous trading and the specialist. Continuous trading differentiated the Open Board from the NYSE, which had two auction sessions per day. The specialist stood at one place in the Open Board's Long

12. The Curb Market
The curb market, c1902, that was a fixture on Wall Street from the 1840s onward. To the left are young boys – the pad shovers and runners who carry completed transactions to be cleared in brokers' offices. In the center are the multitude of curb brokers. (From the collection of Benjamin J. Falk, Library of Congress, Prints and Photographs Division.)

Room – a variant on the trading post that was derived from a broker's position on the curb – and traded in a limited number of companies.[43]

By the end of the decade the curb and the Open Board had become a serious rival to NYSE. While the NYSE was trading about 100,000 shares a day, the curb had its first 1 million-share day.[44] On 29 July 1869, mirroring the concentration and consolidation of industry effected by investment bankers, a merger was consummated among the NYSE, the Open Board of Brokers and a specialized government bond exchange – the Government Bond Department – that produced a new constitution largely in place today. To the 533 members of the NYSE, 354 from the Open Board were added and 173 from the Government Bond Department.[45] The new NYSE thus consisted of over 1,000 members, almost a doubling of its membership, which left it in essential control of some $3 billion of traded securities.[46] This concentration and consolidation of securities trading in the NYSE paralleled the unification of capital in the industrial economy through the trust.

The new 1869 constitution and subsequent procedural changes established trading practices until well into the twentieth century. It required the registration of all securities traded on the NYSE, and by 1873 the NYSE had replaced its two-a-day auction with continuous trading and adopted the specialist system at the 'trading post.'[47] A seat on the consolidated exchange sold for about $4,000 in 1873, even though the word 'seat,' which had come from the previous practice that had brokers sitting in an assigned chair during the two-a-day auctions, was no longer descriptive of the exchange.[48] Now, with continuous trading at specialists' posts, members roamed the floor but did not sit.

Inevitably even this consolidated exchange did not prevent a new curb market from arising almost immediately for the same reasons as before: a conservative attitude toward new companies and industries that could only find a trading home outside the official exchange on the curb. The American Stock Exchange, founded in 1921 again to bring the new curb indoors, greeted members and visitors with these words carved into the facade of its building: 'New York Curb Market.'[49]

WOMEN ON WALL STREET

Women began to play a role on Wall Street for the first time in the decades after the Civil War. Their entrance onto The Street was greeted sarcastically, however, in keeping with the male clubbiness of the place. An early commentator claimed that 'women as a class should keep out of speculation. There may be perhaps a half a dozen of them whose experience and ability and means justify them in speculating in stocks, but they are the exception.'[50] The 'crinoline of Wall Street,' as they were dismissively called, included Victoria Woodhull and her sister, Tennessee Claflin, who opened a brokerage firm at 44 Broad Street in 1870 with the financial backing of Cornelius Vanderbilt. Between 1870 and 1876 the weekly newspaper they founded, *Woodhull and Claflin's Weekly*, which at its peak had a circulation of 20,000, became one of the strongest advocates for woman's suffrage and social reform.[51] In April 1870 Victoria Woodhull announced her candidacy for the presidency in the forthcoming 1872 election (the first woman to run for that office) with this manifesto placed in the New York *Herald*:

While others of my sex devoted themselves to a crusade against the laws that shackle the women of the country, I asserted my individual independence. ... While others sought to show that there was no valid reason why woman should be treated ... as being inferior to man, I boldly entered the arena of politics and business and exercised the rights I already possessed. I therefore claim the right to speak for the unenfranchised woman of the country and ... I now announce myself as a candidate for the Presidency.[52]

Woodhull's journey to her pinnacle of wealth and fame was not easy and not a straight line from her humble origins in Homer, Ohio. Born to the Claflin's, the sixth of ten children, she had a soulless marriage at 15 to Canning Woodhull and then in St. Louis met and married a prosperous railroad owner, the 29-year-old veteran of the Civil War and President of the St. Louis Railroad, James Harvey Blood, who introduced her to the political ideas and reform movements that were to fashion her public profile.[53] With her sister providing the 'magnetic' treatment from 'laying on of hands' and sundry medicinal concoctions, and Victoria's occult speciality in communication through media, the two formed a comprehensive spiritual clinic of sorts for an age that saw such miracles as the transmission of information through the medium of wires across telephone and telegraph.

A 'spiritualist, the high "priestess" of free love, the crusading editor, the San Francisco actress and part-time prostitute, the founder of the first stock exchange brokerage firm for women, the disciple of Karl Marx, the blackmailer, the presidential candidate, the sinner, the saint,' is the way her biographer describes the many sides of Woodhull.[54] Of all these traits, it was her successful endeavors in spiritualism that catapulted Woodhull from drifter to denizen of Wall Street and Manhattan society. An estimated 10 million Americans practiced spiritualism in the late 1860s through media that were available in virtually every town of any substantial size, taking in people from every walk of life, from the poorest to the most prominent, of whom Abraham Lincoln's wife (Mary Todd) was perhaps the most famous. On a Wall Street where faith could quickly turn to despair, contacts with another world were not uncommon. Among the most susceptible was Cornelius Vanderbilt, untutored and unlettered notwithstanding his Dutch establishment last name, yet financially successful beyond the reach of most mortals. The meeting among Vanderbilt, Victoria Woodhull, and her sister Tennessee (Tennie) Claflin fills in some of the missing pieces of the great railroad wars and subsequent gold corner we encountered previously between Vanderbilt and the triad of Fisk, Gould and Drew.[55] Finally, to square the circle, Fisk's mistress and erstwhile actress, Josie Mansfield, takes center stage.

Victoria Woodhull and Josie Mansfield first met in San Francisco in 1858, both living the role of destitute actress seeking care and comfort from comfortably situated men. A decade later their paths crossed again shortly after the sisters, Victoria and Tennie, made their way to Manhattan. Woodhull and Mansfield ran into each other in Annie Wood's brothel. The two sisters met Vanderbilt through the promotion of Victoria's extraordinary spiritual power. With a keen eye for women Vanderbilt took a special liking to Tennie, so much so he asked her to be his wife, but this never materialized. So while Victoria ministered to his spiritual needs, Tennie provided other comforts after the death of Vanderbilt's wife, Sophie.[56] Vanderbilt's financial entanglement with Fisk, Drew and Gould inevitably brought Woodhull into contact with Mansfield with special meaning for the gold corner.

During the gold corner engineered by the triad, Woodhull advised Vanderbilt as to how he should profit from it, no doubt with strategic maneuvers passed to her from Mansfield which she gleaned from Fisk. During a critical juncture in which President Grant signaled his willingness to withhold gold sales from the Treasury, Woodhull advised Vanderbilt to buy gold at the existing $132 per ounce price, which she said she had heard during a trance in which she communicated with the spirit world. Vanderbilt committed his entire liquid fortune of $9.5 million. Shortly thereafter and armed with more spiritually inspired information, she advised him to sell at $150, recounting her vision of the burst of the gold bubble above $150, which coincidentally was the target sale price contemplated by the triad who were executing the gold corner. Vanderbilt promised her half his profits if the vision came true. When the gold price soared to $150 on 24 September 1869, Vanderbilt sold, earning a profit of $1.3 million of which half was given to Woodhull. Was it spiritualism that informed Woodhull of the sort transported through a medium or was it more that form of spiritual nourishment Josie Mansfield provided for James Fisk? It was just such use of the brothel, with which Mansfield was familiar, for the gathering of intelligence that informs this event: 'The world of high finance and the low life of prostitutes,' writes a chronicler of Victorian America, 'converged in the elegant brothels,' which women like Woodhull and Mansfield frequented.[57] It would not be unusual for information spilled on the pillow to find its way into financial speculation. This is probably what happened in this instance.

With their new-found wealth the sisters opened the first Wall Street brokerage house for women, Woodhull, Claflin and Co., on 19 January 1870 and a month later moved to their larger premises at 44 Broad Street, just down the street from the New York Stock Exchange at Broad and Wall and four office doors away from Jim Fisk. This first in the brokerage profession came at a moment when only five of over 40,000 lawyers were women, 67 out of some 44,000 clergy, 525 medical professionals from over 62,000.[58] The New York *Sun* greeted this innovation on The Street with the headline, 'Petticoats Among the Bovine and Irsine Animals.' Victoria Woodhull later reflected on when she opened the office that 'not 100 women in the whole of the United States owned stocks or dared to show independence in property ownership. This step we were induced to take,' she said, was done with the 'view of proving that woman, no less than man, can qualify herself for the more onerous occupations of life.'[59]

Visitors entered a brokerage house appointed like no other. There was a parlor whose walls had luxuriant oil paintings, floor space punctuated with statues, velvet sofas in soft green hues, a piano. The opening was attended by 4,000 people including Vanderbilt, of course, and his rival James Fisk with Josie Mansfield who opened an account with the firm. Victoria Woodhull was only 31 and Tennie 24 when they opened their Wall Street firm, 'gold pens poised on their pretty ears form[ing] a topic of unusual interest for the gouty old war horses of the street,' wrote the New York *Herald*. 'The ladies received their visitors with a coolness and an eye to business that drew forth the plaudits and curses of old veterans.'[60] To accommodate their clientele of women neglected by the traditional Wall Street houses, there was a rear entrance reserved for them which opened into private office space for their exclusive conferences with Woodhull and

Claflin. So taken was Vanderbilt by all this that he gave the sisters a percentage of his company profits in 1870 because of the spiritual guidance and advice of Victoria and the attentions of Tennie.

Armed with this wealth, Victoria Woodhull moved to an impressive four-story brownstone mansion in the fashionable section of Manhattan on 38th Street between Madison and Fifth Avenues to pursue her other ambitions: women's rights, free love, political reform and socialism. Her vehicle was the weekly newspaper she started with her sister Tennie, where the *Communist Manifesto* was published for the first time in the United States, and she featured woman authors such as Georges Sand. In 1871 Victoria Woodhull became the first woman to speak before a committee of the U.S. Congress. These were all firsts for this pioneering duo. This did not, however, gain acceptance among the established and less controversial women's rights advocates, such as Elizabeth Cady Stanton and Susan B. Anthony.[61]

The year 1871 was a heady one for radical politics. This was the year of the Paris Commune and the prominence of the International Workingmen's Association (IWA) founded by Karl Marx. Woodhull headed the American branch, section 12, covered developments in Europe in the *Weekly*, published an interview with Marx, and printed 1,000 copies of his *The Civil War in France*.[62] So prominent was Woodhull's profile in American radical politics that she was denounced by name by Karl Marx at the 1872 meeting of the IWA in the Hague, a propensity of Marx to see anyone not committed to his version of 'scientific socialism' as an opponent drifting into utopian socialist tendencies and to be opposed as forcefully as capitalists. The American organization she led was expelled along with branches from other countries for doctrinal differences of the sort that haunted these meetings. The charge was that the American branch was diverting attention from working-class interests by muddying the water with other extraneous social issues, such as women's rights.

By this time Woodhull's reputation had also peaked in the United States and support among her fellow campaigners for suffrage also foundered on their own version of sectarian squabbles. In addition, she became embroiled in another of her failings, a propensity to blackmail. However, this time Vanderbilt was the target and thus ended the sisters' relationship with him. With their financial resources running low, the *Weekly* suspended publication less than five years after it was inaugurated. The causes for which Woodhull fought ran aground on the shoals of faction-alism and sectarianism, and because of her checkered and controversial past her reputation suffered in this polemical milieu. In 1877 she left the United States for England where she continued to campaign for women's rights and the other issues in which she believed. In that same year Vanderbilt died, leaving 97 per cent of his $100 million estate to his son, William. Vanderbilt's other siblings and Tennie contested the estate and made claims for some of his wealth that were not upheld.

In England Victoria reinvented herself for a time with a new name, Woodhall. Tennie also moved to England, but relations between the sisters became strained and never were reconstituted. Tennie married into aristocracy, Sir James Cook, and died on 18 January 1923. Victoria Woodhull (she reverted back to her original name) reestablished herself, creating a new journal, the *Humanitarian*, which had a nine-year run. She used the new social science of Sociology in her writings to envelop her issues with academic respectability and legitimacy. Newly married to the Englishman and historian of the British banking system, John Martin, Victoria returned to the United States to run for President again in 1892. As before she was abandoned by others in the suffrage movement, such as Susan B. Anthony, who found her past and her views on many issues shocking and unhelpful to the cause. In defeat she said, 'to be frank, I hardly expected to be elected. The truth is I am too many years ahead of this age, and the exalted views and objects of humanitarianism can scarcely be grasped as yet by the unenlightened mind of the average man.'[63] On 10 June 1927, on the edge of a great American reform decade that would see many of her ideas become reality, Victoria Woodhull died at the age of 90. Shortly before her death she wrote that 'I gave America my youth. It was sweet and gallant and fruitful – its memories are buoyant. ... That excellencies pretended to misunderstand and undertook to impugn was their defect, not mine.'[64]

Though only briefly on the national stage, Victoria Woodhull nevertheless left her footprint on history as the first in so many ventures. Her eccentricities, foibles, advocacies such as free love that deflected attention from her main message, and character flaws are typically associated with being a first. It is difficult to maintain that focused pursuit when pushing against so many previously locked doors. Victoria Woodhull and Tennie Claflin were a classy duo whose twin persona embraced a glamorous style and adventurous life in contrast to their rival for fame on Wall Street, Hetty Green, more financially successful than the sisters and the world's top woman financier, who accumulated a fortune worth about $100 million.

Born to New Bedford Quakers, Abby Slocum Howland and Edward Mott Robinson, who accumulated considerable wealth as the owner of a whaling fleet, Hetty was raised by her grandparents following her mother's death. Her education at an austere Quaker school habituated her to modest dress and a firm belief that spending on luxuries bordered on sinfulness.

Reflecting her particular superstitions in a age convulsed by the spiritual, she once remarked that 'I am only comfortable in rags and tatters because I was marked before my birth. While my mother was carrying me she was frightened half to death by a ragged, tattered tramp.'[65]

She traveled to Wall Street on public transport from her modest rented rooms, some days secreting as much as $200,000 in pockets specially stitched into her petticoat. Dressed wholly in black – from black cotton gloves, a plain dress of black alpaca, to black-ribbed stockings – Green entered what amounted to her office: donated rooms and storage space in her favorite bank of the moment, seen sitting 'cross-legged on the cold stone floor ... surrounded ... with portmanteaus and trunks,' according to the bank's staff. A nondescript bonnet, partially covering her gray streaked brownish hair which was twisted into a figure-eight, topped off a public persona that gave her the nickname, the 'witch of Wall Street.'[66] 'I have to wear old clothes,' she told an interviewer. 'I suffer, really, when I'm dressed up.'[67] While Green was commonly known as the 'witch of Wall Street,' her rival Woodhull was called the 'bewitching broker,' and the sisters the 'queens of finance.'[68]

Hetty Green had not always affected this persona, however. At her debutante ball in 1860 she danced with the Prince of Wales (later King Edward VII) at New York's Academy of Music, introducing herself as the Princess of *Whales*. For this occasion she wore the traditional debutante's white Swiss muslin dress with a pink sash, pink slippers and white filigree.[69]

Her nearly $5 million inheritance in 1865 from her father launched her financial career just in time to take advantage of post-Civil War financial opportunities. The death of her father, however, left Green with a lifelong fear of conspirators, assassins and kidnappers, even though there was no evidence to support those suspicions. She believed her father was strangled, that her poisoned aunt swindled her out of part of her father's inheritance, and later that her son was deliberately injured and maimed for life.

She married Edward H. Green in 1867 who was a wealthy trader and made his fortune in the Philippines. He was a meticulous dresser, discerning in choice of food and wine and aware of the comforts of life. Their marriage was a happy one until Edward mishandled some of her wealth. She separated from him, leaving him with seven dollars and a watch, but never severed the marriage and nursed him for several years before his death in 1902.[70] The paranoid Hetty Green then added his name to the list of those close to her who had been murdered.

A contrary view of this humorless, stern and stingy Hetty Green has been left by Anna van Twist, daughter of the manager of a Washington Street boarding house in Hoboken where Hetty rented rooms off and on between

13. Hetty Green
Hetty Green, on left, on the porch of her summer house, with guests, Mr. and Mrs.
M.A. Wilks, contrasting the flower-bearing Mrs. Wilks with the austere Hetty Green.
(Published c1911, Library of Congress, Prints and Photographs Division.)

1895 and her death in 1916. She knew the private Hetty Green and
remembered her as a jovial, gay old lady who got 'more out of life' than
anyone she had encountered, 'lived comfortably and ate well, although
her clothes were funny.'[71] Her gypsy nomadic existence from spare room
to small flat was not merely part of the character she created for herself,
however. It was justified by her imagined pursuit by conspirators and by
the reality of tax assessors who were after a contested tax on her $1.5
million cache of personal property in 1896.[72]

Hetty Green was skeptical of her rival, Victoria Woodhull, and her public
campaigns, leaving this comment on women financiers who involved
themselves with the newly emerging women's rights movement:

> I don't believe much in so-called women's rights ... although I wish
> women had more rights in business and elsewhere than they now have.
> I could have succeeded much easier in my career if I had been a man.[73]

Hetty Green died on 3 July 1916 in a brownstone townhouse at 5 West 19th Street bought for her son, and left an estate worth $100 million.[74]

TECHNOLOGICAL ALTERATIONS

Technology must be added to the elements of financial consolidation that drove the development of a national economy after the Civil War. The ribbons of wires that birthed the industry of telecommunications found their first applications on a Wall Street hungry for more efficient and faster ways to handle the increasing volumes of information. In 1866 the first permanent telegraph cable was laid under the Atlantic by Cyrus Field, connecting the City of London with Wall Street. Within a few years 150 messages a day were being transmitted.[75] The reduction in time of inter-national information transmission produced by the transatlantic telegraph from at least a week to a matter of minutes is relatively more revolution-ary than the transition from telephone or fax to the internet of the late twentieth century. A year later Edward A. Calahan, a telegraph operator for the American Telegraph Company, invented a printing device for stock prices that could be transmitted over telegraph lines. This became known as the *stock ticker* and linked price quotations on the exchange almost instantaneously with offices around the country, wherever there was a telegraph line. Calahan formed the Gold & Stock Telegraph Co. in 1867 to market his device. His company was taken over by the Western Union Telegraph Co. in 1871. The first stock ticker was installed in David Goesbeck & Co., Daniel Drew's headquarters. By 1880, there were some 1,000 stock tickers installed in Wall Street offices.[76] Five years later, after consolidating his fortune from this patented device, Calahan was invited to London where he installed the product on London's exchange and marketed it to City brokerage houses.[77]

Prior to the use of the stock ticker, messengers, known as 'pad shovers,' took down information on bits of paper and raced from the exchange to brokerage houses. Mythological characters imprinted their outline on a street that reveled in the good story told over drinks in the many bars nearby or in one of the fine eateries such as Delmonico's. One was the speedy William Heath, known as the 'American Deer,' who darted from place to place not breaking stride as he hurdled over whatever was in his path.[78] By the 1880s, Wall Street had become an industry, taking its place alongside the great manufacturing institutions. Thousands of messengers, clerks, accountants, cooks and cleaners were employed around the clock to produce The Street's financial products.

The next significant technology was Alexander Graham Bell's telephone, successfully tested in 1876 and installed on the NYSE two years later.[79] The telephone, in just a few years, reduced the time it took to get information from the floor of the exchange to a brokerage house from 15 minutes to 60 seconds.[80] Every technological innovation displaced some Wall Street employees in the short term, but the new inventions extended the possibilities of securities trading and ultimately added employment to Wall Street's operations. These three inventions – Morse's earlier telegraph, the stock ticker that builds on his invention and Bell's telephone – start the industry of telecommunications. They push the human brain's capacity to move information more quickly over space and to handle more of it. This industry is as important to economic transformations of the late nineteenth and twentieth centuries as the machine was to the industrial age, and the railroad to the transport of people and products in the second half of the nineteenth century.

They were a mixed blessing, however. Telecommunications extends the human brain as does manufacturing technology and railroads in extending the capacity of the human body's strength, speed and dexterity. More information can be accumulated and processed, all in faster time and shrunken space. These very attributes of telecommunications technology make speculative crises harder to manage, however. In the midst of a financial crisis managers need to 'buy time,' the conventional phrase used to convey the essence of the problem. The alterations wrought by the telephone, telegraph and stock ticker reduced time and made it more difficult for managers to calm the furies of speculation. In terms economists use, the supply of time has become scarcer due to the speed and scope of information transmissions, as today with further advances in telecommunications: the computer which permits instant moves of money by the nanosecond push of a button and the rapidity with which this information travels the globe. If time is in short supply, its 'price' increases precisely at that crisis moment when the demand for more time is placed on the stability of the system, further increasing its 'price.' Supply of time down, demand for time up, a recipe for a higher cost of time precisely when it needs to be lower during a financial crisis when managers need to buy more of it. But how does one buy more time without increasing demand and its cost? This is the dilemma in which crisis managers find themselves when a financial implosion starts. The speed at which the crisis builds on itself exceeds the time resources available to managers of the crisis. The new technology of telecommunications made this worse in the last decades of the nineteenth century, foreshadowing the even more serious problem this posed in the twentieth century.

The telegraph, stock ticker and telephone comprised a trio of technological changes that not only revolutionized the way business was conducted on The Street but also changed its physical appearance. An early historian of The Street refers to the tangle of wires, connecting office to exchange and office to office, as the 'financial ganglia of this land of national wealth and effort [where] through the air ... hundreds, seemingly thousands, of these wires stretched toward the Exchange. No bird could fly through their network, a man could almost walk upon them.'[81] In 1884 the city adopted a law that required the wires be placed underground.[82]

Discoveries in the new mathematical field of probability statistics led to efforts to predict movements of security prices. The most enduring was the Dow Jones Index, which first appeared on 3 July 1884 consisting of nine railroad stocks and two industrials.[83] The financial journalists, Charles Dow and Eddie Jones, teamed up in 1882 to form the Dow Jones Company at 15 Wall Street. The outgoing Jones, red-haired and angular with 'smiling blue eyes and a dimpled chin,' was the duo's public persona and the more reclusive Dow – dark eyes in deep sockets with a full black beard – the statistical tinkerer of the team.[84] Together they transformed both financial journalism and the tracking of stock movements. Their innovations were subsequently imitated on all of the world's major securities markets. By producing a simple and easy device for assessing stock prices in one composite index, they made investment decisions accessible to a broader public. The essence of the Dow theory, still employed today, is that 'trends in stock prices, once under way, will tend to persist until the market itself sends out a signal that these trends are about to lose their momentum and go into reverse.'[85]

On 8 July 1889 they published the first edition of the *Wall Street Journal*, a successor to their *Afternoon News Letter* – part of a group of so-called 'flimsies' because of the quality of paper on which they were printed – which they had been publishing since 1882. Dow and Jones professionalized financial journalism, and their newspaper identified Wall Street with the center of American finance. The *Journal* became the symbol of Wall Street's preeminence in American finance and prepared the ground for its prominence in worldwide finance in the new century.

PENNSYLVANIA AVENUE RESPONDS

The last decades of the nineteenth century presented a Wall Street poised to assert its worldwide preeminence in the next century. The invention and imposition of the trust by Morgan offered a way to accumulate capital extending beyond regions to the continent just as the railroads were doing the same physically. Both permitted an economy of scale and scope that its stronger competitors in Europe and Great Britain at this time never could achieve and are still trying with the new European Union. The telephone, telegraph and stock ticker were inventions in and of themselves of great import, but it is even more significant that they created the new science and industry of telecommunications that America continues to dominate.

The unification and consolidation of capital at the century's end was not without contest and controversy, however. Responding to these disorienting and radical discontinuities, populist forces opposed such a massing of economic and financial power. Their appeals to the national government for it to act as a representative government of all strata in society went unheeded at this time but were the foundation for impressive reforms in the next century. These admonitions would have to await the next century's economic crises that brought forth the national policies to deal with national capital.

Herein lies the predicament of the last decades of the nineteenth century: while capital was organizing itself on a national foundation, public policy remained largely within the jurisdiction of states, which could not cross borders and keep up with capital's border leaping capabilities. As the telegraph, stock ticker and telephone passed information and money across state boundaries and as railroads moved people and products transcontinentally, public policy was still localized. Pennsylvania Avenue had not kept pace with Wall Street's evolution. Pressures from Main Street on Pennsylvania Avenue to represent a broader public were insufficient to sever the alliance between Pennsylvania Avenue and Wall Street that ratified a privately self-regulated unification of capital markets. Wall Street Barons, and the trusts they administered, acquired power as never before and acted as a private government, answerable only to themselves and to their self-proclaimed 'Gentleman Bankers' Code.'

The initial challenge to their hegemony was the Interstate Commerce Act of 1887 established to deal with preferential freights rates granted to privileged users of railroads. This was the first regulatory regime, pressed on Congress by a coalition of small businesses, farmers and the old Jacksonian populist *mélange*. It set the pattern for America's twentieth-century theory of regulation that set it apart from European and British responses, which took the form of direct national ownership. Under this theory of regulation, capitalists in markets were allowed to play the game but with rules written by supposedly independent parties and refereed by neutral monitors. As in a sporting match the players are called upon to press the match with intensity but within rules detached from the players and refereed by an independent authority responsible for their fair and equal application.

8   The American Century

The twentieth century is known as America's, and it owes this designation as much to Wall Street as to any other institution. Prepared by the developments and innovations of the nineteenth century, Wall Street was poised to become the epicenter of a global financial architecture that framed America's commercial and cultural hegemony in the twentieth century. This did not occur automatically or immediately. First, the country had to overcome two great financial imbroglios – one in 1907 and a second in the 1930s – before its public monetary system and regulatory regime were sufficiently robust to withstand periodic cyclical crises. Second, it had to overcome an isolationist political and cultural legacy forged out of the nation's geographic illusion as a continental island, separated on the east and west from the rest of the world by two great oceans and bordered north and south by friendly nations. Wall Street knew this illusion when it saw it, but the rest of the country did not. Paradoxically, an internationalist Wall Street savored its worldwide reach and battled conservative isolationist tendencies even when it put itself at odds with its natural political allies on the right of the American political spectrum, who did not share this internationalist perspective.

Seen through the lense of Wall Street, American politics consistently presented a dilemma. Should it associate itself with the emerging progressive political alliances of regulatory reformers that were both more internationalist, but at the same time committed to making Pennsylvania Avenue representative of a broader civil society, one of whose targets for reform was the private money center on The Street? Or should it opt for an alliance with an anti-government ideology that would be more convenient for its domestic financial pursuits, but one that was unwilling to assert America's worldwide role and, therefore, was not suited to The Street's international requirements? Wall Street could not have it both ways: support for its international expansion and protection from public regulation. It opted for protection from public regulation, whenever this conundrum surfaced, and aligned itself with the isolationist Republican Party for the most part. It was not until the end of century that this political and doctrinal conundrum was resolved in President Bill Clinton administration's embrace simultaneously of an anti-regulatory posture and an aggressive international presence within the ideological construct of globalization. It fused together two previously competing philosophies into a Washington Consensus that was both internationalist and market-driven *laissez-faire.*

We owe the naming of the twentieth century as 'The American Century' to Henry Luce, founder of the magazine trilogy of *Time, Life,* and *Fortune.* To encourage the United States to abandon its isolationist posture some ten months before the bombing of Pearl Harbor, he wrote an article that conveyed the essence of the American idea that was to dominate the second half of the century. 'Consider the 20th century,' he wrote in *Life* magazine (February 1941) for a mass audience of Americans that spanned all classes: 'it is America's first century as a dominant power in the world.' He drew on the language of a revolution that was rooted in the ideal of a better world and comprised prosperous market economies, democratic political systems and technology – a composite that informs the global era of the twentieth century's *fin de siècle.* He said 'ours is also a revolutionary century, revolutionary ... in science and industry and also revolutionary in politics and the structure of society.' He concluded with a stirring call to arms: 'the world of the 20th century, if it is to come to life in any nobility of health and vigor, must be to a significant degree an American Century.'[1]

In this one brief essay Luce is able to conjure up the imagery of a United States poised to assert its assigned task, one that spoke to American symbols and ideals, a secularized evangelical faith in everything the previous century had been preparing. Set before a reading public, and edged in between *Life*'s photo essays, was a faith in technology, prosperity – read as the American system of manufacturing and what would later come to be called 'the market' – and the political system of democracy that harkens back to the idealism of Woodrow Wilson and his assertion of a right to self-determination as the organizing principle for nations after World War I. It must also be noted that it was possibly a century that could continue beyond the twentieth, because, as he said, it was America's 'first century as a dominant power in the world,' conveying to his audience that it might not be the last.

Luce's metric for assessing the century in 1941 evolved from the nineteenth century's *fin de siècle.* On the eve of the twentieth century, nearly $3 billion of foreign capital was invested in U.S. companies, a 50 per cent increase over the pre-Panic year of 1883. From a net importer of capital Wall Street in the 1890s became an exporter of capital to the rest of the world, a lender and creditor role that reversed its position earlier in the century as a debtor and importer of capital. One hundred million dollars of capital was exported to Canada, $2.2 million to China, to Sweden $10 million, Germany $20 million, Russia $25 million, and the United Kingdom, the largest sum of all, $227 million. It was an index of financial maturity and transformation that produced warnings of an American financial invasion of Europe echoed throughout the century. Count Goluchowski, the Austrian Foreign Minister, warned that 'European nations must close their ranks and fight, shoulder to shoulder, in order to success-fully defend their existence' against the financial threat from Wall Street.[2]

To Luce in 1941 the path from the start of the century, when The Street was poised to assume its international calling, was not linear, however. It was made up of fits and starts, forward and backward movements, zigs and zags. Wall Street had to overcome the financial crisis of 1907 and the crash of 1929. For Pennsylvania Avenue it had to assert its role as the public's agent willing to curb The Street's excesses. For Main Street it had to find its political voice through trade unions, interest groups and a political party ready to take up its program.

MORGAN'S LAST HURRAH

J.P. Morgan's 1895 bailout of the gold-backed U.S. dollar was a prelude to his even bolder intervention in 1907 to save the dollar. The ten-year expansion that had begun in 1897, after the financial crisis of 1895, was sparked by the further expansion of the trust. A wave of mergers and con-solidations occurred that would be unrivaled for nearly a century until the 1980s. The aggressive assertion of the Morgan-inspired Bankers' Code formed the ideology, in which money held by banks in trust for their customers' futures was transformed, almost magically, into great industrial trusts in which assets were privately held on behalf of the nation's future. When Morgan asserted this privilege over the dollar – the coin of the realm – he went too far and the public united against him. Main Street found its voice on Pennsylvania Avenue, asserted its claim to a public authority over national assets, and a place for civil society to regulate the activities of the great trusts if possible and disassemble them if necessary.

In the slightly more than 100 years of its existence, the nation had expe-rienced episodic financial crises of a rather regular nature. As we have seen in this history of Wall Street, the country's birth in 1792 was accompanied by a financial crisis, and nearly every decade thereafter witnessed one. On all of these occasions, Wall Street was situated in the eye of a financial hurricane that tore up enterprises and financial houses by their roots, leaving individual wreckage and re-building in its wake – 'creative destruction,' in the famous formulation of the Austrian-born economist, Joseph Schumpeter. Each of these was preceded by a relatively new economic formation of uncertain market value, whose undertaking was at first attractive but then turned to ashes as speculators drove up valuations and investors attracted to the allure of rapid riches had to dip deeper into the barrel for less valuable investments. Whether it be railroads, new industrial products or commercial shipping, there was Wall Street offering two forms of services: a vehicle for raising funds for the launch of these new ventures and a means for speculative profit-seeking. Each of the functions needed the other but, in reality, the one – the dream of speculative riches – undermined the other. The requirement of a liquid financial market that enabled the bundling of large sacks of financial capital for investment in new products inevitably led to a speculative thrust that undercut the investment's initial purpose in launching a new product. This existential force on The Street reappears regularly, most recently in the dot.com's over-valuation and implosion at the turn of the twentieth century. Thus, the 'street of dreams' of an easy road to riches inevitably unravels and becomes a 'boulevard of broken hearts.' Such was the case with the consummate financial crisis in the nation's history to that moment in 1907.

It was prepared by the overextension of consolidations and mergers into trusts. Between 1895 and 1904 over 3,000 companies disappeared as a result of mergers, peaking in 1899 when some 1,200 enterprises capital-ized at $2.27 billion were absorbed into industrial trusts with company names familiar to the twentieth century: Standard Oil, Carnegie Steel, United Fruit, National Biscuit and Union Carbide.[3] In virtually every one of these, the House of Morgan took the lead and his name on behalf of Wall Street was associated with managing these conglomerations through the legal and operational form of the trust. Morgan did not limit himself solely to private enterprise. He provided $40 million to the government of his sometime friend and other time foe, President Theodore Roosevelt, to purchase the Isthmus of Panama from the French in 1902 and then helped finance the building of the Panama Canal. The Canal was a symbol for an American Century, which embodied its essence: a public building project that overcame physical and medical obstacles such as malaria to become a monument to engineering similar to the monumentalism of the previous century's Erie Canal.

The 1907 financial crisis had its roots planted in these big financial undertakings. However, there was no central bank to manage liquidity expansion. The growth of the money supply was locked into a gold-backed position which limited the expansion of the money supply. This quandary, in which an economic expansion proceeds while money expansion does not, eventually implodes when the fig-leaf of prosperity is removed. Much the same story could be written about Argentina at the beginning of the twenty-first century, when its financial expansion overtook the limitation in liquidity caused by restricting money growth to the base of dollars in its treasury – in effect a dollarized restriction on money growth equating with the gold-based restriction on money growth imposed in the United States in the first decade of the twentieth century.

The signaling marker is debts that accumulate and cannot be serviced, fed by a secondary speculation from those who are interested purely in the financial paper and not in the industrial foundations that underlie money and finance. Typically at this juncture small Main Street investors come in too late, picking on financial crumbs that have fallen off the high table where insiders feast. There is a queuing-up of financial returns and each tranche yields lower returns. The big Street players are there first and pick the ripest fruit. Main Street investors invariably come in later, lured by speculators who bundle funds together, and can only pick fruit that is not yet ripe, not yet ready for harvest, whose returns are too low to justify the inflated speculative price. This motif informs every financial crisis from the first in 1792 to the latest in the dot.coms of the twentieth century's *fin de siècle*.

Leading up to the specific 1907 crisis, the overextension of the trusts was revealed in their increasingly risky undertakings, the high interest rates they had to pay for borrowing as they dove deeper into the financial well, and the use of trust securities as collateral by Wall Street banks for their loans to the same trusts. As much as half of the collateral retained by banks for loans to the trusts were the stocks and bonds of the trusts themselves. The trusts' cash flow required to sustain this fiction of solvency was in excess of their potential and made the whole structure susceptible to runs on it. There was an unhealthy and incestuous relationship between trust debt to Wall Street banks and the trusts themselves. The collateralization of loans with highly leveraged trust securities was a recipe for implosion. It was a financial Potemkin village.

The precipitating event that burst this bubble was the collapse of United Copper, a Morgan-backed venture led by the President of the Knickerbocker Trust, Charles T. Barney. When Morgan turned aside his petition for assistance, he shot himself; this was followed by other suicides among his investors.[4] If Morgan had recognized the consequences of his decision, he probably would have been more forthcoming to Barney. But he did not, and in the wake of this decision confidence collapsed, exposing the rather flimsy facade covering this grand financial edifice. It was only a short time after that on 22 October 1907 that Morgan once again had to preside over the financial rescue of the country from his beloved library, surrounded by one of the great private collections of ancient illustrated manuscripts that revealed to him a physical representation of the civilized world. This fitted nicely into Morgan's appropriation of the mantle of organizer and impresario for a financial world that he considered the highest form of contemporary civilization.

On 22 October the U.S. Secretary of the Treasury, George B. Cortelyou, put $25 million at Morgan's disposal to stabilize the American financial market and quiet fears of a default among foreign investors. Two days later, to avert an impending domestic financial implosion, the President of the New York Stock Exchange, Ransom H. Thomas, visited Morgan, walking across Broad Street from his office to Morgan's and informing him that widespread defaults among brokerage houses were imminent unless he, Morgan, came up with more than $20 million to dam the flood of losses on The Street. Summoned by Morgan, one banker after another strode into his office and by 2:16 in the afternoon, shortly before the market's close at 3 p.m., he had raised $25 million for loans to brokerage houses, thereby performing a central banker's 'lender of last resort' function. A messenger was sent to the floor of the Stock Exchange, and in the mythology that accompanied this drama, it is said that a roar so loud went up from the floor that Morgan could hear it across the street in his office.[5]

This did not immediately end the crisis, but the tide was turned. It took about two weeks for it all to end, during which time depositors lined up to withdraw money from their bank accounts in such numbers that city police handed out numbered chits to manage the queue, as in a bakery today. On 28 October George C. McClellan, the mayor of New York, asked Morgan for a $30 million bailout and was granted it, the first of four Morgan-bank-led bailouts of New York with the most recent occurring in the 1980s.[6] Amassing a total of $80 million in just one week, Morgan rescued Wall Street, New York and the U.S. Treasury's standing in foreign financial markets. Not since Alexander Hamilton had such a feat been accomplished, but this time it was by one private individual.

Morgan was a hero, certainly on Wall Street, in the City of London and other European financial centers and in the city of New York, but less so in other parts of the country. On the many Main Streets people were both in awe of his power, on the one hand, and alarmed, on the other, by the fact that one unelected man could have so much control over the public purse in a democracy. Morgan's finest hour for some – The Street – was his last hurrah for others as Main Street beseeched Pennsylvania Avenue to do something to rein in what came to be called the *Money Trusts*. The spectacle of the U.S. Treasury going to Morgan for a second time in a dozen years to rescue an unstable financial edifice that was largely of his own creation gave the decades-long populist political movement an opening it had not had before. Here was a foe that central casting could not have scripted better to suit its requirements: large and bear-like with a scarred face, bailing out his rich friends while throwing Main Street's small investors to the wolves. It was a melodrama of good and evil, similar to the spectacles played out on the stages of little theaters everywhere across the country in the form of the innocent deceived by the black-coated, bordering-on-demonic, mustachioed villain. Morgan was perfectly cast: aristocratic and contemptuous of popular democracy, flaunting his idea of a Bankers' Code, holding in trust the nation's most iconic asset: its money, the dollar. He also favored black, vested suits. There were no spin doctor's to help Morgan through this political minefield that was laid out on a public tableau with which he was not familiar. He could not forever preside privately from his office or his library in the solitary contemplation he preferred but instead had to appear in an unfamiliar and uncomfortable public milieu. All that was left was a stage and director's set to be composed and a script to be written. The grandeur of the U.S. Congress was the theater, and the stage set was provided by hearings of the House Banking and Currency Committee.

THE PUJO HEARINGS

The aftermath of the 1907 financial crisis and the Morgan-directed rescue was greeted like none other before. Celebrated on Wall Street as the success of a system of privately self-regulated finance, it was received elsewhere as simply further evidence of the concentration of economic power that answered not to a wider public but solely to the interests of the inner circle of finance. Evidence supported this. Morgan and his partners held 72 directorships in 112 corporations, underwrote some $2 billion in securities in the first decade of the century, and 78 major corporations used the Morgan bank. Among this conglomeration of corporate concentration was Morgan's control of banks – Bankers Trust and Guaranty Trust, among others – insurance companies, and securities underwriting, all captured in the emotive 'Money Trust,' whose origins are attributed to Charles A. Lindbergh Sr., a member of Congress from Minnesota.[7] A new progressive alliance forged out of older populist impulses, that had its roots in Andrew

Jackson's opposition to the second National Bank, merged with a new professional belief in the effectiveness of government to modulate private excesses. They found a presidential ally in Theodore Roosevelt.

In 1906 the Pure Food and Drug Act was passed, following on the previous century's Interstate Commerce Act regulating railroad rates, and the Sherman Anti-Trust Act to deal with monopoly power. Wall Street, however, in the form of its concentration of money and finance, was not yet explicitly addressed by these measures. Taken together, these new public agencies began to form a mosaic that decades later would complete an architecture of economic regulation. They fell under the rubric of the 'progressive' movement, an amalgam of the professionalization of public administration, impulses toward 'good government' and were energized by populist political reform. The gathering political direction alarmed The Street, as in this commentary from the *Commercial and Financial Chronicle*:

adverse legislation, national and state, directed against railroads primarily, but also against corporations generally; political attacks against men of wealth and men of capital; the serious advocacy of political and economic doctrines which would completely change the theory of our Government and revolutionize social relations – these and kindred matters had threatened the security and stability of investment values.[8]

Into this breach a Louisiana Democratic Congressman, Arsene Pujo, convened Hearings of the House Banking and Currency Committee to investigate whether there was a conspiracy of money interests and what legislation was needed to regulate this industry. His counsel was Samuel Untermyer, a New York trial lawyer, described by a Morgan biographer as no 'scruffy radical but an affluent lawyer who sported fresh orchids in his lapel ... whose pedigree collies had once beaten Pierpont's in competition.'[9] Hearings of Congressional committees come and go and few become a hinge point in changing public attitudes. The Pujo Hearings were one such event that did and, like most such hearings that become significant, there was a defining moment when the reclusive J.P. Morgan was forced out of his Wall Street office and library at home to present himself to a large public who knew of him but had never seen him in a setting he did not orchestrate.

The colloquy between Untermyer and Morgan pivoted on the issue of competition versus combination, because combinations in restraint of trade were illegal under U.S. anti-trust law at this time and very much in the public's lexicon. 'You are opposed to competition, are you not?' asked

Untermyer. 'No, I do not mind competition,' replied Morgan. 'You are an advocate of combination and cooperation,' pressed Untermyer, 'are you not?' 'Yes: cooperation, I should favor,' replied Morgan ('cooperation' was a less culpable word and one offered by Untermyer, thereby lowering Morgan's guard for a follow up series of questions in which he asked Morgan to explain his view of combination and concentration). 'The question of control,' Morgan began. 'Without ... control, you cannot do anything.' Feigning confusion, Untermyer probed: 'Unless you have got control, you cannot do what?' 'Unless you have got actual control,' expressing annoyance that someone could not understand something so simple, Morgan continued, 'you cannot control anything.' Now Untermyer understood and replied, 'Well, I guess that is right. Is that the reason you want to control everything?' The trap having been laid, Morgan now tried to wriggle out: 'I want to control nothing.' 'What is the point, Mr. Morgan, you want to make?' Untermyer replied, returning to his staged incomprehension by way of exposing Morgan's evasion, 'because I do not quite gather it.'[10]

This series of questions and responses achieved for Untermyer his objective of showing the mindset of Morgan and by extension of the others for whom he spoke. While adhering to an idea of competition, it was not the one associated with *laissez-faire* economics, one approximating competition on Main Street among small businesses and farmers who had to tough it out in markets they did not control, passively respond to price fluctuations, face interest rates and credit conditions controlled in New York's money center banks. The emblematic representative of these money center banks was J.P. Morgan, who was now for the first time sitting before the public and being questioned in a court of public opinion.

Following on this exchange, Untermyer next probed into Morgan's idea of the 'trust,' holding assets in his private control on behalf of the nation. Just what was this all about? How did Morgan see his function, weighing his own private interests and the public's? Untermyer began with a series of questions about why Morgan would want to amalgamate large corporate concentrations, except for reasons of private gain for which the control discussed earlier was essential. 'If it is good business for the interests of the country to do it, I do it,' said Morgan. To which Untermyer nearly leaped out of his chair in a follow-up question: 'But Mr. Morgan, is not a man likely, quite subconsciously, to imagine that things are for the interests of the country when they are good for business?' 'No sir,' shot back Morgan. 'You think that you are able to justly and impartially differentiate, where your own interests are concerned,' asked Untermyer, 'just as clearly as though you had no interest at stake, do you?' 'Exactly, sir,' a now contemptuous Morgan replied. With an incredulity that spoke volumes to his larger public audience, Untermyer concluded, 'And you are acting on that assumption all the time, are you not?' 'I always do, sir,' and Morgan went on to become the questioner, not aware of the conflict between his statements to the committee and his standing at the top of a pyramid of corporate and financial concentration. 'What is your question?' he asked. To which Untermyer replied, 'That the wish to bring these interests together may lead you to believe that the country is not injured by that sort of concentration.' 'I do not think so,' Morgan responded firmly but with a weariness that betrayed his contempt for having to explain his outlook to Untermyer and apparently failing to convey his views effectively.[11] For Morgan it must have been frustrating arguing over a premise which for him was so obvious but not having the language to represent his position in the context of a competing premise accepted by the Committee and by the larger Main Street public it was courting.

Two large points of contention were established by Untermyer which set up a final dialogue. Having constructed the case that revealed Morgan's views of concentration versus competition and Morgan's private interest aligned with his assertion of the public interest, it remained to set up Morgan's core belief in the Bankers' Code, its accord or conflict with historic American values.

As always in such hearings, among the several volumes of text one exchange stands out. Morgan came to describe his philosophy of the Bankers' Code, the preeminence of character in the world of finance, and his beloved idea of 'trust' – trust in the character of the individual with whom you were engaged in a transaction, the trust as warden over the assets of an individual, a company, and indeed the nation's assets. Untermyer asked Morgan, 'is not commercial credit based primarily upon money or property?' 'No, sir, the first thing is character,' Morgan answered. Stacked against Morgan's denials, obfuscation and challenge to the committee's legitimacy, this revelation stood out in stark clarity. To the audience on Main Street it was received with disbelief. Here was a statement that the big banking houses on Wall Street were indeed a closed club where 'character' trumped the transparent balance sheet. For small farmers, shopkeepers and workers who had to provide so much paper to their local bank for a tiny bit of credit, what to Morgan was obvious and innocent was shocking to Main Street. As this colloquy proceeded Untermyer probed into Morgan's underwriting criteria. Does the 'banking house assume no legal responsibility for the value of the bonds it backs?'

'No, sir, but it assumes something else that is still more important, and that is the moral responsibility' of the bond holder to see that the management of the enterprises he holds in trust is performing properly. This confirmed Morgan's interest in protecting the bond holder. In the interpretation of his biographer, by this statement, Untermyer extracted from Morgan 'his rationale for the one-man control of the railroads' and other trusts he sponsored.[12]

The Pujo committee did not conclude there was a Money Trust – a conspiracy that would have been in violation of law – despite considerable circumstantial evidence. Instead they used the term 'community of interest,' born out of the club-like atmosphere among Wall Street bankers, their shared values and common interest in seeing themselves as the most effective custodians of financial wealth, emphatically requiring no regulation from Pennsylvania Avenue. The hearings, however, did irreparable damage to the reputation and awe with which these bankers had previously been endowed. Main Street saw them as rather arrogant men who appropriated great wealth and wielded power over them with a rationale that was at odds with the popular democratic principles taught in Main Street's schools. There seemed also to be a double standard, one for banking on Wall Street and another for banking on Main Street when it came to the criteria for the extension of credit and loans.

Morgan thought he had made a stout defense of his life and his view of the world. 'Father made a magnificent showing,' Morgan's daughter Louisa wrote in her diary, 'Untermyer *nowhere*,' reflecting not just a daughter's fidelity to her father but larger sentiment on Wall Street.[13] It was not received that way by the public, however. In his bewilderment this served only to confirm Morgan's predisposition toward reclusiveness. He went into semi-retirement after the Pujo Hearings and spent his time on his art and manuscript collections, among other interests such as the Episcopal Church and various New York museums he underwrote. He became ill in 1913 during his annual European trip and on 31 March he died in Rome. 'There will be no successor to Morgan,' said the *Wall Street Journal*. 'Now Wall Street is beyond the need or possibility of one-man leadership.'[14] His body was returned at the behest of his erstwhile foe, Secretary of State William Jennings Bryan, the great opponent of Morgan's cherished gold standard, and on 14 April 1913 trading was suspended on the New York Stock Exchange from 10 till noon in his honor and memory, the first time this was done for a private individual. That year also saw the passing of the torch to a new Morgan, John Pierpont Jr. (known as 'Jack'). Symbolically it was marked with the laying of a cornerstone by him on 30

December for a new Morgan headquarters at 23 Wall Street. It contained a copper box with Pierpont's will, a copy of Pierpont's Pujo committee testimony, the articles of partnership for the house of Morgan and, in a nod toward the Morgan's origins in British merchant banking, the form used for a letter of credit.[15]

THE MONEY QUESTION

The year Morgan died, 1913, produced two additional and significant developments on the path to financial reform. It was the year Congress established the Federal Reserve System, thereby resolving a controversy over a national bank that dates back to the founding of the country and Hamilton's first National Bank, carrying through to Jackson's successful challenge to Biddle's second National Bank in the 1830s.[16] It also saw a powerful critique of Wall Street's 'moneyed oligarchy,' as it was labeled, coming from a new source of progressive legal scholar whose writings appeared in the American mainstream media. Louis D. Brandeis, known as the 'people's lawyer' and who later became a Justice of the Supreme Court – whom Morgan's biographer describes as the 'most cunning and resourceful foe the House of Morgan would ever face' – launched a searing critique of The Street's banking rule by a handful of houses and did so in the popular and large circulation *Harper's Weekly*. He coined the phrase, 'other people's money,' to characterize succinctly the issue.[17] 'The development of our financial oligarchy followed ... [a] usurpation,' he wrote for a lettered and influential audience, thus legitimating a critique that had previously been outside the mainstream of elite opinion, 'proceeding by gradual encroachment rather than by violent acts [produced] subtle and often long-concealed concentration of distinct functions, which are beneficent when separately administered and dangerous only when combined in the same person.'[18]

Shortly after the publication of his articles, the editor of *Harper's Weekly*, Norman Hapgood, invited Brandeis to meet Thomas W. Lamont, later Morgan Chairman, at the University Club on Fifth Avenue (December 1913). 'Your are picturing our firm,' Lamont said, 'as having this gigantic power over men and matters,' implying that Brandeis did not really know how the financial world worked – a common ploy between critic and target for critique. 'It has the power, Mr Lamont,' shot back Brandeis. 'You may not realize it, but you are feared, and I believe the effect of your position is toward paralysis rather than expansion.' 'You astonish me beyond measure,' replied a dismissive Lamont. 'How in the world did you arrive at the belief that people are afraid of us, or that we have this terrific power?' 'From my own experience,' a calm Brandeis retorted.[19]

Brandeis perfected the substantive challenge to the concept of the Bankers' Code more effectively than anyone, created the argument for arm's-length banking arrangements that would break the intimate ties between banker and enterprise to which money was lent, and pressed the case for separation among various forms of banking that would inform the later New Deal reforms of the 1930s. This sophisticated attack on financial concentration coincided with the inauguration of the new Federal Reserve System.

The United States did not have a central bank until this moment; instead, Wall Street money-center banks – so called because they were the depository and manager of deposits from banks throughout the country – acted as a *de facto* private central banking system. They controlled the expansion of credit and acted as a lender of last resort as with Morgan in 1907. Morgan's confrontation with the Pujo committee wrote the final chapter on this anomalous arrangement for a country whose financial system was as large and important for worldwide finance as was the United States.

The background to this nearly century-long debate over a national bank is curious in that Wall Street and Main Street held shifting positions on what came to be known as the *money question*. During the Jacksonian period, Main Street opposed the Second National Bank and the alleged oligarchy of money rule from the northeast. They reversed position and came to support a public national bank after the Civil War, however. The reason for this switch was their experience without a public national bank and Wall Street's appropriation of its functions. Wall Street's money-center banks were seen as restricting credit to borrowers on Main Street in favor of large Wall Street and foreign borrowers. The subtext for this dispute was easy or hard money, a rigid adherence to a gold standard or a looser currency backed by a combination of the more expansive combination of silver and gold. Wall Street supported the hard-money, gold-standard position, it argued, to restrain inflation and prudently calibrate the expansion of liquidity in order to solidify its creditworthiness among European bankers. In their conventional role as protectors of the value of existing wealth, The Street's bankers feared inflation above all else and saw themselves as the custodian of a strong dollar. Main Street's soft-money posture offered an alternative argument for economic growth through more liberal credit and the creation of new wealth. Lines were drawn: protect existing wealth (Wall Street) or create new wealth (Main Street). Since Main Street bankers were dependent on Wall Street for their lending capacity, their hands were tied when potential borrowers came to them for loans. Additionally, they were tethered to Wall Street through their deposits in The Street's money-center banks, because these banks paid interest on idle deposits. Consequently, Main Street bankers' interest in the protection of their wealth was coincident with The Street's hard-money, anti-inflation bias for the most part. Main Street's bankers found their prosperity linked to Wall Street's.

The money question figured prominently in the origins of the American populist political movement drawn from outside the northeast and made up of farmers, small businesses on Main Street and an emerging labor movement. Although difficult to pinpoint in its origins, a likely candidate for the formal establishment of the populist political movement was a meeting held in Lampass County, Texas in 1877 when the Knights of Reliance was organized. It warned against an impending future 'when all the balance of labor's products become concentrated into the hands of a few, there to constitute a power that would enslave posterity.'[20] The Knights were reconstituted in a few years as the Farmers Alliance, which a decade later spread from the Dakotas in the west to the Carolinas in the east.

Money was not a commodity for management by experts on Wall Street, argued these Populist Alliances, but was at its core a political question open to democratic adjudication by all classes and mediated through the political system. Says a chronicler of the Federal Reserve, 'money' was a

political question – a matter of deliberate choice made by the state. ... Money was an everyday argument among competing interests, in which some would benefit and some would lose ... a social plan that rewarded or punished, stimulated or restrained. Money might encourage democratic aspirations or thwart them.[21]

Nineteenth-century discourse was rife with these debates; ordinary citizens were familiar with the nuances and the polemics of the arguments, unlike the muted discussions over what had become an abstraction in the twentieth century. The money question exercised the nation's politics in the three decades leading up to the establishment of the Federal Reserve. In 1886 the various Farmers Alliance chapters meeting in Cleburne, Texas drew up a platform plank with principles that embodied federal regulation of the banking system and a national currency whose expansion was not constrained by gold. This was refined further at the St. Louis Alliance convention in 1889 where these principles were elaborated into detail that framed the architecture of a central bank. This movement powered the

14. The 'Money Question'
Another view of the bulls and bears (and lambs – lower right) of Wall Street, published in 1916. Here the powerful images of Main Street in the person of from left, the miner, farmer, African-American share-cropper, Hispanic rancher and generic factory worker challenge The Street's claim that it is the source of American wealth creation. Meekly the bulls and bears (and lamb) are portrayed as supplicants to the 'real' creators of wealth symbolized by the factory, mining car and oil rig (to the right). (By William Allen Rogers for the New York *Herald*, 16 October 1916, Library of Congress, Prints and Photographs Division.)

trajectory toward its realization, which, however, looked quite different from the ultimate Federal Reserve.

The St. Louis plan envisioned a central bank administered by an elected board with broad representation and decentralized to take account of distinct regional requirements. The 1913 Federal Reserve system accepted the idea of regional adjuncts of the central bank but placed them under direct ownership and control of private banks in a region. Rather than directly elected governors, it imposed an indirect democratic process in which governors of the Federal Reserve were appointed by the President with Senate approval. 'The money creation system that was adopted in 1913,' argues an historian of the Federal Reserve System, 'preserved the banking system as the intermediary that controlled the distribution of new money and credit.'[22] This was not what its originators had in mind.

Money-center banks on Wall Street lost little influence after the creation of a Federal Reserve they initially opposed. They prospered in two ways. First, the U.S. government and the Treasury now assumed the burden of lender-of-last-resort when bail-outs of the financial system were required, relieving The Street's banks of this expensive and troublesome obligation. Second, this Federal Reserve system ultimately de-personalized the money question and placed a cloud of mystification around the banking system. There no longer was an individual such as Morgan who could so readily be identified with Main Street's complaints. The melodrama faded and its villainous heavy was replaced by a modern, ambiguous and professional managerial class which was less easy to target by a political opposition. As a peculiar American institution of the reformist twentieth century, the Fed, as it came to known, was a mixture of the private and the public, blurring the lines between the political and private spheres of activity. It was the quintessential representative of the Progressive era in which professional public administration would manage national assets presumably for a public's interest while tied closely to and dependent upon a powerful private interest – The Street's banks. Modified twice by Congress – in 1935 and 1980 – the Federal Reserve became, in alliance with Wall Street, one of the most powerful forces in the consolidation of the American Century.

THE GREAT CRASH AND ITS AFTERMATH

The Federal Reserve and Morgan's death in 1913 were but two of the prophetic events of that year. The third was the ensuing consequence of World War I for Wall Street. From a net debtor of more than $3 billion in 1914 it became a net creditor of $5 billion to the rest of the world by 1917. As the *Manchester Guardian* editorialized, 'It can hardly be doubted that under these circumstances, New York will enter the lists for the financial leadership of the world. ... American bankers will have acquired the experience they have hitherto lacked in the international money market and all this strengthened financial fabric will rest upon an economic fabric which the war will have much expanded.'[23] It was a role, however, that produced an ambivalence. Was the country better off as an island enclave disengaged from the world or should it assert its ordination to spread the American idea?

Wall Street was given a crude example of what this dilemma implied on 16 September 1920 when a horse-drawn wagon loaded with 500 pounds of iron sash-weights and explosives parked on The Street between Morgan's building and the U.S. Assay Office on the other side. In the explosion which ensued the iron weights traveled like machine gun projectiles through a lunchtime crowd, killing 38 and wounding 300, narrowly missing the young Joseph Kennedy, father of the Kennedy dynasty. The Morgan building's Tennessee marble was scarred and damaged with pockmarks that have been kept unrepaired to this day as a memorial to the two bank employees who died.[24] This incident was as alarming to Wall Street in 1920 as the attack on the World Trade Center in 2001. A wave of anti-immigrant sentiment engulfed the nation. The bombing itself was associated with immigrants. As great as the shock was to the nation and to Wall Street, the bombing came to symbolize the dilemma faced by a nation unsure of whether it wanted to join the world or remain apart from it. The decision to enter World War I evoked this controversy, and incidents such as this were seen as extensions of that decision, confirming the isolationist predisposition of many Americans.

In the aftermath of the war and the ensuing decade of the 1920s an aggressive bull market engulfed Wall Street. With the automobile transforming the way Americans moved about, electricity coming into its own

15. Bombing
In the aftermath of the bombing on Wall Street that was directed at the Morgan building, as police officers and citizens survey the damage to an over-turned automobile. (Library of Congress, Prints and Photographs Division.)

in changing the way people lived in their houses and worked in the nation's factories, and the telephone expanding into homes and workplaces speeding up the flow of information, the country seemed to be set upon a path to permanent prosperity. No one saw the flimsy base upon which this edifice was constructed, as is always the case with a classic bubble economy.

When the bubble burst on Thursday, 24 October 1929, it started on Wall Street with the failure of the unfortunately named Bank of United States, the fourth largest in New York with 450,000 depositors, whose name gave it more importance than it actually had.[25] This started a minor run on banks and symbolically was the trigger for the crash. One unresolved question surrounding the collapse of the Bank of United States is why the Morgan bank did not intervene to stem the run. There has always been speculation that it was due to prejudice against Jews on Wall Street, because the Bank of United States was Jewish-owned and catered to a Jewish clientele. As Morgan's biographer conjectures,

with so many Morgan rescues occurring in those years, all backed by high-flown rhetoric about saving the banking system, it's hard to believe religion wasn't a major factor behind Wall Street's refusal to act. Hundreds of thousands of Jewish depositors were not worth one Charles Mitchell. [National City Bank] Jews were always a blind spot in the [Jack] Morgan vision, no less than in the days when Pierpont Morgan had vied with Jacob Schiff.[26]

The panic moved on the next day to the Stock Exchange where a wave of selling attacked share values. Heavily margined holders of stocks – the practice of buying stocks with leveraged debt – saw their brokers call in loans, and a cascade of falling share values followed as everyone needed to sell to cover these margin calls. No one was buying. The actual losses for the economy were small but the symbolic value was large. The best estimates are that in 1928 only some 3 million individuals out of a population of 120 million owned securities, concentrated in 600,000 margin accounts in the large cities with few such accounts among workers, farmers or small business people.[27] They held their savings in banks, which also began to fail, or purchased stocks with cash. The fall-out from brokers calling in loans from margined stock holders on Wall Street caused The Street's banks to run short of cash. They then called in their loans to banks around the country on Main Street which were tied into the money-center banks on Wall Street. The resulting domino effect produced a withdrawal

16. Anticipating the Crash of 1929

In the expressionist style of this period, the artist in 1926 foreshadows a Wall Street in panic that occurs three years later, with prices falling (upper left), aside a broker about to shoot himself, and the stock ticker machine from center to bottom left, where the tape is in the hand of a dark somber face. Accompanying this lithograph is a poem by Vachel Lindsay: 'What will you trading frogs do on a day when Armageddon thunders through the land, when each sad patriot rises, mad with shame, his ballot or his musket in his hand.' (By William Gropper, *New Masses*, v. 1, October 1926. Library of Congress, Prints and Photographs Division.)

of money from the economy, a contraction of liquidity – the very opposite of what was required. The Federal Reserve was created to handle precisely these sorts of financial problems.

Facing its first management crisis, the Federal Reserve defaulted. They followed the lead of a Wall Street ever fearful of inflation, not understanding that the problem was deflation, and placed priority on calming the fears of foreign clients and protecting bond holders. Instead of expanding liquidity to cover the market's contraction of liquidity by pumping money into the system, they adopted a *laissez-faire* position, allowing the financial system to contract. The subsequent contraction of liquidity in the banking system spread beyond the financial to the manufacturing sector and a vicious downward cycle of deflation and depression ensued. Its origins were in a financial bubble in which share values were driven up by speculation on leveraged margin accounts, all motored by an inequality in income that produced idle funds at the top and inadequate resources for consumption in the middle to bottom. However, the Fed was culpable, too, in following Wall Street's lead against aggressive intervention, in bending with the hurricane-like forces of the wind instead of standing against them. Main Street's suspicions were confirmed: the Federal Reserve was not on its side, but had instead been appropriated by The Street to do its bidding. This set the stage for a confrontation between Pennsylvania Avenue and Wall Street unique in the nation's history. It followed on Franklin D. Roosevelt's election to the presidency in 1932.

A NEW AND BETTER DEAL

Franklin D. Roosevelt's election heralded a New Deal for the ordinary American and a new wave of regulatory constraints for Wall Street. Shortly after his inauguration in March 1933 he asked Congress for banking legislation that would be based on the 'ancient truth that those who manage banks, corporations, and other agencies handling or using other people's money are trustees acting for others,' with an obvious nod to J.P. Morgan's philosophy and Brandeis's critique, but now asserting Pennsylvania Avenue's role in assuming and defending trusteeship over the value of the nation's money. This clear statement followed on another challenge to bankers in his inaugural address: 'the money changers have fled from their high seats in the temple of our civilization [and] we now restore that temple to the ancient truths.'[28] These were words Wall Street had never before heard from Pennsylvania Avenue but their defenses were down, having been shattered by a financial and economic reality and decades-long public debate. Now the representatives of a popular politics on Main Street had the upper hand, and The Street found itself in an unfamiliarly defensive position. In the summer of 1932, alarmed by Roosevelt's embrace of banking reform making its way through Congress, Russell Leffingwell – a Morgan bank top manager, later Chairman of its board and one of those few in the House who had voted for Roosevelt – wrote to 'Frank': 'You and I know that we cannot cure the present deflation and depression by punishing the villains, real or imaginary ... and when it comes down to the day of reckoning nobody gets very far with all this prohibition and regulation stuff.' Undeterred, Roosevelt, who by now was seen by many on The Street as a traitor to the New York aristocracy from which he came, bluntly replied by saying, 'I wish we could get from the bankers themselves an admission that in the 1927 to 1929 period there were grave abuses and that bankers themselves now support whole-heartedly methods to prevent recurrence thereof.'[29]

As before after the 1907 crisis, Congress convened hearings, this time in the Senate Subcommittee on Banking and Currency under the direction of chief committee counsel, Ferdinand Pecora, former Assistant District Attorney from New York. As a representative of a new class of immigrants, who made their way to power through the city's political machine, Pecora knew well the haughtiness and disdain with which he and his fellow immigrants were held by The Street's denizens. He was born in Sicily and his thick, wavy, peppered gray hair betrayed his origins. As Assistant District Attorney, he had tangled with Wall Street's operations, from bucket shops to money-center banks. His investigation started before Roosevelt's inauguration in January 1933 and carried through May 1934, filling eight volumes and 10,000 pages.[30] In the popular idiom bankers were transformed into 'banksters' by the hearings.

Three decades earlier in the Pujo hearings, the central confrontation was between the committee's counsel, Untermyer, and the head of the House of Morgan – J.P. This was to be repeated in the colloquy between J.P.'s son, Jack Morgan, and Pecora, whom he once in private called a 'dirty little wop.' Now J.P.'s son was engaged in verbal sparring with another ethnic. After Morgan's initial refusal to cooperate with the committee and open its records to investigators, the Senate ordered the House of Morgan to comply. For the first time outsiders were able to examine the files at 23 Wall Street. By extension the public was able to peer into the workings of the great House of Morgan and its operations. Finally on 23 May 1933 the awaited showdown occurred between Jack Morgan, now 66, and the

53-year-old Pecora, the 'imperturbable Bourbon and the assertive immigrant,' in the characterization of Morgan's biographer.[31]

Jack Morgan's opening prepared statement took its lineage from his father's: 'The private banker is a member of a profession which has been practiced since the middles ages,' he began.

> In the process of time there has grown up a code of professional ethics and customs, on the observation of which depends his professional reputation ... if in the exercise of his profession, the private banker disregards this code, which could never be expressed in any legislation, but has a force far greater than any law, he will sacrifice his credit.

Thus once again a reversion to the Bankers' Code, Morgan's birthright, as having more strength in exercising trusteeship than any act of Congress. Here we see the core point of dispute. Should Wall Street remain a self-regulating private organization or be subject to the rule of law enacted by elected members of Congress? Would The Street be subject to regulation by a democratically elected Congress or would it be construed as a voluntary organization regulated by markets? Would Pennsylvania Avenue assert its rule-making and refereeing claims on Wall Street on behalf of a Main Street that had no access to influence on The Street?

As the hearings wore on, Morgan dug himself into a deeper hole by his testimony. Take this exchange with Senator Duncan U. Fletcher of Florida and Chairman of the committee. Fletcher wanted to know whether Morgan and his kind would accept anyone's business, in just the way it was done on Main Street. 'I suppose if I went there [to Morgan's bank], even though I had never [seen] any member of the firm, and had $100,000 I wanted to leave with the bank, you would take it, wouldn't you?' 'No; we should not do it.' 'You would not?' an incredulous Fletcher asked. 'Not unless you came in with some introduction, Senator.' It did not end there at this colloquy on the Bankers' Code. Pecora was able to show from the investigation of Morgan's records that he and his partners held 126 directorships in 89 corporations with $20 billion in assets. Yet Jack had paid no income tax between 1930 and 1932 and all 20 Morgan partners likewise paid no income tax in either 1931 or 1932. The flood gates were open. Nothing could protect The Street's defense of its code from Congressional legislation, not even a public relations stunt, designed to 'humanize' Morgan and promoted by Charles Leef of the Ringling Brothers Circus. He had the 27-inch, 32-year-old midget, Lya Graf, brought to Capital Hill from the circus and sat her on Morgan's knee. A photo of this appeared in virtually every newspaper the next day and became a signature Depression photo. Morgan actually appeared bemused and fatherly toward the adult on his lap, but the unintended subtext was of a large man of power and a fragile tiny woman, the one sitting throne-like and the other a supplicant on his lap. The man of power, the banker, could obviously at any moment throw the significantly weaker Graf off his lap onto the ground. It summed up main Street's understanding of the distortion of power between itself and Wall Street and, once again, personified it in a Morgan.

Morgan was frustrated by his inability to convince the public of his and his house's fidelity to the country and its financial morality. The consequence of the hearings became for Morgan a form of psychologically and self-imposed internal exile in his own country, albeit still with immense wealth and power. He could never overcome his sense that he let his father down and was the personification of the defeat and demise of the Bankers' Code. Lya Graf's fate was far more tragic, however. Projecting her into a celebrity spotlight produced humiliation and jokes about her minute size that she could not tolerate. Half Jewish – her real name was Lia Schwarz – she returned to her native Germany in 1935 and two years later was sent to Auschwitz where she died, a victim of the dual stigma of being Jewish and stunted in her growth. Morgan was to know nothing of this or how his meeting with her for a public relations stunt to smarten up his image was to be the cause of this tragedy.

In quick order and in the midst of these epochal hearings the first legislation regulating Wall Street's securities markets was passed by Congress: the Securities and Exchange Act of 1934, forcefully opposed by Jack Morgan on behalf of The Street. The essence of this act was transparency, a truth-in-securities law that required registration and full disclosure with enforcement powers in the SEC (Securities & Exchange Commission) and the Federal Trade Commission, whose existing powers were expanded to cover new issues of securities. *Caveat vendor* supplanted *caveat emptor* as a regulatory principle that has performed imperfectly but certainly provided a degree of protection for buyers of securities they would otherwise not possess. A year earlier the Glass–Steagall Act (1933) had offered coordinate protection for ordinary bank depositors by, first, prohibiting commercial and savings banks from investing in the stock market's securities, and second, establishing a bank insurance fund for protection of depositors: the Federal Deposit Insurance Corporation. In essence, this legislation took direct aim at the House of Morgan, segmenting the banking industry between commercial bank short-term lending and long-term capital financing through investment banks' underwriting of stocks and bonds.

A financial institution had to choose which of these it wanted to pursue – investment banking or large, customer-based commercial banking – and a firewall was erected between the two functions of banking. The Morgan's chose investment banking, harking back to its origins in the merchant banking system of the City of London.

The intellectual source for the conceptualization of all this legislation was attributed to the now Supreme Court Justice, Louis Brandeis, and his famous work of 20 years earlier, encapsulated in 'Other People's Money.' This phrase found its way into President Roosevelt's speeches and its use was not lost on the Morgans. Early in 1934 after a re-issue of Brandeis's book, Russell C. Leffingwell – Morgan partner and conduit to the Democratic Party – wrote to Thomas W. Lamont, Chairman of the Morgan house, placing responsibility for the Glass–Steagall banking reform legislation on the pen of Brandeis in less-than-flattering terms. 'I have no doubt that he inspired it, or even drafted it. The Jews do not forget. They are relentless.' Leffingwell understood the depth of the political problem facing the Morgans and the banking oligarchy on Wall Street. 'I believe we are confronted with the profound politico-economic philosophy,' he told Lamont, 'matured in the wood for twenty years, of the finest brain and the most powerful personality in the Democratic party, who happens to be a Justice of the Supreme Court.'[32]

Brandeis was no doubt influential, more through his writings than direct drafting. The actual designer of banking legislation, particularly Federal Reserve reform, was an unlikely luminary who emerged from far outside The Street in the person of Marriner Eccles: a Mormon from Ogden (Utah), owner of the First National Bank in Ogden, who mounted one of the few successful ploys to stem the run on banks in the early 1930s. Folksy, like Jimmy Stewart in Frank Capra's 1946 film, *It's a Wonderful Life*, when lines started to form among depositors wanting to withdraw their money from his bank, he made a display of the cash his bank had on hand, so they could see the reserves he possessed. 'Many of you have been in line for a considerable time,' he said to the throng waiting at the bank's teller windows. 'Instead of closing at the usual three o'clock, we have decided to stay open just as long as there is anyone who desires to withdraw his deposit or make one.' To make this work, Eccles had arranged for the regional Federal Reserve in Salt Lake City to bring a large amount of dollars to the Ogden bank, and he showed this off proudly. With a transparency unusual for banks, he said to the crowd, 'As all of you can see, we have just brought up from Salt Lake City a large amount of currency that will take care of all your requirements. There is plenty more where that came from.'[33] This exercise taught him another lesson: when the Federal Reserve assumed its rightful role as lender-of-last-resort, it could plug leaks and the dam would hold out against a potential flood of depositors' withdrawals.

Roosevelt named Eccles Chairman of the Federal Reserve in 1934, a position he held for 14 years. An unlikely choice, drawn far from the geography and ideology of Wall Street, Eccles was the populist's dream: a banker of solid probity from the West, unburdened by the East's albatross of the Bankers' Code, and tutored in the banking needs of small borrowers on Main Street – much like the clientele he served in Ogden, Utah. He steered banking legislation he had drafted through the Congress. He reformed the Federal Reserve by placing control of monetary policy in a new Open Market Committee, thereby removing it from the control of The Street's money-center banks where it had been since 1913.

Taken together, these and other measures for the first time inserted Pennsylvania Avenue into the triad that included Main and Wall Streets, placing Pennsylvania Avenue on the side of Main Street and relegating Wall Street to a defensive position in which, for the first time since 1792, it began to lose the argument that it was a private, self-regulating membership organization and knew how to protect the public better than Pennsylvania Avenue. We hear echoes of this at the turn of the twenty-first century in the self-regulated accounting industry's assertion of precisely this point after the collapse of Enron, WorldCom and others and the revelations of accounting misfeasance and malfeasance. Of course, this idea goes back to the very origins of Wall Street when it used exactly this defense in 1792 against prospective regulation by the state legislature of New York.[34]

During Eccles's tenure and supported by Roosevelt's equally populist Secretary of the Treasury, Henry Morgenthau, Jr., monetary and financial policy began to approximate to what Main Street sought from Pennsylvania Avenue: an honest hearing and attention to its requirements, persistent challenges to Wall Street hegemony on behalf of Main Street, and credit policies that placed them as co-equal with bond holders on The Street. This did not last beyond a decade or two, as Wall Street regrouped and adapted to a new political reality, but at least for a time the nation was exposed to the way a balanced and proportional financial system could function, leaving it an historical record against which prior and subsequent arrangements could be measured. The far-reaching banking and monetary reforms of the New Deal framed public policy for nearly half a century until the deregulatory thrust of the 1980s undid them. From Pennsylvania Avenue as rule-maker and umpire for the game of money and finance, it retrogressed after the 1980s to its pre-1930s role as cheerleader on the sidelines, but ever ready to bail out the banks when they overextended themselves.

THE ERA OF GLOBAL FINANCE

The regulatory regime established during the 1930s prevailed until its undoing in the deregulatory movement of the 1980s. In that half-century the American economy grew faster than in any other comparable period in its history. It was also the only such half-century span without a major or even minor financial crisis on Wall Street, which had become accustomed to one every ten years or so from its origins in 1792 to the 1930s. The first pre-1930s-style financial crisis occurred in October 1987 and a more serious one 15 years later in 2002. Many on The Street would deny that the financial regime constructed during the 1930s had anything to do with this half-century record of stable economic growth. While grudgingly accepting and adapting to Pennsylvania Avenue's attention during the 1930s, The Street resisted any further incursions into its private self-regulating world, notwithstanding the advantages of the stability brought to Wall Street by the Roosevelt reforms and the post-World War II international financial regime.

At the end of World War II, Wall Street and the nation now assumed the worldwide leadership role the United States could objectively claim. It was the moment for Luce's American Century, and with some fits and starts the country had asserted its title by the 1950s. This was prepared for by an extraordinary conference toward the end of World War II at Bretton Woods, New Hampshire – convened in a turn-of-the-century grand hotel that backed onto the White Mountains – where some 730 delegates from 44 countries met to plan for the post-war world economy, which had been laid to rubble, initially by the breakdown of the world economy during the Great Depression, and, secondly, reduced literally to ruins by the war itself. The lone remaining economy left standing after these twin disasters was that of the United States. The conference planning had actually begun shortly after America's entry into the war. On 14 December 1941 – a week after the Japanese attack on Pearl Harbor – President Roosevelt wrote to his Secretary of the Treasury, Henry Morgenthau, Jr., 'to think about and plan for an Inter-Allied Stabilization Fund [that would] provide the basis for post-war international monetary stabilization arrangements; and to provide a post-war "international currency".'[35] In this endeavor Roosevelt involved both the Soviet Union and Great Britain, the three principal allied governments during the war. The Soviet Union took little interest in this project. The British, however, did, and Churchill assigned the task of developing a plan to John Maynard Keynes, the most important living economist. Morgenthau gave the portfolio to one of his deputies, Harry Dexter White, the son of Jewish immigrants from Lithuania and virtually unknown when he was given this assignment. White, however, came to be every bit as clever as Keynes in the negotiations over the institutions that would govern the world economy, and, of course, he was aided by the fact that the U.S. held most of the strong cards in the deck by virtue of its relative economic and financial strength.

What came out of Keynes's and White's exchange of memos and proposals were institutions that for the first time represented a publicly established set of boundaries over the operations of the world economy and finance to accompany the New Deal's inspired boundaries around the domestic financial regime. At Bretton Woods two new international institutions were established: the World Bank (officially called the International Bank for Reconstruction and Development) to raise and channel capital to where it was needed, and the International Monetary Fund, whose original function was to assist in the stabilization of foreign exchange rates and act as a lender-of-last-resort when they fluctuated beyond some agreed band. These arrangements effectively extended the policy architecture for the domestic U.S. financial system in several ways. First, transparent rules were written. They were next enforced and supported by an international organization that was governed both by national governments and by independent managers, drawn from many countries and, supposedly, answerable to neutral financial principles, rather than to national governments. In short, this was in essence an extension of the Progressive movement's faith in public administration and the application of objective theories to empirical information. Second, the Bretton Woods system asserted a public role in managing worldwide financial markets to complement the public's function in doing the same in domestic financial markets.

Put into operation in 1946, the Bretton Woods system represents the zenith of this set of ideas. It had roughly a 25-year run before it began to unravel between 1971 and 1973, largely for lack of imagination on the part of governments in the 1960s and their unwillingness to update the Bretton Woods institutions and adapt them to a set of new economic conditions.[36] Nonetheless, during that quarter-century the world economy grew faster than during any 25-year stretch before or since. And there was no financial crisis during that period, either.

Wall Street, as always, opposed the Bretton Woods arrangements even though its residents came to benefit enormously from it. In fact, it is fair to say the system established in New Hampshire in 1944 was the enabling device that established The Street as the uncontested leader of world finance. The dollar became the world's reserve currency, to the dismay of Keynes and the British who tried to forestall this by advocating a new world currency separate from any one nation's. White and the U.S. opposed this and prevailed over Keynes's objections. The Street, however, was stuck in its ideology of opposition to any public role in finance, which they continued to construe as a private market affair arranged among a self-regulated membership organization, whether it be formal – as with the New York Stock Exchange – or informal as among friends and family.

The American Bankers' Association reacted to Bretton Woods, by proclaiming in one of the worst forecasts ever made that '[we] find provisions which, in our opinion, are financially unsound and, if adopted, might retard rather than promote enduring recovery.' Morgenthau replied with characteristic bluntness: 'Is it better for us to take the risk and spread it among forty-four partners or to have five banks in New York dictate foreign exchange rates ... and having London lead us around by the nose, which they have done in the last one hundred years.'[37]

A new composite governing economic philosophy was emerging, one in which a publicly established envelope of rules created regulatory boundaries that banded economic and financial instability, not so much that innovation was stifled, but just enough to allow more investment and creativity to be launched. A degree of stability and predictability that reduced risk and uncertainty, bounded by and guaranteed by the public, would allow the private market economy to function better by encouraging investment and innovation within a range of constrained risk. In this way the tables were turned on conventional economic thinking in a way that is at odds with the prevailing philosophy today which re-emerged in the 1980s atmosphere of privatization and de-regulation, namely that unbounded risk freed from the nuisance of public regulation is required for investment and innovation. What has also reappeared, however, is financial instability and crises that were all but obliterated during the quarter-century of the Bretton Woods regime. An editorial comment from the *Christian Science Monitor* in February 1945 sums up the distinction in these viewpoints:

At the heart of the matter is the fact that this machinery [Bretton Woods] would be put into the hands of public servants, paid executives of the governments involved, rather than in the group of private and powerful international bankers in 'The City' in London, and in lower Manhattan in New York. You can see at once why there is a row involved. It depends on whether you think public servants can do the international job better than big private banks ... who have been doing it in the past.[38]

The evolution from an international economy between 1946 and 1971 – that was made up of one part public and the other part private – to a global one was incubated in the early 1970s with control centered in the private market. It came in bits and pieces with no grand plan. It was hastened along by the 1970s epochal changes in the technologies of communications and information – comparable to the role of the telephone and telegraph a century earlier.

During the Bretton Woods period Wall Street became one of the essential governors over a new international economic order that was not yet 'global' but was setting the conditions for a new global economy. The distinction between these two terms – 'international' and 'global' economy – turns on one important difference. An international economy reflects arrangements among nation-states in which countries set the rules and enforce them. This is the Bretton Woods financial regime. A global economy is a set of arrangements among private non-state actors – corporations, banks, media, technology and information systems – that circumvent, supersede, and eviscerate nation-state boundaries and public policies. They are supranational, transcending the boundaries of countries and their public policy reach in the first instance. Secondly, they resist effectively any envelope of regulation emanating from an international organization or country unless they conform to and reinforce the direction laid down by the private arrangements of markets. In effect, a global economy takes us back to the future with a new form of Morgan's Bankers' Code now written for a global era of communications and information management, whose speed, capacity and scope would have been unimaginable in Morgan's era.[39]

STREET OF DREAMS – BOULEVARD OF BROKEN HEARTS

In many ways Wall Street in the year 2000 would be unrecognizable to the Wall Street of 1800 or 1900. In other ways it would. It has always physically been an anachronism among American cities – 'an old city of Europe, with narrow, irregular streets and random congestion of its buildings,' is an apt description, where the 'essence of finance was ... an exchange across time

... between the past and the future ... the surplus accumulated from past endeavors was made available to new ventures, with the promise of future rewards for both.'[40] Nor is the revolution in telecommunications and information processing wrought by the computer and digitalization of the last quarter of the twentieth century not comparable to that of the telephone and telegraph a century earlier if measured by the degree of change relative to where Wall Street was in each of those quarter-centuries. Going from the speed with which an individual could physically move information by foot or horse to the transfer of information by telephone or telegraph is arguably a more dramatic transformation than the one associated with the computer and satellite communications that either replaced or supplemented the telephone and telegraph.

At some point, however, these quantitative changes in The Street metamorphose into something qualitatively distinct, and that is what would immediately confront the visitor from a century ago. The dazzling pace of transactions across such a multitude of financial products and tens of millions of investors, moved instantaneously to any spot on the globe would, to a nineteenth-century observer, leap forward into the realm of science fiction, a literary genre that had not yet been invented in that earlier century. From another perspective, however, the pace of nineteenth-century Wall Street was equally frenetic. Recall the curb market with its legions of brokers dressed flamboyantly to distinguish one from another as they relayed transactions to their clerks hanging from window ledges. Or the scurrying about of hundreds of runners – pad shovers – taking bits of paper from one office to another non-stop through the night, so that all buys and sells could be recorded before markets opened the next morning. Perhaps the difference is more perceptual: the one moving in physical and observable space, the other operating across abstract ethereal space.

There is one incontestable difference in today's Wall Street, however, compared to previous centuries. More financial activity has moved beyond The Street. The concentration is no longer exclusively situated in that small neighborhood of lower Manhattan. The target for 11 September 2001 was American global finance, but the attack was on the Twin Towers of the World Trade Center not Wall Street itself. There have been recurrent predictions of the end of Wall Street in its more than two-century history, but all of them have been shown to be as unreliable as the predictions of the markets' ups and downs. A wave of these appeared in 1992 on The Street's two-hundredth anniversary as in this faulty forecast on the occasion of the anniversary celebration. 'After the hoopla was over, the pesky question lingering on many minds was whether the Big Board, in anything like its current form, will still be round for No. 210.'[41] After a decade of unsurpassed expansion in the markets and subsequent collapse, Wall Street has remained the hub. Wall Street understood this better and in its anniversary proclamation it took out three full pages of newspaper ads, leading with just these words on the first page superimposed on the great columns of its building, 'This is not Just A Place,' and continuing onto the next double page: 'It's A Way Of Doing Business.'[42]

The explanation for The Street's persistence, therefore, is to be found not solely in the mechanics of buying and selling stocks and bonds. More significantly, The Street retains the iconographic mantle for America's global financial reach. It is the symbol, the keeper of the mythology, the metaphorical place from which the great power of American capital bestrides the planet. It is the custodian of the imagination that sums up everything the American Century brought to the world through the force of its financial invention. Newscasts end with a shot of the New York Stock Exchange's podium, with the bell clanging and some dignitary pounding the podium with an oversized gavel, while flashing across the screen are the market's closings with voice over from the news anchor reading out scores as if from a sports event. There is much symbolism here: a harkening back to a presumably more manageable and comforting past (the bell and the gavel), while enduring the hectic present with numbers in the billions of transactions whose dimensions are hard to grasp. Even though other markets challenge The Street – as they did in the nineteenth century – none can replace it in its monopoly over the American imagination, the country's infatuation with money as idol and the quixotic attachment to this one place that embodies the gambler's illusions that are scattered about the many Main Streets of America.

In this drama Wall Street needed a Main Street, for two reasons: first, as a source of supply of money from small investors that, when packaged together, became large bundles of capital for investment in the grand undertakings that powered the American economy from virtually nowhere to the supreme economy in the world in not much more than a century. Second, The Street needed Main Street to provide it with the popular political cover and support against a potential challenge from Pennsylvania Avenue. Main Street was invested in Wall Street both in the form of financial capital and in the guise of 'political' capital: that crucial identification with an individualist-based economy of which Wall Street was the premier emblem. Wall Street constructed the ideology of 'people's capitalism,' in which everyone could effortlessly participate in the big economic show. It put teeth into this with the formation of mechanisms for accomplishing its ideological objective, starting with Cooke's mass sale of bonds during the Civil War and continuing through the invention of small accounts for individual investors throughout the country in the twentieth century. The Street's ability to adapt itself and absorb political challenges are all part of the unique American creation of a financial market that reached from the loftiest towers of capital on and around Wall Street to the smallest Main Street in the smallest town in the United States. It was in the business not only of marketing securities but of manufacturing dreams.

As in the past, these longings continue to become broken hearts, renewed periodically by a new slate of seductive scoundrels and scandals. The American Century's *fin de siècle* of dot.coms that came and went, powered by overwrought IPOs (Initial Public Offerings), the inevitable follow-on of discoveries of scandal wrapped in a deceptive opaqueness – Enron, WorldCom, Arthur Andersen accounting practices and The Street's own contribution in the form of misleading investment reports – is not terribly dissimilar to what transpired in the past, starting with the very origins of Wall Street in 1792. But scandals and scoundrels are not the only history of Wall Street. It is a remarkable place that has adapted to change and survived longer than any other non-governmental institution in the United States. More than any such organization, it has helped shape the nation.

When infatuation turns to betrayal after a bubble's burst, there is always talk of the end of Wall Street. Main Street will never touch it again, proclaim the pundits. Pennsylvania Avenue will see to it that power is divested from The Street. This has been wrong in the past and will be wrong in the future. After all, we all need dreams – that pile of gold at the end of the rainbow – as in Judy Garland's plaintive rendition of E.Y. Harburg's, 'Somewhere Over the Rainbow.'[43] It doesn't matter that hearts have been broken in the past. Main Street and the nation will continue to be guided in their dreams by the walk with The Street's leaders, parting company for a time when it becomes a boulevard of broken hearts, only to return again when elapsed time obliterates a bad memory.

Notes

PREFACE

1. A.C. Grayling, 'Reflections on the Spirit of an Age,' *Financial Times* (14–15 June 1997), p. vi.
2. Ibid.
3. Charles Mackay, *Extraordinary Popular Delusions and the Madness of Crowds* (London: Richard Bentley, 1841).
4. Forrest McDonald, *Alexander Hamilton. A Biography* (N.Y.: W.W. Norton & Co., 1979), p. 164.

CHAPTER 1

1. It was erected under William Kieft, the colony's third governor. He had gone bankrupt in his merchant business in Amsterdam before his appointment. Known as having an 'irascible temper' and for his 'hasty judgment,' he left a $200,000 debt for his successor, Peter Stuyvesant. [Bank of America, *A History of Fifty Feet in New York at Wall & William Streets* (N.Y.: Bank of America, 1926), p. 63.] Kieft's wall consisted principally of 'untrimmed trees felled at the edge of the adjoining forest and piled together to form a sort of barricade.' [Frederick Trevor Hill, *The Story of a Street* (N.Y.: Harper & Brothers, 1908), reprinted: (Wells, VT.: Fraser Publishing Co., 1969.]
2. For a discussion of the origins of Manhattan in New Amsterdam, see: Edwin G. Burrows and Mike Wallace, *Gotham: A History of New York City to 1898* (New York and Oxford: Oxford University Press, 1999), chaps. 1–5. Manhattan takes its name from the Lenape Indian name for the river Manhattes that flows into the bay at the tip of the island, (pp. 18–19).
3. Bank of America, *A History of Fifty Feet in New York at Wall & William Streets*, p. 15. At Broadway there was a heavy wooden gate, the Land Gate, and at Pearl Street, the Water Gate. A large gun emplacement was at the northwest corner of Wall and William Streets.
4. Oswald Garrison Villard, 'The Early History of Wall Street, 1653–1789,' speech before the New York Historical Society (2 May 1905), New York Historical Society, Box 10, No. 4, p. 2.
5. John Steele Gordon, *The Scarlet Woman of Wall Street: Jay Gould, Jim Fisk, Cornelius Vanderbilt, the Erie Railway Wars, and the Birth of Wall Street* (N.Y.: Weidenfeld & Nicolson, 1988), p. 10; and Villard, 'The Early History of Wall Street,' p. 2. In common with other colonies, the inhabitants of New Amsterdam frequently complained of inadequate capitalization, which limited their economic success and led, at times, to small rebellions against the home country. [Robert M. Sharp, *The Lore and Legends of Wall Street* (Homewood, IL.: Dow Jones-Irwin, 1989), p. 36; Villard, 'The Early History of Wall Street,' p. 3;

Maxine Friedman, *Wall Street: Changing Fortunes* (N.Y.: Fraunces Tavern Museum, 1990), pp. 13–14; and Hill, *The Story of a Street*, pp. 10–13.]

6. Johan de Vries, *A Century of Stocks and Shares* (Amsterdam: Amsterdam Stock Exchange, 1991), p. 3; and Burrows and Wallace, *Gotham*, p. 19.

7. The deep waters of the bay provided a natural harbor and rivers provided relatively easy passage to New England through Long Island Sound and to Albany via the Hudson River Valley (Friedman, *Wall Street*, p. 11).

8. John Pomeroy Townsend, 'Wall Street. Portrait,' Chauncey M. Depew, ed., *One Hundred Years of American Commerce*, vol. I (N.Y.: D.O. Haynes & Co., 1895); reprinted: (N.Y.: Greenwood Press, Publ., 1968), p. 67.

9. Villard, 'The Early History of Wall Street,' p. 1.

10. Hill, *The Story of a Street*, p. 18.

11. Sharp, *The Lore and Legends of Wall Street*, p. 36.

12. James E. Buck, ed., *The New York Stock Exchange: The First 200 Years* (Essex, Conn.: Greenwich Publishing Group, Inc., 1992), p. 14; William Worthington Fowler, *Ten Years in Wall Street* (Hartford: Worthington, Dustin & Co., 1870), p. 21; and Bank of America, *A History of Fifty Feet in New York at Wall & William Streets*, p. 19.

13. Friedman, *Wall Street*, p. 15.

14. The City Hall is on the corner of what is now Wall and Nassau Streets (Bank of America, *A History of Fifty Feet in New York at Wall & William Streets*, pp. 19, 21).

15. Friedman, *Wall Street*, p. 15; and Hill, *The Story of a Street*, p. 29.

16. Edmund C. Stedman, *The New York Stock Exchange* (N.Y.: Stock Exchange Historical Co., 1905), reprinted: (N.Y.: Greenwood Press, 1969), p. 34; and Villard, 'The Early History of Wall Street,' pp. 9, 18.

17. Robert Sobel, *Panic on Wall Street: A History of America's Financial Disasters* (N.Y.: The Macmillan Co., 1968), p. 9.

18. Thomas K. McCraw, 'The Strategic Vision of Alexander Hamilton,' *The American Scholar* (Winter, 1994), p. 47.

19. Forrest McDonald, *Alexander Hamilton: A Biography* (N.Y.: W.W. Norton & Co., 1979), pp. 7, 15, 62; and Hill, *The Story of a Street*, p. 99.

20. The most prominent of the retrospectives was Wall Street's commission of its own official history, a lavishly illustrated and otherwise excellent historical treatment that sidesteps the contentious issues surrounding The Street's origins: Buck, *The New York Stock Exchange*.

21. Quoted in McDonald, *Alexander Hamilton*, p. 164.

22. Charles A. Beard, *An Economic Interpretation of the Constitution of the United States* (N.Y.: The Macmillan Co., 1913), p. 33.

23. Burrows and Wallace, *Gotham*, p. 302.

24. Ibid., p. 302.

25. Villard, 'The Early History of Wall Street,' pp. 17–18.

26. Stedman, *The New York Stock Exchange*, p. 36.

27. Prior to the agreement, securities were exchanged in individual broker's offices in an auction-like setting, for example, as in this notice in a local newspaper, *Loudon's Register* (March 1792): 'the stock exchange office was opened at 22 Wall Street' for the purpose of holding a daily public sale of stock at noon. [Robert Sobel, *The Curbstone Brokers: The Origins of the American Stock Exchange* (N.Y.: The Macmillan Co., 1970), p. 1.]

28. Charles T. Gehring, 'New Netherland – Translating New York's Dutch Past,' *Humanities*, 14, 6 (November–December, 1993), pp. 27–8.

29. Joseph S. Davis, *Essays in the Earlier History of American Corporations* (Cambridge: Harvard University Press, 1917), p. 139.

30. Sharp, *The Lore and Legends of Wall Street*, p. 69; and Hill, *The Story of a Street*, p. 100.

31. Notes taken from present building on Central Park West.

32. He had a brief marriage in 1799 to an Anglican, Catherine Brett, before his marriage to Rebecca Seixas in 1806. The birth of his son by that earlier marriage, Henry Hart, was followed almost immediately by separation and divorce in 1800. The significance of this is that Henry's son was Bret Harte – one of the great early American writers, chronicler of the west, and arguably an originator of the American short story who took his subject matter largely from California in the mid-nineteenth century.[Interview with New York Stock Exchange Archivist, Steven Wheeler (5 October 1992); Walter Barrett, *The Old Merchants of New York* (N.Y.: M. Doolady, 1870), vol. II, pp. 122–9; and George R. Stewart, Jr., *Bret Harte: Argonaut and Exile* (Boston: Houghton Mifflin Co., 1931), pp. 6, 7, 10.]

33. Barrett, *The Old Merchants of New York*, vol. II, pp. 2, 55.

34. Stedman, *The New York Stock Exchange*, p. 36.

35. Robert Sobel, *The Big Board: A History of the New York Stock Market* (N.Y.: The Free Press, 1965), p. 11.

36. Lois Severini, *The Architecture of Finance: Early Wall Street* (Ann Arbor: UMI Research Press, 1983), p. 82.

37. In well-preserved documents on the Tontine at the New York Historical Society, one can examine the original agreement with each shareholder's designated survivor, and a log book kept by the House's lawyer – Frederick de Peyster – which contains an X-mark beside a designee's name when he or she dies, a date of death, and sometimes an obituary glued alongside a name (Sobel, *The Big Board*, pp. 11, 26; 'Tontine Coffee House, 1789–1823,' New York Historical Society).

38. Sharp, *The Lore and Legends of Wall Street*, p. 1.

39. Davis, *Essays in the Earlier History of American Corporations*, p. 180.

40. Stedman, *The New York Stock Exchange*, p. 50.

41. Gerard Bancker, '1792 – the Memorial of Gerard Bancker, Treasurer of the State of N.Y.,' New York Historical Society, Box 14, No. 8.

42. Humphrey B. Neill, *The Inside Story of the Stock Exchange* (N.Y.: B.C. Forbes & Sons Publishing Co., Inc., 1950), pp. 13–14.

43. The charges against Hamilton reached such a crescendo in 1793 that the House of Representatives conducted an inquiry that vindicated Hamilton on some charges but, as the historian Charles Beard points out, the investigation did not look into Hamilton's dealings with brokers and others who were involved with his bond transactions (Beard, *An Economic Interpretation of the Constitution of the United States*, pp. xv, 104, 108). The debate continues: a prominent history textbook of the 1960s and 1970s concluded that many of Hamilton's colleagues and associates in lower Manhattan 'had known that his report would contain such a recommendation and had begun buying up certificates when they could be found.' [John M. Blum et al., *The National Experience: A History of the United States*, fourth edition (N.Y.: Harcourt Brace Jovanovich,

1977), p. 134.] More recent Hamilton scholars dispute this allegation. [See, for example, Forrest McDonald, *Alexander Hamilton*; and Jacob Ernest Cooke, *Alexander Hamilton* (N.Y.: Charles Scribner's & Sons, 1982).]

44. Peter Anspach, 'Anspach & Rogers Papers,' New York Historical Society, 3 boxes.
45. Burrows and Wallace, *Gotham*, p. 302.
46. Buck, *The New York Stock Exchange*, p. 16. This version appears in the officially commissioned 1992 New York Stock Exchange history of Wall Street. Another recent history has the deal struck at a dinner among Hamilton, James Madison and Thomas Jefferson. [Kenneth R. Bowling, *The Creation of Washington, D.C.: The Idea and Location of the American Capital* (Fairfax: George Mason University Press, 1991).]
47. Burrows and Wallace, *Gotham*, p. 304.
48. McDonald, *Alexander Hamilton*, p. 176.
49. Blum, et al., *The National Experience: A History of the United States*, pp. 134–5; and Beard, *An Economic Interpretation of the Constitution of the United States*, p. 126.
50. Cooke, *Alexander Hamilton*, p. 78.
51. McDonald, *Alexander Hamilton*, pp. 39, 189; and Stedman, *The New York Stock Exchange*, p. 50.
52. Broadus Mitchell, *Alexander Hamilton: A Concise Biography* (N.Y. and Oxford: Oxford University Press, 1976), p. 225.
53. Harold C. Syrett and Jacob E. Cooke, eds, *The Papers of Alexander Hamilton, 1757–1804*, 27 vols. (N.Y.: Columbia University Press, 1961–87), vol. V, pp. 452, 454.
54. Mitchell, *Alexander Hamilton*, p. 223.
55. Broadus Mitchell, *Alexander Hamilton, vol. II: The National Adventure, 1788–1804* (N.Y.: The Macmillan Co., 1962), p. 160.
56. Syrett and Cooke, *The Papers of Alexander Hamilton*, vol. V, p. 517.
57. Ibid., vol. IX, pp. 31, 92, 404.
58. This is used, for example, in two recent Hamilton biographies – Cooke, *Alexander Hamilton* and McDonald, *Alexander Hamilton* – as proof of his innocence and as sufficient to dismiss the allegations against him, as it is broadly cited as exculpatory evidence in the earlier 1962 two-volume biography by Broadus Mitchell, *Alexander Hamilton*.
59. Henry Lee's letter to Hamilton in Syrett and Cooke, *The Papers of Alexander Hamilton*, vol. IX, p. 31.
60. Mitchell, *Alexander Hamilton*, McDonald, *Alexander Hamilton*, and Cooke, *Alexander Hamilton*, the latter one of the editors of Hamilton's collected papers. Hamilton's reputation has had cyclical fluctuations. It suffers after his death in a duel with Aaron Burr in 1804 and reaches its nadir during the Jacksonian period. His reputation is rehabilitated and resurrected after the Civil War, peaking between 1890 and 1920, especially with Herbert Croly's influential work, *The Promise of American Life* (N.Y.: The Macmillan Co.,1909). After World War I, and the collapse of the Progressives, it once again falters, only to be restored after World War II. [Michael Lind, 'Hamilton's Legacy,' *Wilson Quarterly* (Summer 1994), vol. 18, no. 3, pp. 40–52.]
61. Burrows and Wallace, *Gotham*, p. 302.

62. Beard, *An Economic Interpretation of the Constitution of the United States*, pp. 103–4. The Reynolds and Hamilton correspondence are in: Syrett and Cooke, *The Papers of Alexander Hamilton*, vol. X, pp. 376–9, 387–90, 396, 401, 503, 519–20.

63. Beard, *An Economic Interpretation of the Constitution of the United States*, p. xv. The Willing evidence is contained in the private journals of Senator W. Maclay, an opponent of Hamilton's. Since the journals were private and not meant for public consumption, they were not made available until well after his death. However, the contemporaneous documentary record of Maclay's must carry some weight as to their veracity.

64. Cooke, *Alexander Hamilton*, p. 78.

65. Beard, *An Economic Interpretation of the Constitution of the United States*, pp. 111–12.

66. In a letter to William Duer, Hamilton refers to 'Bank Script getting so high as to become a bubble, ... "tis a South Sea dream"' (Syrett and Cooke, *The Papers of Alexander Hamilton*, vol. IX, p. 74). Writings about the South Sea Bubble and Tulipomania extend from the classic, Charles Mackay, *Extraordinary Popular Delusions and the Madness of Crowds* (London: Richard Bentley, 1841), pp. 46–97 to a collection edited by Ross B. Emmett, *Great Bubbles*, vol. 1, pp. 82–161 and vol. 3 (London: Pickering & Chatto, 2000) and to Edward Chancellor, *Devil Take the Hindmost: A History of Financial Speculation* (N.Y.: Farrar, Straus, Giroux, 1999), chap. 3.

67. Mitchell, *Alexander Hamilton*, p. 172 (emphasis in original).

68. Burrows and Wallace, *Gotham*, p. 310.

69. Ibid., p. 302.

70. Davis, *Essays in the Earlier History of American Corporations*, pp. 174, 176, 177.

71. Ibid., p. 191.

72. Burrows and Wallace, *Gotham*, p. 304.

73. McDonald, *Alexander Hamilton*, pp. 244–7; David L. Sterling, 'William Durer, John Pintard and the Panic of 1792,' Joseph R. Freese, S.J. and Jacob Judd, eds, *Business Enterprise in Early New York* (Tarrytown: The Sleepy Hollow Press, 1979), pp. 106–13; Robert F. Jones, 'William Duer and the Business of Government in the Era of the American Revolution,' *William and Mary Quarterly*, 32 (1975), pp. 393–416; and Walter Werner and Stephen T. Smith, *Wall Street* (N.Y.: Columbia University Press, 1991), pp. 15–16.

74. New York Historical Society, Pintard Papers. A day after Pintard was awarded the broker's license he took out this ad in the newspaper of record, the New York *Daily Advertiser* (26 November 1790), which reads in part:

> The opinion of many respectable characters has confirmed his own idea of the utility of establishing an office in this city upon the principle of a sworn broker in Europe. The advantages of negotiating through the medium of an agent, no ways interested in purchases or sales on his own account, is too evident to every person of discernment to need any comment. (Sterling, 'William Durer, John Pintard and the Panic of 1792', p. 102)

75. Davis, *Essays in the Earlier History of American Corporations*, p. 287; Sterling, 'William Durer, John Pintard and the Panic of 1792', pp. 101, 122; and Barrett, *The Old Merchants of New York*, Vol. II, p. 219.

76. Sterling, *Business Enterprise in Early New York*, pp. 102–7.
77. New York Historical Society, Pintard Papers.
78. The full text of the ad and citation is provided in note 74.
79. Frederick L. Collins, *Money Town* (N.Y.: G.P. Putnam & Sons, 1946), p. 236.
80. Davis, *Essays in the Earlier History of American Corporations*, p. 206. Emphasis in original.
81. McDonald, *Alexander Hamilton*, p. 247.
82. 'The Panic of 1792,' New York Historical Society, Box 14, No. 1.
83. Sterling, 'William Durer, John Pintard and the Panic of 1792', p. 109.
84. Davis, *Essays in the Earlier History of American Corporations*, pp. 295–6; and Sterling, 'William Durer, John Pintard and the Panic of 1792', p. 115.
85. Sterling, 'William Durer, John Pintard and the Panic of 1792', p. 114. Seth Johnson wrote to Andrew Craigie, a competitor of Duer's, on 25 March 1792 saying that 'Pintard has gone off without clearing up his character & from all appearances he has been a perfect swindler' (Davis, *Essays in the Earlier History of American Corporations*, p. 296).
86. Sterling, 'William Durer, John Pintard and the Panic of 1792', pp. 118, 123.
87. Ibid., pp. 114, 121, 122.
88. The decision was printed in the 16 May 1792 issue of Francis Childs's New York *Daily Advertiser*, a major daily newspaper and one that was fairly objective by the standards of the time.
89. Davis, *Essays in the Earlier History of American Corporations*, p. 304.
90. From 1793 to 1794 he kept a daily horticultural diary concerning the garden he started in Newark. While in Newark prison, he maintained a detailed reading diary, making notes and comments on a voluminous literature in Greek, Latin, some Italian, as well as English. [John Pintard, 'Diary and Garden Calendar of John Pintard at Newark, New Jersey (April 1793–May 1794),' New York Historical Society, Box 2A; and John Pintard, 'Miscellaneous Papers Relating to John Pintard and His Family,' New York Historical Society, Box 2.]
91. John Pintard, 'Diary,' New York Historical Society, entries during 1798 and 1799.
92. Pintard, 'Diary,' New York Historical Society, Sept. 17, 1799. Pintard's employment as agent for Duer is not in dispute. But the extent of his culpability is. Was it naivete, as his defenders claim, or deliberate abuse of his agent's role as Duer and his defenders claim? Among members of the financial community, who were not direct participants on either side, the tendency is to charge Pintard with naivete. As Ebenezer Hazard told Jeremy Belknap in 1792, Pintard has his 'amiable qualities, though I never thought him possessed of either prudence or steadiness sufficient for a man of business.' The historian, David L. Sterling, who has made a study of these events from original documents, has perhaps the clearest fix on both Duer and Pintard. Of Duer, he writes, that he was the 'most important figure in the panic, that he devised the scheme and directed Macomb, Livingston, and Pintard in its execution. He formed the plan to buy up the stocks of the Bank of New York and the Bank of the United States.' Of Pintard, Sterling concludes that 'he must have known what a 5 per cent per month interest rate represented to their investments, [and] as Duer's agent, John Pintard knew what he was doing, but his ambition overwhelmed him.' A contemporaneous testimony from Seth Johnson said 'Mr. Pintard must be mortified at his folly. If he is not, his friends

and even those who dislike him, pity his want of prudence' (Sterling, 'William Durer, John Pintard and the Panic of 1792', pp. 106, 117, 123, 124).

93. Werner and Smith, *Wall Street*, pp. 24–5. At least four of the Buttonwood signers had been involved with Duer, including the very prominent Leonard Bleecker and Benjamin Seixas.

94. Davis, *Essays in the Earlier History of American Corporations*, p. 308; and Hill, *The Story of a Street*, p. 139.

95. Peter Eisenstadt, 'How the Buttonwood Tree Grew: The Making of a New York Stock Exchange,' *Prospects: An Annual of American Cultural Studies*, (19), p. 79.

96. The first reference to the Buttonwood story is in an 1885 article in *Harper's Monthly* (ibid., p. 82).

97. Eisenstadt, 'How the Buttonwood Tree Grew,' p. 84.

98. Pintard, 'Diary,' New York Historical Society, July 27, 1801.

99. Barrett, *The Old Merchants of New York*, Vol. II, p. 237.

CHAPTER 2

1. Jacob Ernest Cooke, *Alexander Hamilton* (N.Y.: Scribner's & Sons, 1982), p. 114. This point is also made in: Gordon S. Wood, *The Radicalism of the American Revolution* (N.Y.: Alfred A. Knopf, 1992), pp. 105–6; and Charles Sellers, *The Market Revolution: Jacksonian America, 1815–1846* (Oxford: Oxford University Press, 1991), p. 4.

2. Robin M. Williams, Jr., *American Society: A Sociological Interpretation* (N.Y.: Alfred A. Knopf, 1970), p. 464.

3. Sean Willentz, *Chants Democratic: New York City and the Rise of the American Working Class 1788–1850* (Oxford: Oxford University Press, 1984), p. 62.

4. Ibid, p. 61.

5. Forrest McDonald, *Alexander Hamilton: A Biography* (N.Y.: W.W. Norton & Co., 1979), pp. 35–7, 121–2.

6. Quotations in the paragraph from: Cooke, *Alexander Hamilton*, pp. 6, 21, 86.

7. James E. Buck, ed., *The New York Stock Exchange: The First 200 Years* (Essex, Conn.: Greenwich Publishing Group Inc., 1992), p. 25; Edmund C. Stedman, *The New York Stock Exchange* (N.Y.: The Stock Exchange Historical Co., 1905), reprinted: (N.Y.: Greenwood Press, 1969), p. 52; and John Pomeroy Townsend, 'Wall Street Portrait,' C.M. Depew, ed., *100 Years of American Commerce*, vol. I (N.Y.: D.O. Haynes & Co., 1895), reprinted: (N.Y.: Greenwood Press, 1968), p. 68. Soon after the funds were raised for the Manhattan Company, Burr lost interest in the water purification project and concentrated his energies on the Bank. [Bray Hammond, *Banks and Politics in America: From the Revolution to the Civil War* (Princeton: Princeton University Press, 1957), p. 155.]

8. Interview with descendant of the lawyer who argued this case.

9. Edwin W. Burrows and Mike Wallace, *Gotham: A History of New York City to 1898* (New York and Oxford: Oxford University Press, 1999), p. 361.

10. Ibid., p. 322.

11. Cooke, *Alexander Hamilton*, pp. 231, 240.

12. Burrows and Wallace, *Gotham*, pp. 331–2.

13. Sellers, *The Market Revolution*, p. 22; and U.S. Department of Commerce, Bureau of the Census, *Historical Statistics of the United States: Colonial Times to 1970*, Part 2 (Washington: Government Printing Office, 1975), p. 886.
14. Burrows and Wallace, *Gotham*, pp. 333–4.
15. Ibid. pp. 410–11.
16. Joseph Edward Hedges, *Commercial Banking and the Stock Market Before 1863* (Baltimore: The Johns Hopkins Press, 1938), p. 29; and Curtis P. Nettels, *The Emergence of a National Economy: 1775–1815* (N.Y.: Holt, Rinehart and Winston, 1962), reprinted: (Armonk, N.Y.: M.E. Sharpe Publishers, 1989), p. 291. Other states contributed to the growth of new corporations, too. Between 1800 and 1817 close to 1,800 charters had been issued throughout the nation. Many of these charters were for banks, which were a favorite of the states. Until the failure to re-charter the First Bank of the United States in 1811 – due in part to the states' opposition and their desire to capture deposits held in the national bank – there were 62 state banks. By 1816, 246 had been chartered and by 1820 the number exceeded 300 (Wood, *The Radicalism of the American Revolution*, pp. 316, 321).
17. George Rogers Taylor, *The Transportation Revolution: 1815–1860* (N.Y.: Holt, Rinehart and Winston, 1951), reprinted: (Armonk, N.Y.: M.E. Sharpe Publishers, 1977), p. 28.
18. Sellers, *The Market Revolution*, pp. 15–16; Robert Sobel, *The Big Board: A History of the New York Stock Market* (N.Y.: The Free Press, 1965), p. 28; and U.S. Department of Commerce, *Historical Statistics of the United States*, p. 886.
19. Ralph Catterall, *The Second Bank of the United States* (Chicago: University of Chicago Press, 1902), p. 2.
20. Sellers, *The Market Revolution*, p. 68.
21. Walter Werner and Stephen T. Smith, *Wall Street* (N.Y.: Columbia University Press, 1991), pp. 37, 85.
22. Sobel, *The Big Board*, p. 30.
23. The identity of this individual is sometimes referred to as William Lawton and elsewhere as William Lamb, so we are not certain of his name. We do know, however, that he returned in mid-February 1817 with a set of by-laws and a constitution from the Philadelphia exchange, which inspired the New York brokers to push ahead with their plans for a new Wall Street securities organization. [James Medbery, *Men and Mysteries of Wall Street* (Boston: Fields, Osgood & Co., 1870), reprinted: (Wells, VT.: Fraser Publishing Co., 1968), pp. 287–8; and Sobel, *The Big Board*, p. 30.]
24. Sobel, *The Big Board*, p. 30.
25. 'Constitution of the New York Stock Exchange Board, 1817,' New York Stock Exchange Archives.
26. Werner and Smith, *Wall Street*, p. 28.
27. Wood, *The Radicalism of the American Revolution*, p. 325.
28. Buck, *The New York Stock Exchange*, p. 19; Werner and Smith, *Wall Street*, p. 20; and Medberry, *Men and Mysteries of Wall Street*, pp. 288–9.
29. Walter Barrett, *The Old Merchants of New York*, (N.Y.: M. Doolady, 1870), Vol. I, p. 11. The fall-off in interest and activity on The Street is seen in the paucity of newspaper reports on securities activities in 1795, for example, compared to 1792 – just before the financial crisis of that year. Virtually all dailies and weeklies had extensive reporting on securities prices and the comings and

goings on The Street in 1792. But not in 1795 (Werner and Smith, *Wall Street*, p. 50).

30. Lois Severini, *The Architecture of Finance: Early Wall Street* (Ann Arbor: UMI Research Press, 1983), p. 38.

31. Nathaniel Prime, 'Prime Family Correspondence & Papers of Nathaniel Prime and His Sons,' New York Historical Society.

32. Werner and Smith, *Wall Street*, p. 51.

33. Ibid., pp. 52–3.

34. Sobel, *The Big Board*, p. 33.

35. Sellers, *The Market Revolution*, p. 20.

36. Barrett, *The Old Merchants of New York*, Vol. I, p. 12; and Werner and Smith, *Wall Street*, p. 54.

37. Werner and Smith, *Wall Street*, p. 37; and Taylor, *The Transportation Revolution*, p. 52.

38. Taylor, *The Transportation Revolution*, pp. 28, 33; Burrows and Wallace, *Gotham*, p. 430; and Sellers, *The Market Revolution*, p. 42.

39. Burrows and Wallace, *Gotham*, p. 431.

40. Steamboats had been operating on the Hudson to Albany since Robert Fulton successfully tested his *Clermont* in 1807. Subsequent technical refinements had improved their design, so that by 1817 ferrying freight by steamboat was common and financially viable.

41. Taylor, *The Transportation Revolution*, p. 35.

42. Alfred D. Chandler, Jr., *The Visible Hand: The Managerial Revolution in American Business* (Cambridge: Harvard University Press, 1977), p. 24.

43. Sellers, *The Market Revolution*, pp. 41–2.

44. Taylor, *The Transportation Revolution*, pp. 34, 52.

45. John M. Blum, et al., *The National Experience: A History of the United States*, fourth edn (N.Y.: Harcourt Brace Jovanovich, 1977), p. 198.

46. Stedman, *The New York Stock Exchange*, pp. 79–80.

47. David R. Goldfield and Blaine A. Brownell, *Urban America: A History*, second edn (Boston: Houghton Mifflin Co., 1990), p. 102.

48. Burrows and Wallace, *Gotham*, pp. 341–2.

49. Ibid., p. 433

50. Sellers, *The Market Revolution*, pp. 40–1.

51. Burrows and Wallace, *Gotham*, p. 433.

52. Ibid., p. 336.

53. Ibid., p. 653.

54. Goldfield and Brownell, *Urban America*, p. 102.

55. Ibid., p. 435.

56. Burrows and Wallace, *Gotham*, pp. 446–7.

57. Stedman, *The New York Stock Exchange*, pp. 84–5.

58. John Pintard, 'Pintard Diary 1800–1801,' Pintard Papers, Box 2A, New York Historical Society. It was under President Jefferson, for example, that the number of banks expanded from 29 to 246 even though his biting words about banks have been immortalized in populist circles. He proposed using budget surpluses in 1806 not only for tax reduction but for the 'great purposes of the public education, roads, rivers, canals.' Only the Congress stopped him, and later Madison, from initiating a major federal expenditure program for what

today we call *infrastructure* (Nettels, *The Emergence of a National Economy*, p. 340).

59. Wood, *The Radicalism of the American Revolution*, p. 230.
60. Burrows and Wallace, *Gotham*, p. 447.
61. Material in this paragraph drawn from Burrows and Wallace, *Gotham*, chapter 28. The quote at the end of the paragraph is from p. 467.
62. Severini, *The Architecture of Finance*, pp. 1, 5, 6, 30, 36.
63. Buck, *The New York Stock Exchange*, pp. 14, 27.
64. 'Merchants' Exchange,' New York Historical Society.
65. Doris Faber, *Wall Street: A Study of Fortunes and Finance* (N.Y.: Harper & Row Publishers, 1979), p. 42.
66. New York *Mirror*, vol. xiv. (1836), p. 135.
67. Townsend, 'Wall Street Portrait,' p. 68.
68. William Worthington Fowler, *Ten Years in Wall Street* (Hartford: Worthington, Dustin & Co., 1870), pp. 19–20.
69. Louis D. Auchincloss, ed., *The Hone and Strong Diaries of Old Manhattan* (N.Y.: Abbeville Press, 1989), p. 51.
70. Stedman, *The New York Stock Exchange*, p. 96; and Buck, *The New York Stock Exchange*, p. 15.
71. Auchincloss, *The Hone and Strong Diaries of Old Manhattan*, p. 54.

CHAPTER 3

1. James A. Hamilton, *Reminiscences of James A. Hamilton; or, Men and Events, at Home and Abroad, During Three Quarters of a Century* (N.Y.: Charles Scribner & Co., 1869), p. 70.
2. Ibid., p. 69.
3. Edwin W. Burrows and Mike Wallace, *Gotham: A History of New York City to 1898* (New York and Oxford: Oxford University Press, 1999), p. 444.
4. Bray Hammond, *Banks and Politics in America: From the Revolution to the Civil War* (Princeton: Princeton University Press, 1957), pp. 287–9.
5. Ibid., p. 293.
6. Ibid., pp. 298–9.
7. Lois Severini, *The Architecture of Finance: Early Wall Street* (Ann Arbor: UMI Research Press, 1983), pp. 29–30.
8. Alfred D. Chandler, Jr., *The Visible Hand: The Managerial Revolution in American Business* (Cambridge: Harvard University Press, 1977), p. 42.
9. James E. Buck, ed., *The New York Stock Exchange: The First 200 Years* (Essex, Conn.: Greenwich Publishing Group, Inc., 1992), p. 220.
10. Charles Sellers, *The Market Revolution: Jacksonian America, 1815–1846* (Oxford: Oxford University Press, 1991), pp. 72, 321.
11. Ralph Catterall, *The Second Bank of the United States* (Chicago: University of Chicago Press, 1902), p. 184. The South Sea Bubble refers to the speculation that surrounded the British South Sea Company in 1720. The Company was granted a monopoly on trade with the south seas – especially the east coast of South America – in return for a government tax on imports that was used to reduce England's national debt. Excessive speculation in South Sea's stock in the Spring of 1720 quickly led to the bubble bursting in June. [See: Robert M.

Sharp, *The Lore and Legends of Wall Street* (Homewood, IL.: Dow Jones-Irwin, 1989), pp. 51–3.] Additional writings about the South Sea Bubble can be found in: Ross B. Emmett, ed., *Great Bubbles*, vol. 3, *The South Sea Bubble* (London: Pickering & Chatto, 2000) and Edward Chancellor, *Devil Take the Hindmost: A History of Financial Speculation* (N.Y.: Farrar, Straus, Giroux, 1999), pp. 14–27.
12. Hamilton, *Reminiscences*, p. 86 (emphasis in original).
13. Hammond, *Banks and Politics in America*, p. 150. The quotations in the paragraph above are from the same source.
14. New York *Commercial Advertiser*, 15 December 1829.
15. Hamilton, *Reminiscences*, p. 167.
16. Hammond, *Banks and Politics in America*, p. 352.
17. Ibid., p. 353.
18. Ibid., pp. 387, 443.
19. Ibid., p. 354.
20. John M. Blum et al., *The National Experience: A History of the United States*, fourth edn (N.Y.: Harcourt Brace Jovanovich, 1977), p. 222.
21. Catterall, *The Second Bank of the United States*, pp. 19, 252; and in Blum et al., *The National Experience*, p. 221 (emphasis in original).
22. New York *Commercial Advertiser* (12 and 13 July 1832).
23. The custom of the day was for a newspaper to reprint other's editorials. This from the *American Daily Advertiser* and the quotation from the *U.S. Gazette* in the next paragraph appear in the New York *Commercial Advertiser* (14 July 1832).
24. New York *Commercial Advertiser* (13 July 1832).
25. Edward Pessen, *Riches, Classes, and Power Before the Civil War* (Lexington, MA.: D.C. Heath and Co., 1973), p. 33.
26. Hammond, *Banks and Politics in America*, p. 419.
27. Margaret G. Myers, *A Financial History of the United States* (N.Y.: Columbia University Press, 1970), p. 90.
28. Sellers, *The Market Revolution*, pp. 336–7.
29. Burrows and Wallace, *Gotham*, p. 573.
30. Hamilton, *Reminiscences*, pp. 252–8.
31. Ibid., pp. 261–5 (emphasis in original).
32. This is discussed in Chapter 1.
33. Burrows and Wallace, *Gotham*, pp. 573–5.
34. Allan Nevins, ed., *The Diary of Philip Hone, 1828–1851* (N.Y.: Dodd, Mead and Co., 1927), pp. 112–13.
35. Peter Temin, *The Jacksonian Economy* (N.Y.: W.W. Norton & Co., 1969), p. 88.
36. Burrows and Wallace, *Gotham*, p. 571.
37. Myers, *A Financial History of the United States*, p. 98; and Temin, *The Jacksonian Economy*, p. 119.
38. State of New York, 'Memorial and Remonstrance of the Board of Stock and Exchange Brokers of the City of New York,' no. 291, 23 March 1836. New York Public Library, Manuscript Collection.
39. Sellers, *The Market Revolution*, p. 356; and Doris Faber, *Wall Street: A Story of Fortunes and Finance* (N.Y.: Harper & Row Publishers, 1979), p. 43.
40. Robert Sobel, *The Big Board: A History of the New York Stock Market* (N.Y.: The Free Press, 1965), p. 49.

41. Louis Auchincloss, ed., *The Hone & Strong Diaries of Old Manhattan* (N.Y.: Abbeville Press, 1989), p. 63.

42. Hammond, *Banks and Politics in America*, p. 526.

CHAPTER 4

1. See Chapter 1.

2. Edwin G. Burrows and Mike Wallace, *Gotham: A History of New York City to 1898* (New York and Oxford: Oxford University Press, 1999), pp. 596–9.

3. Barbaralee Diamonstein, *The Landmarks of New York* (N.Y.: Harry N. Abrams Inc., Publishers, 1988), p. 85. The new Merchants' Exchange was remodeled and enlarged in 1907 when it became a Citibank building at 55 Wall Street. [Robert Sobel, *The Big Board: A History of the New York Stock Exchange* (N.Y.: The Free Press, 1965), p. 16; and James E. Buck, ed., *The New York Stock Exchange: The First 200 Years* (Essex, Conn.: Greenwich Publishing Group, Inc., 1992), p. 30.] In its latest reincarnation it is now a hotel.

4. Citibank, *55 Wall Street: A Working Landmark* (N.Y.: Citibank, 1979), p. 5.

5. Sereno S. Pratt, *The Work of Wall Street* (N.Y.: D. Appleton & Co., 1912), p. 156.

6. Edward K. Spann, *The New Metropolis: New York City, 1840–1857* (N.Y.: Columbia University Press, 1981), pp. 10–11.

7. Allan Nevins, ed., *The Diary of Philip Hone, 1828–1851* (N.Y.: Dodd, Mead and Co., 1927), pp. 610–11.

8. Lois Severini, *The Architecture of Finance: Early Wall Street* (Ann Arbor: UMI Research Press, 1983), pp. 43, 44, 49.

9. William Worthington Fowler, *Ten Years in Wall Street* (Hartford: Worthington, Dustin & Co., 1870), p. 90.

10. Edmund C. Stedman, *The New York Stock Exchange* (N.Y.: The Stock Exchange Historical Co., 1905), reprinted: (N.Y.: Greenwood Press, 1969), p. 105.

11. Robert Sobel, *The Curbstone Brokers: The Origins of the American Stock Exchange* (N.Y.: The Macmillan Co., 1970), pp. 35, 53; and James K. Medberry, *Men and Mysteries of Wall Street* (Boston: Fields, Osgood, & Co., 1870); reprinted: (Wells, VT.: Fraser Publishing Co., 1968), p. 275. None of these survived, however, as some of their functions were absorbed by the NYS&EB, while others could not withstand the downside of the business cycle.

12. Walter Werner and Stephen T. Smith, *Wall Street* (N.Y.: Columbia University Press, 1991), p. 30; and John Pomeroy Townsend, 'Wall Street Portrait,' Chauncey M. Depew, ed., *One Hundred Years of American Commerce*, vol. I (N.Y.: D.O. Haynes & Co., 1895), reprinted: (N.Y.: Greenwood Press, 1968), p. 70.

13. Fowler, *Ten Years in Wall Street*, p. 81.

14. Ibid., p. 53. Hart was a leader on Wall Street socially as well as financially. At Baker's Hotel near Wall and New Streets he presided as President over evening meetings of the 'House of Lords,' where many important financial transactions were arranged (Pratt, *The Work of Wall Street*, pp. 30–1). The role of Hart and Seixas in the early days of Wall Street is discussed in Chapter 1.

15. John Steele Gordon, *The Scarlet Woman of Wall Street: Jay Gould, Jim Fisk, Cornelius Vanderbilt, the Erie Railway Wars, and the Birth of Wall Street* (N.Y.: Weidenfeld & Nicolson, 1988), p. 14.

16. This legal issue was not settled until the early decades of the twentieth century with the formation of the curb's descendant – the American Stock Exchange – which in 1921 carved the words 'New York Curb Market' above the portico on its first permanent building (Sobel, *The Curbstone Brokers*, photo opposite p. 172).

17. Stedman, *The New York Stock Exchange*, p. 100; and Fowler, *Ten Years in Wall Street*, p. 96.

18. Burrows and Wallace, *Gotham*, p. 569.

19. Fowler, *Ten Years in Wall Street*, pp. 40, 117.

20. Margaret G. Myers, *A Financial History of the United States* (N.Y.: Columbia University Press, 1970), p. 125.

21. Allan Nevins and Milton Halsey Thomas (abridged by Thomas J. Pressly), *The Diary of George Templeton Strong* (Seattle: University of Washington Press, 1988), p. 20.

22. Buck, *The New York Stock Exchange*, p. 46.

23. This picture is now in the permanent collection of Washington, D.C.'s Corcoran Gallery.

24. William Drozdiak, 'Monet's Lasting Impression,' *Washington Post*, 2 June 1992, p. D4. His work as a portrait painter receives more attention today from art critics. One of Morse's portraits can be seen hanging in the permanent collection of the New York Public Library.

25. Musée Américain (Giverny), *Lasting Impressions: American Painters in France, 1865–1915* (Evanston, IL.: Terra Foundation for the Arts, 1992), pp. 126–7.

26. Ibid. The essay on Morse in this catalogue was written by Jochen Wierich.

27. Sobel, *The Big Board*, p. 52.

28. Werner and Smith, *Wall Street*, pp. 39–40.

29. Ron Chernow, *The House of Morgan: American Banking and the Rise of Modern Finance* (N.Y.: Simon and Schuster, 1990), p. 12.

30. These institutional and technological achievements happened during the severe economic crisis of the late 1830s and early 1840s. The anomaly of creativity in the midst of economic despair would re-occur in the nation's history.

31. Burrows and Wallace, *Gotham*, pp. 420–1 (the quotation is from p. 420).

32. Ibid., p. 422.

33. Ibid., p. 586.

34. Spann, *The New Metropolis*, pp. 15, 23 and 407; Burrows and Wallace, *Gotham*, p. 487; and Sean Willentz, *Chants Democratic: New York City and the Rise of the American Working Class, 1788–1850* (Oxford: Oxford University Press, 1984), p. 110.

35. Nevins and Thomas, *The Diary of George Templeton Strong*, p. 785.

36. Edward Pessen, *Riches, Classes, and Power Before the Civil War* (Lexington, MA.: D.C. Heath and Co., 1973), p. 34.

37. Louis Auchincloss, ed., *The Hone & Strong Diaries of Old Manhattan* (N.Y.: The Abbeville Press, 1989), p.150.

38. Spann, *The New Metropolis*, p. 135.

39. Nevins and Thomas, *The Diary of George Templeton Strong*, pp. 49–51; and Spann, *The New Metropolis*, p. 235.

40. Spann, *The New Metropolis*, p. 235.

41. Nevins and Thomas, *The Diary of George Templeton Strong*, pp. 866–70; and Lawrence W. Levine, *Highbrow/Lowbrow: The Emergence of Cultural Hierarchy in America* (Cambridge: Harvard University Press, 1988), pp. 63–9.
42. Nevins and Thomas, *The Diary of George Templeton Strong*, pp. 467–8.
43. Spann, *The New Metropolis*, pp. 114, 285.
44. Diamonstein, *The Landmarks of New York*, p. 23.
45. Nevins and Thomas, *The Diary of George Templeton Strong*, p. 87.
46. Spann, *The New Metropolis*, pp. 289, 293–4.
47. In 1846 the idea for moving people over a subway-like rail conveyance appeared in a visionary proposal by John Randel, Jr. who foresaw an elevated railroad above Broadway that powered coaches with a pulley arrangement. The city council even considered an underground rail system before it opted for the horse-drawn, surface rail system (Spann, *The New Metropolis*, pp. 288–9).
48. See Chapter 1.
49. Spann, *The New Metropolis*, pp. 117–19.
50. The most recent scholarship on the Park attributes the idea to Robert Browne Minturn and his wife, Anna Mary Welden Minturn, who returned from a trip to Europe with the vision of a great park for New York. It was then energized with a campaign led by the poet and *Evening Post* editor, William Cullen Bryant, and was given impetus by the suburban landscape architect, Andrew Jackson Downing, who also edited the influential magazine, *Horticulturist*. [Roy Rosenzweig and Elizabeth Blackmar, *The Park and the People: A History of Central Park* (Ithaca: Cornell University Press, 1992), pp. 15–17.]
51. Spann, *The New Metropolis*, pp. 164–5, 176. There was a conflict between wealthy downtowners around Wall Street who generally opposed the park and uptowners who had speculated in land near the proposed park (Rosenzweig and Blackmar, *The Park and the People*, chaps. 1 and 2).
52. Rosenzweig and Blackmar, *The Park and the People*, pp. 22, 32.
53. Spann, *The New Metropolis*, pp. 185–6, 256–7.
54. Richard L. Bushman, *The Refinement of America: Persons, Houses, Cities* (N.Y.: Alfred A. Knopf, 1992), p. 365.
55. Ibid., pp. 245–9.
56. Spann, *The New Metropolis*, p. 98.
57. Ibid., pp. 97–8; and Diamonstein, *The Landmarks of New York*, p. 93.
58. Burrows and Wallace, *Gotham*, p. 668.
59. Diamonstein, *The Landmarks of New York*, pp. 82–3.
60. Charles Sellers, *The Market Revolution: Jacksonian America, 1815–1846* (Oxford: Oxford University Press, 1991), pp. 217, 230, 237.
61. Burrows and Wallace, *Gotham*, pp. 497, 530–31.
62. Spann, *The New Metropolis*, pp. 243–4.
63. Sellers, *The Market Revolution*, pp. 267–8.
64. Burrows and Wallace, *Gotham*, pp. 533–4, 612.
65. Ibid., pp. 552, 557, 559.
66. Medbery, *Men and Mysteries of Wall Street*, p. 319.
67. Ibid.
68. William Warren Sweet, *The Story of Religion in America* (N.Y.: Harper & Brothers Publishers, 1930), pp. 310–11.
69. Spann, *The New Metropolis*, p. 415.

CHAPTER 5

1. Edwin G. Burrows and Mike Wallace, *Gotham: A History of New York City to 1898* (New York and Oxford: Oxford University Press, 1999), p. 865.
2. Ernest A. McKay, *The Civil War and New York City* (Syracuse: Syracuse University Press, 1990), p. 24.
3. The reference to 'Tri-Insula' is from: Dana L. Thomas, *The Plungers and the Peacocks: An Update of the Classic History of the Stock Market* (N.Y.: G.P. Putnam & Sons, 1967), p. 25; and the quote from Wood is from: Charles Burr Todd, *The Story of the City of New York* (N.Y. : G.P. Putnam & Sons, 1888), p. 446.
4. Burrows and Wallace, *Gotham*, p. 849. The reforms and building program of Wood in the 1850s are discussed in Chapter 4.
5. Ibid., pp. 866–7.
6. Todd, *The Story of the City of New York*, p. 445.
7. On Gazzaway Bugg Lamar (p. 94), see McKay, *The Civil War and New York City*, pp. 33–6. The quote from Wood and Lincoln's response is also in McKay, p. 45.
8. Edmund C. Stedman, *The New York Stock Exchange* (N.Y.: The Stock Exchange Historical Co., 1905); reprinted: (N.Y.: Greenwood Press, 1969), pp. 144–5. The quote following is also in Stedman.
9. Louis Auchincloss, ed., *The Hone and Strong Diaries of Old Manhattan* (N.Y.: Abbeville Press, 1989), p. 203.
10. McKay, *The Civil War and New York City*, p. 59.
11. Ibid., p. 31.
12. Bray Hammond, *Banks and Politics in America: From the Revolution to the Civil War* (Princeton: Princeton University Press, 1957), p. 718.
13. McKay, *The Civil War and New York City*, p. 28.
14. Ibid., p. 29. (Emphasis in original.)
15. Burrows and Wallace, *Gotham*, p. 875.
16. This quote and the one above is from: Auchincloss, *The Hone and Strong Diaries of Old Manhattan*, pp. 208, 225.
17. Jean Strouse, *Morgan: American Financier* (N.Y.: HarperCollins, 1999), p. 109.
18. Burrows and Wallace, *Gotham*, pp. 893, 895; Auchincloss, *The Hone and Strong Diaries of Old Manhattan*, p. 219; and McKay, *The Civil War and New York City*, pp. 208–9.
19. Auchincloss, *The Hone and Strong Diaries of Old Manhattan*, p. 222; and McKay, *The Civil War and New York City*, p. 204.
20. Burrows and Wallace, *Gotham*, pp. 886–7.
21. See Chapter 3.
22. Ron Chernow, *The House of Morgan: An American Banking Dynasty and the Rise of Modern Finance* (N.Y.: Simon & Schuster, 1990), pp. 21–2; and Strouse, *Morgan*, pp. 93–4. The reference to clothing and the quote on boots is from Burrows and Wallace, *Gotham*, p. 875.
23. A composite quotation from: William Worthington Fowler, *Ten Years in Wall Street* (Hartford: Worthington, Dustin & Co., 1870), pp. 156–7, 364–5.
24. McKay, *The Civil War and New York City*, p. 220.
25. Bray Hammond, *Sovereignty and an Empty Purse: Banks and Politics in the Civil War* (Princeton: Princeton University Press, 1970), p. 78.
26. Ibid., pp. 44–5.

27. James A. Hamilton, *Reminiscences of James A. Hamilton; or Men and Events at Home and Abroad, During Three Quarters of a Century* (N.Y.: Charles Scribner & Co., 1869), pp. 538–47.

28. Ellis Paxson Oberholtzer, *Jay Cooke: Financier of the Civil War*, vol. 1 (Philadelphia: George W. Jacobs & Co., 1907), p. 102; Hammond, *Sovereignty and an Empty Purse*, p. 43; and McKay, *The Civil War and New York City*, pp. 94–5.

29. Susan Strasser, *Satisfaction Guaranteed: The Making of the American Mass Market* (N.Y.: Pantheon Books, 1989).

30. Oberholtzer, *Jay Cooke*, p. 252 (emphases in original).

31. Thomas, *The Plungers and the Peacocks*, p. 28.

32. Oberholtzer, *Jay Cooke*, pp. 61, 159–61.

33. Stedman, *The New York Stock Exchange*, p. 140; Hammond, *Sovereignty and an Empty Purse*, p. 252; and Oberholtzer, *Jay Cooke*, p. 178.

34. Fowler, *Ten Years in Wall Street*, pp. 150–51 (emphasis in original).

35. Oberholtzer, *Jay Cooke*, p. 500.

36. John Steele Gordon, *The Scarlet Woman of Wall Street: Jay Gould, Jim Fisk, Cornelius Vanderbilt, the Erie Railway Wars, and the Birth of Wall Street* (N.Y.: Weidenfeld & Nicolson, 1988), p. 258.

37. Oberholtzer, *Jay Cooke*, pp. 235–6, 575–6, 617. The quotation from the 'Irish woman' is from p. 596.

38. Ibid., pp. 575–6, 617. The quotation is from p. 599.

39. Thomas, *The Plungers and the Peacocks*, p. 31.

40. Oberholtzer, *Jay Cooke*, p. 289.

41. Ibid., p. 596.

42. Fowler, *Ten Years in Wall Street*, pp. 134–5.

43. Wayne W. Westbrook, *Wall Street in the American Novel* (N.Y.: New York University Press, 1980), p. 20.

44. J. Armory Knox, *The Man from the West: 'From Chaparral to Wall Street'* (N.Y.: Pollard & Moss Publishers, 1889). The quotations are from pp. 6, 12. This 245-page novel sold for 50 cents and was part of 'a weekly literary library of standard fiction, consisting mostly of novels not procurable in any other series,' touts the blurb on the book.

45. McKay, *The Civil War and New York City*, p. 221; and Oberholtzer, *Jay Cooke*, p. 489.

46. Oberholtzer, *Jay Cooke*, pp. 259–60.

47. Ibid., p. 396.

48. Ibid., p. 619.

49. See chapter 3.

50. Jerome W. Sheridan, *Financing Industrial Growth: The Transformation of Bank Investment from Antebellum State Banking to the National Bank of the United States, 1840–1890*, doctoral dissertation (Washington, D.C.: American University, 1990), pp. 35, 75–6, 128, 138.

51. Hammond, *Banks and Politics in America*, pp. 360, 726.

CHAPTER 6

1. Edmund C. Stedman, *The New York Stock Exchange* (N.Y.: The Stock Exchange Historical Co., 1905); reprinted (N.Y.: Greenwood Press, 1969), p. 168.

2. John Steele Gordon, *The Scarlet Woman of Wall Street: Jay Gould, Jim Fisk, Cornelius Vanderbilt, the Erie Railroad Wars, and the Birth of Wall Street* (N.Y.: Weidenfeld & Nicolson, 1988), pp. 15–17.
3. Henry Clews, Drew's contemporary broker-competitor, described him as 'bland, good-natured, with affected but well-dissembled humility, which was highly calculated to disarm any resentment and enable him to move smoothly in society. ... He was often mistaken for a country deacon' (ibid., pp. 24–5).
4. James K. Medberry, *Men and Mysteries of Wall Street* (Boston: Fields, Osgood & Co., 1870); reprinted: (Wells, VT.: Fraser Publishing Co., 1968), p. 169.
5. Charles Francis Adams, Jr. and Henry Adams, *Chapters of Erie* (Ithaca: Cornell University Press, 1956), pp. 3, 107; and W.A. Swanberg, *Jim Fisk: The Career of an Improbable Rascal* (N.Y.: Charles Scribner's Sons, 1959), p. 29.
6. Stedman, *The New York Stock Exchange*, p. 199.
7. William Worthington Fowler, *Ten Years in Wall Street* (Hartford: Worthington, Dustin & Co., 1870), pp. 120, 126; Frederick L. Collins, *Money Town* (N.Y.: G.P. Putnam & Sons, 1946), p. 21; and Gordon, *The Scarlet Woman of Wall Street*, p. 50.
8. Stedman, *The New York Stock Exchange*, p. 170.
9. Gordon, *The Scarlet Woman of Wall Street*, pp. 39, 41.
10. Charles Sellers, *The Market Revolution: Jacksonian America, 1815–1846* (N.Y. and Oxford: Oxford University Press, 1991), p. 392.
11. Fowler, *Ten Years in Wall Street*, pp. 351–2. William Fowler wrote about this episode from personal experience. He lost $24,000 on his short position.
12. Charles P. Kindleberger, *Manias, Panics and Crashes: A History of Financial Crises*, third edn (N.Y.: John Wiley & Sons, 1996) chaps. 2 and 3.
13. Kenneth D. Ackerman, *The Gold Ring: Jim Fisk, Jay Gould and Black Friday, 1869* (N.Y.: Dodd, Mead & Co., 1988), pp. 3–6; and Gordon, *The Scarlet Woman of Wall Street*, pp. 156–8.
14. Adams and Adams, *Chapters of Erie*, p. 19.
15. Robert M. Sharp, *The Lore and Legends of Wall Street* (Homewood, IL.: Dow Jones-Irwin, 1989), pp. 87–90; Swanberg, *Jim Fisk*, p. 45; and Gordon, *The Scarlet Woman of Wall Street*, pp. 15–17.
16. Gordon, *The Scarlet Woman of Wall Street*, pp. 363–4.
17. Ibid., pp. 162–8; and Swanberg, *Jim Fisk*, pp. 40–2.
18. Adams and Adams, *Chapters of Erie*, p. 33; and Fowler, *Ten Years in Wall Street*, pp. 502–3.
19. Fowler, *Ten Years in Wall Street*, p. 428. Testimony to the fame and importance of Delmonico's restaurant is reflected in the existence of a book about this successful importation of French culinary attractions and its impressive wine cellar with some of the finest French vintages. [Lately Thomas, *Delmonico's: A Century of Splendor* (N.Y.: Houghton Mifflin Co., 1967).]
20. Gordon, *The Scarlet Woman of Wall Street*, p. 181.
21. Ibid., p. 181; and Adams and Adams, *Chapters of Erie*, pp. 48–9.
22. Gordon, *The Scarlet Woman of Wall Street*, p. 183.
23. Swanberg, *Jim Fisk*, p. 60.
24. Adams and Adams, *Chapters of Erie*, p. 53; and Gordon, *The Scarlet Woman of Wall Street*, p. 186.
25. Fowler, *Ten Years in Wall Street*, p. 504.

26. Adams and Adams, *Chapters of Erie*, pp. 58–9; and Ackerman, *The Gold Ring*, p. 15.
27. Gordon, *The Scarlet Woman of Wall Street*, pp. 189, 192–3; Fowler, *Ten Years in Wall Street*, p. 506; and Ackerman, *The Gold Ring*, p. 15.
28. Sharp, *The Lore and Legends of Wall Street*, p. 115.
29. Adams and Adams, *Chapters of Erie*, p. 95.
30. Stedman, *The New York Stock Exchange*, p. 282.
31. Gordon, *The Scarlet Woman of Wall Street*, p. 377; Edmund C. Stedman, *The New York Stock Exchange*, pp. 282–3; and Louis Auchincloss, ed., *The Hone & Strong Diaries of Old Manhattan* (N.Y.: Abbeville Press, 1989), p. 253.
32. Ron Chernow, *The House of Morgan: American Banking and the Rise of Modern Finance* (N.Y.: Simon & Schuster, 1990), p. 42.
33. Ackerman, *The Gold Ring*, p. 48.
34. Stedman, *The New York Stock Exchange*, p. 219.
35. Swanberg, *Jim Fisk*, pp. 1–2, 11–17.
36. Ibid., pp. 1–2; and Allen Nevins and Milton Halsey Thomas (abridged by Thomas J. Pressly), *The Diary of George Templeton Strong* (Seattle: University of Washington Press, 1988), p. 379.
37. This composite portrait of Gould is drawn from: Edward Chancellor, *Devil Take the Hindmost: A History of Financial Speculation* (N.Y.: Farrar, Strauss, Giroux, 1999), p. 178; and Swanberg, *Jim Fisk*, pp. 11–17.
38. James E. Buck, ed., *The New York Stock Exchange: The First 200 Years* (Essex, Conn.: Greenwich Publishing Group, Inc., 1992), p. 59.
39. Stedman, *The New York Stock Exchange*, p. 349.
40. Gordon, *The Scarlet Woman of Wall Street*, pp. 231–2; Fowler, *Ten Years in Wall Street*, p. 512; and Swanberg, *Jim Fisk*, pp. 2–3.
41. Ackerman, *The Gold Ring*, p. 36.
42. Jean-Christophe Agnew, *Worlds Apart: The Market and the Theater in Anglo-American Thought, 1550–1750* (Cambridge: Cambridge University Press, 1986), p. x.
43. Nevins and Thomas, *The Diary of George Templeton Strong*, p. 379; Auchincloss, *The Hone & Strong Diaries of Old Manhattan*, p. 266; and Swanberg, *Jim Fisk*, p. 6.
44. Gordon, *The Scarlet Woman of Wall Street*, p. 292.
45. Buck, *The New York Stock Exchange*, p. 58.
46. Adams and Adams, *Chapters of Erie*, p. 116.
47. Ackerman, *The Gold Ring*, pp. 59, 279.
48. Buck, *The New York Stock Exchange*, p. 58.
49. Ackerman, *The Gold Ring*, pp. 84–5.
50. Ibid., p. 93.
51. Ibid., pp. 87–8, 99.
52. Ibid., pp. 126–7.
53. Buck, *The New York Stock Exchange*, p. 60.
54. Ackerman, *The Gold Ring*, p. 164.
55. Ibid., p. 106.
56. Buck, *The New York Stock Exchange*, p. 62.
57. Ackerman, *The Gold Ring*, p. 269.
58. Gordon, *The Scarlet Woman of Wall Street*, p. 310.
59. Stedman, *The New York Stock Exchange*, p. 245.

60. Gordon, *The Scarlet Woman of Wall Street*, p. 325.
61. Ibid., pp. 328, 338–9.
62. Ackerman, *The Gold Ring*, pp. 279, 284.
63. Ibid., p. 280.
64. Medberry, *Men and Mysteries of Wall Street*, p. 196.
65. Adams and Adams, *Chapters of Erie*, p. 96.
66. Harry S. Quire, *Wall Street in Paradise: An Original and Musical Extravaganza* (N.Y.: George F. Nesbitt & Co., 1869), pp. 1, 4, 10.

CHAPTER 7

1. I have borrowed this formulation from: Ron Chernow, *The House of Morgan: American Banking and the Rise of Modern Finance* (N.Y.: Simon and Schuster, 1990), Part I.
2. Jean Strouse, *Morgan: American Financier* (N.Y.: HarperPerennial, 2000), p. 230.
3. Chernow, *The House of Morgan*, pp. 34, 46.
4. See Chapter 2.
5. Joseph Wechsberg, *The Merchant Bankers* (Boston: Little, Brown and Company, 1966), p. 11.
6. Chernow, *The House of Morgan*, p. 23 and the quotation from p. 43; and James A. Meeker, *The Work of The Stock Exchange* (N.Y.: The Ronald Press Co., 1922), p. 440.
7. Chernow, *The House of Morgan*, pp. 24–5.
8. Garet Garret, *Where the Money Grows* (N.Y.: Harper & Brothers, 1911), p. 49.
9. Ibid, pp. 49–50.
10. Chernow, *The House of Morgan*, p. 108.
11. Strouse, *Morgan*, p. 3.
12. Chernow, *The House of Morgan*, p. 117. Chernow says that Morgan was 'oblivious to Impressionists and modern American artists, [and] he favored objects with long, romantic histories.' Paintings made up only 5 per cent of his collection (p. 51).
13. Edmund C. Stedman, *The New York Stock Exchange* (N.Y.: The Stock Exchange Historical Co., 1905); reprinted: (N.Y.: Greenwood Press, 1969), p. 261.
14. Stedman, *The New York Stock Exchange*, p. 265.
15. Chernow, *The House of Morgan*, p. 35.
16. Margaret G. Myers, *A Financial History of the United States* (N.Y.: Columbia University Press, 1970), p. 224; Chernow, *The House of Morgan*, p. 68; and Frederick L. Collins, *Money Town* (N.Y.: G.P. Putnam's Sons, 1946), p. 279.
17. Chernow, *The House of Morgan*, pp. 67–8. At the turn of the century, the country's rail network was consolidated into six large systems, controlled primarily by the Wall Street firms of J.P. Morgan and Kuhn, Loeb.
18. This discussion is based on Chernow, *The House of Morgan*, pp. 30–8. The quote is from p. 32.
19. Ibid., pp. 13, 88.
20. Ibid. p. 89.
21. Ron Chernow, *The Warburgs: The 20th-Century Odyssey of a Remarkable Jewish Family* (N.Y.: Random House, 1993), p. 50.

22. Chernow, *The House of Morgan*, pp. 90–91. This was the largest block purchase to this date.
23. Stedman, *The New York Stock Exchange*, p. 395.
24. Chernow, *The House of Morgan*, p. 93.
25. Ibid., p. 93.
26. Ibid., pp. 71–8.
27. Some of the opposition was anti-semitic. The New York *World* characterized the gold cabal as a group of 'blood-sucking Jews and aliens,' and William Jennings Bryan inserted in the *Congressional Record* a reading on Shylock from Shakespeare's *Merchant of Venice*. [Chernow, *The House of Morgan*, p. 76.]
28. William Greider, *Secrets of the Temple: How the Federal Reserve Runs the Country* (N.Y.: Simon and Schuster, 1987), pp. 271–3.
29. The exchange's first home was the Tontine Coffee House at Wall and Water Streets. In 1827 it moved into the first Merchants' Exchange at Wall and Hanover Streets. After it was destroyed by the 1835 fire, the NYS&EB moved into the Jauncey Building at 43 Wall Street until the second Merchants' Exchange was completed in 1842 at Wall, Hanover, and Exchange Place. [Mutual Life Insurance Company of New York, *King's View of the New York Stock Exchange* (N.Y.: Moses King, 1897), p. 70.]
30. Deborah Gardner, *Marketplace: A Brief History of the New York Stock Exchange* (N.Y.: New York Stock Exchange, 1982), p. 9; and James E. Buck, ed., *The New York Stock Exchange: The First 200 Years* (Essex, Conn.: Greenwich Publishing Group, Inc., 1992), p. 54.
31. Lois Severini, *The Architecture of Finance: Early Wall Street* (Ann Arbor: UMI Research Press, 1983), pp. 9, 56–7.
32. James K. Medberry, *Men and Mysteries of Wall Street* (Boston: Fields, Osgood & Co., 1870), p. 15; reprinted: (Wells, VT.: Fraser Publishing Co., 1968).
33. Gardner, *A Brief History of the New York Stock Exchange*, p. 10.
34. Robert Sobel, *The Curbstone Brokers: The Origins of the American Stock Exchange* (N.Y.: The Macmillan Co., 1970), p. 31.
35. Buck, *The New York Stock Exchange*, p. 56.
36. Ibid., p. 57; and Sereno S. Pratt, *The Work of Wall Street* (N.Y.: D. Appleton & Co., 1912), p. 134.
37. Medberry, *Men and Mysteries of Wall Street*, pp. 130–31. The curb was dominated by Jews and Irish Catholics, who found it difficult to gain entrance into the NYSE, which was controlled by Episcopal Trinity Church members.
38. Robert M. Sharp, *The Lore and Legends of Wall Street* (Homewood, IL.: Dow Jones-Irwin, 1989), pp. 159–61.
39. Sobel, *The Curbstone Brokers*, pp. 107–9.
40. Medberry, *Men and Mysteries of Wall Street*, p. 130.
41. John Steele Gordon, *The Scarlet Woman of Wall Street: Jay Gould, Jim Fisk, Cornelius Vanderbilt, the Erie Railway Wars, and the Birth of Wall Street* (N.Y.: Weidenfeld & Nicolson, 1988), p. 115.
42. Sobel, *The Curbstone Brokers*, pp. 83–4.
43. There appears to be no evidence to support Wall Street legend about the specialist, which is based on a story about someone named Boyd who broke his leg and had to remain at one post to trade securities. The Boyd fable is put in 1875 when we know the specialist and the trading post appeared earlier.

[Robert Sobel, *Inside Wall Street: Continuity and Change in the Financial District* (N.Y.: W.W. Norton & Co., 1977), p. 29.]

44. Sobel, *The Curbstone Brokers*, p. 31.
45. Stedman, *The New York Stock Exchange*, p. 214; and Medberry, *Men and Mysteries of Wall Street*, p. 15.
46. Gardner, *A Brief History of the New York Stock Exchange*, p. 10.
47. Stedman, *The New York Stock Exchange*, p. 214; and Gardner, *A Brief History of the New York Stock Exchange*, p. 10.
48. Pratt, *The Work of Wall Street* , p. 134.
49. Sobel, *The Curbstone Brokers*, photo before p. 173.
50. Pratt, *The Work of Wall Street*, p. 89.
51. Francine du Plessix Gray, 'Sex, Scandals, and Suffrage: The Misadventures of an Unlikely Feminist,' *The New Yorker*, 20 April 1998, p. 95.
52. Barbara Goldsmith, *Other Powers: The Age of Suffrage, Spiritualism, and the Scandalous Victoria Woodhull* (N.Y.: Alfred A. Knopf, 1998), p. 212.
53. Mary Gabriel, *Notorious Victoria: The Life of Victoria Woodhull, Uncensored* (Chapel Hill, NC.: Algonquin Books of Chapel Hill, 1998), pp. 22–3.
54. Goldsmith, *Other Powers*, p. 7.
55. See Chapter 6.
56. This and what follows is drawn from: Goldsmith, *Other Powers*, pp. 146–62, 188–92.
57. Ibid., p. 159.
58. Gabriel, *Notorious Victoria*, p. 39.
59. Ibid., pp. 1, 39.
60. Ibid., p. 2.
61. Ibid., p. 3.
62. Ibid., p. 125.
63. Lois Beachy Underhill, *The Woman Who Ran for President: The Many Lives of Victoria Woodhull* (Bridgehampton, N.Y.: Bridge Works Publishing Co., 1995), p. 294. John Martin's, *The Grasshopper of Lombard Street*, on the National Bank of England became a classic and still is used today as an important historical reference work on the Bank (p. 292).
64. Gabriel, *Notorious Victoria*, p. 301.
65. Boyden Sparkes and Samuel Taylor Moore, *Hetty Green: The Witch of Wall Street* (Garden City, N.Y.: Doubleday, Doran & Co., 1935), pp. 11, 34, 35. The quote is from p. 265.
66. Buck, *The New York Stock Exchange*, p. 66; and Sobel, *The Curbstone Brokers*, p. 107. Photographs and contemporary accounts generally support this depiction of Hetty Green. [Sharp, *The Lore and Legends of Wall Street*, pp. 147–50; and Kenneth L. Fisher, *100 Minds that Made the Market* (Woodside, CA.: Business Classics, 1993), pp. 413–16.] The quote is from Sparkes and Moore, *Hetty Green*, p. 224.
67. Sparkes and Moore, *Hetty Green*, pp. 8, 265, 267.
68. Goldsmith, *Other Powers*, p. 192.
69. Sparkes and Moore, *Hetty Green*, pp. 64–5.
70. Ibid., pp. 10, 117, 250, 266.
71. Ibid., p. 269.
72. Ibid., p. 218.
73. Ibid., p. 231.

74. Ibid., p. 337.
75. Buck, *The New York Stock Exchange*, pp. 44–5; and Medberry, *Men and Mysteries of Wall Street*, p. 195.
76. Gardner, *A Brief History of the New York Stock Exchange*, p. 11.
77. Horace L. Hotchkiss, 'The Stock Ticker,' Edmund C. Stedman, ed., *New York Stock Exchange* (N.Y.: The Stock Exchange Historical Co., 1905); reprinted: (N.Y.: Greenwood Press, 1969), pp. 433, 437.
78. Buck, *The New York Stock Exchange*, p. 48.
79. Ibid, pp. 44–5.
80. Gardner, *A Brief History of the New York Stock Exchange*, p. 11.
81. Stedman, *New York Stock Exchange*, pp. v–vi.
82. Buck, *The New York Stock Exchange*, p. 68.
83. The material on Dow and Jones is from: Peter L. Bernstein, *Capital Ideas: The Improbable Origins of Modern Wall Street* (N.Y.: The Free Press, 1992), pp. 24–7. Dow changed his Index in 1896 from a mixture of railroads and industrials to a pure industrial index, originally consisting of twelve companies of which two remain in today's index.
84. Ibid., p. 25.
85. Ibid., p. 26.

CHAPTER 8

1. Henry R. Luce, 'The American Century,' *Life* (17 February 1941), p. 64.
2. The statistics in this paragraph and quote are from: Robert Sobel, *The Big Board: A History of the New York Stock Market* (N.Y.: The Free Press, 1965), pp. 150–51.
3. Ibid., p. 156.
4. Ron Chernow, *The House of Morgan: An American Banking Dynasty and the Rise of Modern Finance* (N.Y.: Simon & Schuster, 1990), pp. 122–4.
5. Ibid., pp. 124–5.
6. Ibid., p. 126.
7. Ibid., pp. 147, 152.
8. Sobel, *The Big Board*, p. 188.
9. Chernow, *The House of Morgan*, pp. 150, 154.
10. Jean Strouse, *Morgan: American Financier* (N.Y.: HarperCollins, 1999), pp. 12–13.
11. Ibid., p. 12.
12. The quotations from the hearings are in: Chernow, *The House of Morgan*, pp. 154–5.
13. Strouse, *Morgan*, p. 671 (emphasis in original).
14. Sobel, *The Big Board*, pp. 200–1.
15. Chernow, *The House of Morgan*, p. 165.
16. See Chapters 1, 3.
17. Chernow, *The House of Morgan*, p. 176.
18. Louis D. Brandeis, *Other People's Money and How the Bankers Use It* (N.Y.: Frederick A. Stokes & Co., 1914); reprinted: (Fairfield, NJ.: Augustus M. Kelley, 1986), p. 6.
19. Chernow, *The House of Morgan*, pp. 179–80.
20. William Greider, *Secrets of the Temple: How the Federal Reserve Runs the Country* (N.Y.: Simon and Schuster, 1987), p. 243.

21. Ibid., p. 242.
22. For a discussion of this, see: Ibid., pp. 253–63. The quotation is from p. 263.
23. Sobel, *The Big Board*, p. 221.
24. Chernow, *The House of Morgan*, pp. 212–13.
25. Ibid., p. 326.
26. Ibid., p. 327.
27. Sobel, *The Big Board*, p. 252 and Chernow, *The House of Morgan*, p. 303.
28. Sobel, *The Big Board*, pp. 289, 290, 293.
29. Chernow, *The House of Morgan*, pp. 354–5.
30. Ibid., pp. 355, 360.
31. This and what follows is from: ibid., pp. 355, 361, 363, 365–9.
32. Ibid., pp. 378–9.
33. Greider, *Secrets of the Temple*, pp. 304–5.
34. See Chapter 1.
35. Howard M. Wachtel, *The Money Mandarins: The Making of a New Supranational Economic Order* (N.Y.: Pantheon Books, 1986), p. 24.
36. For an analysis of the breakdown of Bretton Woods, see: Ibid., Chapter 4.
37. Ibid., p. 43.
38. Ibid., p. 43.
39. For more on this, see: Howard M. Wachtel, 'World Trade Order and the Beginning of the Decline of the Washington Consensus,' *Politik Und Gesellschaft* (3, 2000), pp. 247–53.
40. Greider, *Secrets of the Temple*, pp. 23, 30.
41. Robert J. McCartney, 'Big Board, Big Birthday, Big Questions,' *Washington Post* (19 May 1992), p. C1. Another example of this is: 'The Next Hundred Years,' *The Economist* (9 May 1992), p. 97.
42. *Washington Post* (24 March 1992), pp. A9–A11.
43. E.Y. ('Skip') Harburg was a democratic socialist who used his creative talents not only to entertain but to promote progressive ideas. His 'Brother, Can You Spare a Dime,' became the anthem of the Great Depression. The lyrics for many of his songs in *The Wizard of Oz* – in which 'Somewhere Over the Rainbow' appears – and *Finian's Rainbow* are layered with multiple meanings.

Bibliography

Ackerman, Kenneth D. *The Gold Ring: Jim Fisk, Jay Gould and Black Friday, 1869* (N.Y.: Dodd, Mead & Company, 1988)

Adams, Charles Francis, Jr. and Henry Adams. *Chapters of Erie* (N.Y.: Henry Holt, 1886), reprinted: (Ithaca: Cornell University Press, 1956)

Agnew, Jean-Christophe. *Worlds Apart: The Market and the Theater in Anglo-American Thought, 1550–1750* (Cambridge: Cambridge University Press, 1986)

Auchincloss, Louis D. *The Hone and Strong Diaries of Old Manhattan* (N.Y.: Abbeville Press, 1989)

Bank of America. *A History of Fifty Feet in New York at Wall & William Streets* (N.Y.: Bank of America, 1926)

Barrett, Walter [né: Scoville, Joseph Alfred]. *The Old Merchants of New York*, 2 volumes (N.Y.: M. Doolady, 1870)

Beard, Charles A. *An Economic Interpretation of the Constitution of the United States* (N.Y.: The Macmillan Co.,1913)

Bernstein, Peter L. *Capital Ideas: The Improbable Origins of Modern Wall Street* (N.Y.: The Free Press, 1992)

Birmingham, Stephen. *Our Crowd: The Great Jewish Families of New York* (N.Y.: Dell Publishing Co., 1967)

Blackermar, Elizabeth. *Manhattan for Rent, 1785–1850* (Ithaca: Cornell University Press, 1989)

Blum, John M., et al. *The National Experience: A History of the United States*, fourth edn (N.Y.: Harcourt Brace Jovanovich, 1977)

Blumin, Stuart. 'Explaining the New Metropolis,' *Journal of Urban History*, v. 11, n. 1 (November 1984), pp. 9–38

Bogin, Ruth. 'Measures so Glaringly Unjust: A Response to Hamilton's Funding Plan by William Manning,' *William and Mary Quarterly*, v. 46, n. 2 (April 1989), pp. 315–31

Booth, Mary L. *History of the City of New York* (N.Y.: E.P. Dutton, 1880)

Botkin, B.A. *New York City Folklore* (N.Y.: Random House, 1956)

Bowling, Kenneth R. *The Creation of Washington, D.C.: The Idea and Location of the American Capital* (Fairfax: George Mason University Press, 1991)

Brandeis, Louis D. *Other People's Money and How the Banks Use It* (N.Y.: Frederick A. Stokes & Co., 1914)

Browder, Clifford. *The Money Game in Old New York: Daniel Drew and His Times* (Lexington: The University Press of Kentucky, 1986)

Buck, James E., ed. *The New York Stock Exchange: the First 200 Years* (Essex, Conn.: Greenwich Publishing Group, Inc., 1992)

Burrows, Edwin G. and Mike Wallace. *Gotham: A History of New York City to 1898* (N.Y. and Oxford: Oxford University Press, 1999)

Bushman, Richard L. *The Refinement of America: Persons, Houses, Cities* (N.Y.: Alfred A. Knopf, 1992)

Cantor, Eddie. *Caught Short: A Saga of Wailing Wall Street* (N.Y.: Simon and Schuster, 1929)

Catterall, Ralph. *The Second Bank of the United States* (Chicago: University of Chicago Press, 1902)

Chancellor, Edward. *Devil Take the Hindmost: A History of Financial Speculation* (N.Y.: Farrar, Straus, Giroux, 1999)

Chandler, Alfred D., Jr. *The Visible Hand: The Managerial Revolution in American Business* (Cambridge: Harvard University Press, 1977)

Chernow, Ron. *The House of Morgan: American Banking and the Rise of Modern Finance* (N.Y.: Simon & Schuster, 1990)

—. *The Warburgs: The 20th-Century Odyssey of a Remarkable Jewish Family* (N.Y.: Random House, 1993)

Citibank, *55 Wall Street: A Working Landmark* (N.Y.: Citibank, 1979)

Clews, Henry. *Fifty Years in Wall Street* (N.Y.: Irving Publishing, 1908)

—. *The Wall Street Point of View* (N.Y.: Silver, Burdett & Co., 1900)

Collins, Frederick L. *Money Town* (N.Y.: G.P. Putnam and Sons, 1946)

Cooke, Jacob Ernest. *Alexander Hamilton* (N.Y.: Charles Scribner's & Sons, 1982)

Croly, Herbert. *The Promise of American Life* (N.Y.: The Macmillan Co., 1909)

Davis, Joseph S. *Essays in the Earlier History of American Corporations* (Cambridge: Harvard University Press, 1917)

Depew, Chauncey M. *My Memories of Eighty Years* (N.Y.: Charles Scribner's Sons, 1922)

Diamonstein, Barbaralee. *The Landmarks of New York* (N.Y.: Harry N. Abrams, Inc., Publishers, 1988)

Dorfman, Joseph. *The Economic Mind in American Civilization, 1606–1865*, 2 vols. (N.Y.: The Viking Press, 1946)

Dos Passos, John R. *A Treatise on the Law of Stock-Brokers and Stock-Exchanges* (N.Y.: Harper and Bros., 1882)

Drozdiak, William. 'Monet's Lasting Impression,' *Washington Post* (2 June 1992), p. D4

Eames, Francis L. *The New York Stock Exchange* (N.Y.: Thomas G. Hall, 1894)

The Economist, 'The Next Hundred Years' (9 May 1992), pp. 97–8

Ehrlich, Judith Ramsey and Barry J. Rehfeld. *The New Crowd: The Changing of the Jewish Guard on Wall Street* (N.Y.: Little, Brown and Co., 1989)

Eisenstadt, Peter. 'How the Buttonwood Tree Grew: The Making of the New York Stock Exchange,' *Prospects: An Annual of American Cultural Studies* (19), pp. 75–98

Emmett, Ross B. *Great Bubbles*, 3 vols. (London: Pickering & Chatto, 2000)

Faber, Doris. *Wall Street: A Story of Fortunes and Finance* (N.Y.: Harper & Row Publishers, 1979)

Fisher, Kenneth L. *100 Minds that Made the Market* (Woodside, CA.: Business Classics, 1993)

Fowler, William Worthington. *Ten Years in Wall Street* (Hartford: Washington, Dustin & Co., 1870)

Friedman, Maxine. *Wall Street: Changing Fortunes* (N.Y.: Fraunces Tavern Museum, 1990)

Freese, Joseph R., S.J. and Jacob Judd, eds, *Business Enterprise in Early New York* (Tarrytown: The Sleepy Hollow Press, 1979)

Fuller, Robert H. *Jubilee Jim: The Life of Colonel James Fisk, Jr.* (N.Y.: The Macmillan Co., 1928)

Gabriel, Mary. *Notorious Victoria: The Life of Victoria Woodhull, Uncensored* (Chapel Hill, NC.: Algonquin Books of Chapel Hill, 1998)

Gabriel, Ralph Henry. *The Course of American Democratic Thought* (N.Y.: The Ronald Press Co., 1956)

Gardner, Deborah S. *Marketplace: A Brief History of the New York Stock Exchange* (N.Y.: New York Stock Exchange, 1982)

Garret, Garet. *Where the Money Grows* (N.Y.: Harper & Brothers, 1911)

Gehring, Charles T. 'New Netherland – Translating New York's Dutch Past,' *Humanities*, v. 14, n. 6 (November–December 1993)

Geist, Charles R. *Wall Street: A History* (N.Y. and Oxford: Oxford University Press, 1997)

Goldfield, David R. and Blaine A. Brownell, *Urban America: A History* (Boston: Houghton Mifflin Co., 1990)

Goldsmith, Barbara. *Other Powers: The Age of Suffrage, Spiritualism, and the Scandalous Victoria Woodhull* (N.Y.: Alfred A. Knopf, 1998)

Gordon, John Steele. 'The Founding Wizard,' *American Heritage*, v. 41, n. 5 (July 1990), pp. 41–56.

—. *The Scarlet Woman of Wall Street: Jay Gould, Jim Fisk, Cornelius Vanderbilt, the Erie Railway Wars, and the Birth of Wall Street* (N.Y.: Weidenfeld & Nicolson, 1988)

Gray, Francine du Plessix. 'Sex, Scandals, and Suffrage: The Misadventures of an Unlikely Feminist,' *The New Yorker* (20 April 1998), pp. 94–8

Grayling, A.C. 'Reflections on the Spirit on an Age,' *Financial Times* (14–15 June 1997), p. vi

Greider, William. *Secrets of the Temple: How the Federal Reserve Runs the Country* (N.Y.: Simon & Schuster, 1987)

Hamilton, James A. *Reminiscences of James A. Hamilton; or Men and Events, at Home and Abroad, During Three Quarters of a Century* (N.Y.: Charles Scribner & Co., 1869)

Hammond, Bray. *Banks and Politics in America: From the Revolution to the Civil War* (Princeton: Princeton University Press, 1957)

—. *Sovereignty and an Empty Purse: Banks and Politics in the Civil War* (Princeton: Princeton University Press, 1970)

Hedges, Joseph Edward. *Commercial Banking and the Stock Market Before 1863* (Baltimore: The Johns Hopkins Press, 1938)

Hickling, John. *Men and Idioms of Wall Street* (N.Y.: John Hickling & Co., 1875)

Hill, Frederick Trevor. *The Story of a Street* (N.Y.: Harper & Brothers, 1908)

Hotchkiss, Horace L. 'The Stock Ticker,' Edmund C. Stedman, ed., *The New York Stock Exchange* (N.Y.: The Stock Exchange Historical Co., 1905), reprinted: (N.Y.: Greenwood Press, 1969)

Hunter, Gregory S. 'The Water Company that Turned to Money,' *Harvard Business Review*, v. 68, n. 4 (July 1990), pp. 204–5

Jackson, Frederick. *A Week in Wall Street by One Who Knows* (N.Y.: J.F. Trow, 1841)

Jennings, Robert M., et al, 'Alexander Hamilton's Tontine Proposal,' *The William and Mary Quarterly*, v. 53, n. 45 (January 1988), pp. 107–15

Jones, Robert F. 'William Duer and the Business of Government in the Era of the American Revolution,' *William and Mary Quarterly*, v. 32 (1975), pp. 393–416.

Judis, John B. *Grand Illusion: Critics and Champions of the American Century* (N.Y.: Farrer, Strauss, & Giroux, 1992)

Kammen, Michael. *Colonial New York: A History* (Oxford: Oxford University Press, 1975)

Kindlerberger, Charles P. *Manias, Panics and Crashes: A History of Financial Crises*, third edn (N.Y.: John Wiley & Sons, 1996)

Knox, J. Armory. *The Man from the West: 'From the Chaparral to Wall Street'* (N.Y.: Pollard & Moss, Publishers, 1889)

Lamb, Martha J. *Wall Street in History* (N.Y.: Funk & Wagnalls, 1883)

LeFevre, Edwin. *The Making of a Stockbroker* (N.Y.: George H. Doran Company, 1925)

—. *Reminiscences of a Stock Operator* (Larchmont, N.Y.: American Research Council, 1923)

Lerner, Max. *America as a Civilization: Life and Thought in the United States Today* (N.Y.: Simon & Schuster, 1957)

Levine, Lawrence. *Highbrow/Lowbrow: The Emergence of Cultural Hierarchy in America* (Cambridge: Harvard University Press, 1988)

Levinson, Leonard Lewis. *Wall Street: A Pictorial History* (N.Y.: Ziff-Davis Publishing Co. 1961)

Lind, Michael. 'Hamilton's Legacy,' *Wilson Quarterly*, v. 18, n. 3 (Summer 1994), pp. 40–52

Luce, Henry R. 'The American Century,' *Life* (17 February 1941), pp. 61–5

Mackay, Charles. *Extraordinary Popular Delusions and the Madness of Crowds* (London: Richard Bentley, 1841)

Marshall, Matthew (a.k.a. Thomas Hitchcock). 'The Functions of the Stock Exchange,' Edmund C. Stedman, ed., *The New York Stock Exchange* (N.Y.: The Stock Exchange Historical Co., 1905)

Martin, Joseph. *A Century of Finance* (Boston: Joseph Martin, 1898)

Mayer, Martin. *Wall Street: Men and Money* (N.Y.: Harper & Brothers, 1955)

Medberry, James K. *Men and Mysteries of Wall Street* (Boston: Fields, Osgood & Co., 1870), reprinted: (Wells, VT.: Fraser Publishing Co., 1968)

Meeker, James A. *The Work of the Stock Exchange* (N.Y.: The Ronald Press Co., 1922)

Meinig, D.W. *The Shaping of America: A Geographical Perspective on 500 Years of History*, vol. 1, *Atlantic America: 1492–1800* (New Haven: Yale University Press, 1986)

Miller, Nathan. *The Enterprise of a Free People* (Ithaca: Cornell University Press, 1962)

Mitchell, Broadus. *Alexander Hamilton: A Concise Biography* (N.Y. and Oxford: Oxford University Press, 1976)

—. *Alexander Hamilton: The National Adventure, 1788–1804* (N.Y.: The Macmillan Co., 1962)

Moody, John. *The Masters of Capital* (New Haven: Yale University Press, 1919)

Morgan, Christopher. *The Documentary History of the State of New York* (Albany: Weed, Parsons & Co., 1849)

Musée Américain (Giverny). *Lasting Impressions: American Painters in France, 1865–1915* (Evanston, IL.: Terra Foundation for the Arts, 1992)

Mutual Life Insurance Company of New York. *King's View of the New York Stock Exchange* (N.Y.: Moses King, 1897)

Myers, Margaret G. *A Financial History of the United States* (N.Y. Columbia University Press, 1970)

—. *The New York Money Market*, vol. 1: *Origins and Development* (N.Y.: Columbia University Press, 1931)

McCartney, Robert J. 'Big Board, Big Birthday, Big Questions,' *Washington Post* (19 May 1992), pp. C1 & C4

McCraw, Thomas K. 'The Strategic Vision of Alexander Hamilton,' *American Scholar*, v. 63, n. 1 (Winter 1994), pp. 31–57

McDonald, Forrest. *Alexander Hamilton: A Biography* (N.Y.: W.W. Norton & Co., 1979)

McKay, Ernest A. *The Civil War and New York City* (Syracuse: Syracuse University Press, 1990)

Neill, Humphrey B. *The Inside Story of the Stock Exchange* (N.Y.: B.C. Forbes & Sons Publishing Co., Inc., 1950)

Nelson, John R. Jr. 'Alexander Hamilton and American Manufacturing: A Reexamination,' *Journal of American History*, v. 65, n. 4 (March 1979), pp. 971–95

Nettels, Curtis P. *The Emergence of a National Economy: 1775–1815* (N.Y.: Holt, Rinehart & Winston, 1962)

Nevins, Allen and Milton Halsey Thomas (Abr. Thomas J. Pressly). *The Diary of George Templeton Strong* (Seattle: University of Washington Press, 1988)

—. *The Diary of Philip Hone, 1828–1851*, 2 vols. (N.Y.: Dodd, Mead & Co., 1927)

New York *Commercial Advertiser* (12–14 July 1832)

New York *Mirror*, vol. xiv (1836)

Noyes, Alexander Dana. *Forty Years of American Finance* (N.Y.: G.P. Putnam's Sons, 1909)

Oberholtzer, Ellis Paxson. *Jay Cooke: Financier of the Civil War*, 2 vols. (Philadelphia: George W. Jacobs & Co., 1907)

Pecora, Ferdinand. *Wall Street Under Oath: The Story of Our Modern Money Changers* (N.Y.: Simon & Schuster, 1939)

Pemberton, Edgar T. *The Life of Bret Harte* (London: C. Arthur Pearson, Limited, 1903)

Perkins, Edwin J. *American Public Finance and Financial Services, 1700–1815* (Columbus: Ohio State University Press, 1994)

Pessen, Edward. *Riches, Classes, and Power Before the Civil War* (Lexington, MA.: D.C. Heath and Co., 1973)

—. 'The Social Configuration of the Antebellum City: An Historical and Theoretical Inquiry,' *Journal of Urban History*, v. 2, n. 3, pp. 267–306

Pratt, Sereno S. *The Work of Wall Street* (N.Y.: D. Appleton & Co., 1912)

Quire, Harry S. *Wall Street in Paradise: An Original and Musical Extravaganza* (N.Y.: George F. Nesbitt & Co., 1869)

Ripley, William Z. *Main Street and Wall Street* (Boston: Little, Brown, & Company, 1927)

Rodemeyer, John. 'The New York Stock Exchange,' Edmund C. Stedman, ed., *The New York Stock Exchange* (N.Y.: The Stock Exchange Historical Co., 1905)

Rosenzweig, Roy and Elizabeth Blackmar. *The Park and the People: A History of Central Park* (Ithaca: Cornell University Press, 1992)

Sellers, Charles. *The Market Revolution: Jacksonian America, 1815–1846* (N.Y. and Oxford: Oxford University Press, 1991)

Severini, Lois. *The Architecture of Finance: Early Wall Street* (Ann Arbor: UMI Research Press, 1983)

Sharp, Robert M. *The Lore and Legends of Wall Street* (Homewood, IL.: Dow Jones-Irwin, 1989)

Sheridan, Jerome. *Financing Industrial Growth: The Transformation of Bank Investments from Antebellum State Banking to the National Banks of the United States, 1840–1890* (Ph.D. dissertation, American University, 1990)

Simmons, Edward Henry Harriman. *Financing American Industry, and Other Addresses by E.H.H. Simmons* (New York: 1930. No publisher identified)

Smith, Walter B. *20 years Among the Bulls and Bears at Wall Street* (Hartford: J.B. Burr, 1871)

Sobel, Robert. *The Big Board: A History of the New York Stock Market* (N.Y.: The Free Press, 1965)

—. *The Curbstone Brokers: The Origins of the American Stock Exchange* (N.Y.: The Macmillan Co., 1970)

—. *Inside Wall Street: Continuity and Change in the Financial District* (N.Y.: W.W. Norton & Co., 1977)

—. *Panic on Wall Street: A History of America's Financial Disasters* (N.Y.: The Macmillan Co., 1968)

Spann, Edward K. *The New Metropolis: New York City, 1840–1857* (N.Y.: Columbia University Press, 1981)

Sparkes, Boyden and Samuel Taylor Moore. *Hetty Green: The Witch of Wall Street* (Garden City, N.Y.: Doubleday, Doran & Co., Inc, 1935)

Stedman, Edmund C. *The New York Stock Exchange* (N.Y.: The Stock Exchange Historical Co., 1905), reprinted: (N.Y.: Greenwood Press, 1969)

Sterling, David L. 'William Duer, John Pintard and the Panic of 1792,' Joseph R. Freese, S.J. and Jacob Judd, eds, *Business Enterprise in Early New York* (Tarrytown, N.Y.: The Sleepy Hollow Press, 1979), pp. 99–132

Stewart, George R., Jr. *Bret Harte: Argonaut and Exile* (Boston: Houghton Mifflin, Co., 1931)

Stokes, I. N. Phelps. *The Iconography of Manhattan Island, 1498–1909* (N.Y.: Robert H. Dodd, 1916)

Strasser, Susan. *Satisfaction Guaranteed: The Making of the American Mass Market* (N.Y.: Pantheon Books, 1989)

Strouse, Jean. *Morgan: American Financier* (N.Y.: HarperPerennial, 1999)

Swanberg, W.A. *Jim Fisk: The Career of an Improbable Rascal* (N.Y.: Charles Scribner's Sons, 1959)

Swanson, Donald F. *The Origins of Hamilton's Fiscal Policies* (Gainesville: University of Florida Press, 1963)

— and Andrew P. Trout. 'Alexander Hamilton, Conversion, and Debt Reduction,' *Explorations in Economic History*, v. 29, n. 4 (October 1992), pp. 417–29

— and Andrew P. Trout. 'Alexander Hamilton, "the Celebrated Mr. Neckar," and Public Credit,' *William and Mary Quarterly*, v. 47, n. 3 (July 1990), pp. 422–30

— and Andrew P. Trout. 'Alexander Hamilton's Sinking Fund,' *William and Mary Quarterly*, v. 49, n. 1 (January 1992), pp. 108–16

— and Andrew P. Trout. 'Alexander Hamilton's Invisible Hand,' *Policy Review*, n. 59 (Winter 1992), pp. 86–7

— and Andrew P. Trout. 'Alexander Hamilton's Report on the Public Credit (1790) in a European Perspective,' *Journal of European Economic History*, v. 19, n. 3 (Winter 1990), pp. 623–33

Sweet, William Warren. *The Story of Religion in America* (N.Y.: Harper & Brothers Publishers, 1930)

Syrett, Harold C. and Jacob E. Cooke, eds, *The Papers of Alexander Hamilton, 1757–1804*, 27 vols. (N.Y.: Columbia University Press, 1961–87)

Taylor, George Rogers. *The Transportation Revolution: 1815–1860* (N.Y.: Holt, Rinehart and Winston, 1951), reprinted: (Armonk, N.Y.: M.E. Sharpe Publishers, 1977)

Temin, Peter. *The Jacksonian Economy* (N.Y.: W.W. Norton & Co., 1969)

Thomas, Dana L. *The Plungers and the Peacocks: An Update of the Classic History of the Stock Market* (N.Y.: G.P. Putnam & Sons, 1967)

Thomas, Lately. *Delmonico's: A Century of Splendor* (N.Y.: Houghton Mifflin Co., 1967)

Todd, Charles Burr. *The Story of the City of New York* (N.Y.: G.P. Putnam & Sons, 1888)

Townsend, John Pomeroy. 'Wall Street. Portrait,' Chauncey M. Depew, ed., *One Hundred Years of American Commerce*, vol. I (N.Y.: D.O. Haynes & Co., 1895), pp. 67–75

Tuckerman, Bayard, ed. *The Diary of Philip Hone*, 2 vols. (N.Y.: Dodd, Meade & Co., 1910)

Underhill, Lois Beachy. *The Woman Who Ran for President: The Many Lives of Victoria Woodhull* (Bridgehampton, N.Y.: Bridge Works Publishing Co., 1995)

U.S. Department of Commerce, Bureau of the Census. *Historical Statistics of the United States: Colonial Times to 1970*, Part 2 (Washington: Government Printing Office, 1975)

de Vries, Johan. *A Century of Stocks and Shares* (Amsterdam: Amsterdam Stock Exchange, 1991)

Wachtel, Howard M. *The Money Mandarins: The Making of a New Supranational Economic Order* (N.Y.: Pantheon Books, 1986)

—. 'World Trade Order and the Beginning of the Decline of the Washington Consensus,' *Politik und Gessellschaft* (3, 2000), pp. 247–53

Warshaw, Robert Irving. *The Story of Wall Street* (N.Y.: Greenberg Publishers, 1929)

Wechsberg, Joseph. *The Merchant Bankers* (Boston: Little, Brown & Company, 1966)

Werner, Walter and Stephen T. Smith. *Wall Street* (N.Y.: Columbia University Press, 1991)

Westbrook, Wayne W. *Wall Street in the American Novel* (N.Y.: New York University Press, 1980)

White, Bouck. *The Book of Daniel Drew* (N.Y.: Doubleday & Co., 1910)

Willentz, Sean. *Chants Democratic: New York City and the Rise of the American Working Class, 1788–1850* (Oxford: Oxford University Press, 1984)

Williams, Robin M., Jr. *American Society: A Sociological Interpretation* (N.Y.: Alfred A. Knopf, 1970)

Wilson, John Grosvenor. 'The Stock Exchange Clearing House,' Edmund C. Stedman, ed., *The New York Stock Exchange* (N.Y.: The Stock Exchange Historical Co., 1905)

Wood, Gordon S. *The Radicalism of the American Revolution* (N.Y.: Alfred A. Knopf, 1992)

MANUSCRIPTS AND PAPERS

New York Historical Society

1792. 'The Panic of 1792'

Allen, Stephen A. 'Letters'

Anspach, Peter. 'Anspach & Rogers Papers,' 3 boxes

Bancker, Gerard. '1792 – The Memorial of Gerard Bancker, Treasurer of the State of New York,' Box 14, Mo. 8

Bank of the United States. 'Letter from Christopher Hughes to Albert Gallatin on rumors of "deals" in U.S. bank stock' (16 December 1817)

—. 'Letters of Nicholas Biddle to Daniel Parker'

Bleecker Family. 'Bleecker Family Notes,' 1 box

Constable, William. 'Wm. Constable Letters,' Constable-Pierrepont Papers

Hardenbrook, John A. 'Misc. Papers of John A. Hardenbrook and his wife … 1789–1829'

Merchants Exchange. Manuscript Collection

Pintard, John. 'Deposition to Transact Business as a Stock Broker' (25 November 1790)

—. 'Diary and Garden Calendar of John Pintard at Newark, New Jersey (April 1793–May 1794)'

—. 'Letters from John Pintard to his Daughter, 1816–1833'

—. 'Miscellaneous Papers relating to John Pintard and his Family…'

—. 'Pintard Diary 1800–1801'

Prime, Nathaniel. '1810–1846 Prime Family'

—. 'Prime Family Correspondence & Papers of Nathaniel Prime and His Sons'

Robinson, Robert S. 'Reminiscences of Wall Street as it Was in 1785–1790'

Robinson, William Henry. 'Robinson Family NYC and Ossining NY, Legal and Business Papers,' 2 boxes

State of New York. 'Memorial and Remonstrance of the Board of Stock and Exchange Brokers of the City of New York,' No. 291, 23 March 1836

Tailer, Edward N. 'Diaries,' 57 volumes

Tontine Coffee House. 'Tontine Coffee House, 1789–1823'

Villard, Oswald Garrison. 'The Early History of Wall Street, 1653–1789,' speech before New York Historical Society (2 May 1905)

Wilde, Richard Henry. 'Letters to Verplanck, 1833–1834'

Other Archives

'Buttonwood Agreement,' New York Stock Exchange Archives

'Constitution of the New York Stock Exchange Board 1817,' New York Stock Exchange Archives

Index

Compiled by Auriol Griffith-Jones

accounting industry, 186, 193
Adams, Charles Francis, 123
Adams, Evangeline, astrologer, 138
Adams, John, feud with Hamilton, 33
advertising, 104
Alexander, Kitty (wife of William
  Duer), 21
American Anti-Slavery Society, 91
American Bankers' Association, and
  Bretton Woods, 189
American Bible Society, 91
American Daily Advertiser, 63
American Express, 128
American Stock Exchange (New York
  Curb Market), 149, 206*n*
American Tract Society, 90, 91
Amsterdam, 2
Anspach, Peter, 10, 14
Anthony, Susan B., 153, 154
anti-trust law, 169–70
arbitrage strategy, speculation in
  Continentals, 8
architecture
  Broadway stores, 89
  classical Greek style, 50, 54–5, 145
  geometric ordering, 81–2
  investment banking houses, 137–8
  Italianate palazzo style, 145
  Merchants' Exchange Building, 50
  new NYSE building (1863), 145–6
  rebuilding after 1835 fire, 72, *73*
  Second National Bank, 54–5
  Tontine Coffee House, 10
  Trinity Church, 89
Armstrong, General John, 54
Arthur Andersen, 193
arts, patronage of, 79, 136, 138
Astor House hotel, 88
Astor, John Jacob, 38, 60, 84
Astor Place Opera House, 84
Astor Place Riot (1849), 83–6
auction markets, 48, 72–3, 149

Austrian Empire, 164
automobiles, 178–9

Baker's Hotel, 205*n*
Balcom, Ransom, Judge, 121
Baltimore & Ohio Railroad Company,
  48
Bancker, Gerard, New York Treasurer,
  13
Bank of New York, 21–2, 34, 42
  and panic of 1792, 24–5
bankers' balances, 77, 111
Bankers Code *see* Gentleman Bankers
  Code
Bankers Trust bank, 168
bankruptcy
  1800 law, 27
  National Bankruptcy Act, 111–12
  as state prerogative, 26
Baring Brothers, 42
Barnard, George C., Supreme Court
  Judge, 120–1, 122, 123, 132
  impeached, 132
Barney, Charles T., 166
Barnum, P.T., 24
Bayard, Nicholas, 4
Bayard, William, 14, 48, 49, 50
Beawes, Wyndham, *Lex Mercatoria*,
  32–3
Beebe, Samuel, Buttonwood signatory,
  10, 39
Beekman, James, 87
Belknap, Jeremy, 199*n*
Bell, Alexander Graham, 158
Bellows, Henry W., evangelical
  minister, 90
Belmont, August, 100, 144
Benedict, Erastus, 88
benevolent societies, 88
Bennett, James Gordon, 100
Benson, John, and NYS&EB, 39

Biddle, Nicholas
    death, 69
    and Second National Bank, 54–7,
        61–2, 63–4
    Whig party support for, 66–7
Bingham, William, 18–19
Black Ball Line, transatlantic trade, 47
black population (New York), and draft
    riots, 99–100
Blackwell, Dr Elizabeth, 88
Bleecker, Leonard, Buttonwood
        signatory, 9, 10, 21, 23, 200n
    and NYS&EB, 39
    and Pintard, 27
Blood, James Harvey, 150
bonds
    5-20s war bonds (1862), 106
    canal issues, 41, 45
    federal government (interest-
        bearing), 7
    to finance 1812 war, 38
    government war, 102–3, 104–7
    issued by Hamilton, 6–7
    mass marketing of, 106–7, 140
Boston, 4
Botta, Anne Lynch, 88
Boudinot, Elias, 15
Boutwell, George S., Treasury Secretary,
        124, 129, 130
Bowery Theatre, 83
Boyd, William, broker, 14, 35
brand identification, 103–4
Brandeis, Louis D.
    challenge to Bankers' Code, 173–4,
        181
    Other People's Money, 185
Brett, Catherine, 196n
Bretton Woods system, 187–90
bridges, construction innovations, 45
Broad Street
    new NYSE building (1863), 145
    Open Board of Brokers, 148–9
Broadway, 71, 194n
    Church of the Divine Unity, 90
    fashion stores, 89
Broadway Theatre, 84
brokers see stockbrokers
Bronson, Isaac, 48, 65, 67
Brooklyn Female Academy, 88

Brooklyn Refining Company, 132
Brooks Brothers, clothiers, 97, 99, 102
brothels, 152
Bryan, William Jennings, 172
Bryant, William Cullen, 49
bucket shop market, 147
Buffalo, Erie canal terminus, 43
Buffalo, Bradford & Pittsburgh
    Railroad, 119–20
Bull's Head Tavern, cattle yards, 120
Buntline, Ned, journalist, 84
Burr, Aaron, 23, 29
    Manhattan Company and Bank,
        34–5
    quarrel with Hamilton, 34, 35, 87,
        197n
    water purification scheme, 34–5, 71
Butterfield, General Daniel, 128, 130
Butterfield, John, American Express,
    128
Buttonwood Agreement (1792), xiv, 1,
        8–10, 27–8, 28
    and NYS&EB, 39
buttonwood trees, 8
'buying on margin', 77

Calahan, Edward A., 157
call loans, 77
Callender, J.T., 18
Canada, 164
canals, 42, 43–4, 46
    see also Erie canal
capital investment
    from Britain, 42, 72, 138
    international (by Wall Street), 163–4,
        177
    and stock valuation, 118–19
car bombing (1920), 177–8, 178
Carnegie, Andrew, 98, 139
Carnegie Steel, 165
cartoons, political, 139
Century Club, 96
Chapin, William A., 129
chartered banks, national, 110–11
Chase Manhattan Bank, 34–5
Chase, Salmon B., Treasury Secretary,
        101, 102
    and National Bank Act, 110–11
    national currency, 105–6

and war bond sales, 107, 109–10
wartime financing, 102–3
Chatham Street Theatre, 90
Cheeves, Langdon, 54
Chesapeake and Ohio Railroad, 141
Chestnut Street, Philadelphia, 46, 50
see also Second National Bank
Childs, Francis, 199n
China, 164
cholera, 87
epidemics, 62, 83
Christian Science Monitor, on Bretton
Woods, 189–90
City Bank, 72
city banks, reserve, 111
City Hall, 4
civic works, 12, 29–30, 49–51, 202–3n
Civil War, 95–6, 104–5
and development of national
financial market, 135
draft riots (1863), 98–100, 99
government financing, 100–2
prelude, 93–4
profiteering, 101–2
Claflin, Tennessee, 150, 151, 154
class
and Civil War draft, 98–100
discontent, 94
and exclusivity of NYS&EB, 74–5
extremes in New York, 81–5
and Wall Street–Main Street
tensions, 145, 160
Clay, Edward Williams, 64
Clay, Senator Henry, 62, 63
Cleveland, Grover, President, 144
Clews, Henry, 210
climate control, Astor House Hotel, 88
Clinton, Bill, President, 162–3
Clinton, General De Witt, 43
Clymer, George, 15
Coffee House Slip, 4
Colden, H.M., 26
Cole, Thomas, 49
commerce, conflict with republican
virtues, 31–2
Commercial Advertiser, 62–3
commercial banking, customer-based,
184–5
Commercial and Financial Chronicle, 169

Communist Manifesto (Marx), 153
competition, and anti-trust law,
169–70
Congregation Shearith Israel, 10
Congress, xii, 30
debate on Hamilton's Continentals
project, 14–16
Hearings of the House Banking and
Currency (Pujo) Committee,
169–73
modifications to Federal Reserve,
177
and Roosevelt's banking reforms,
182, 184
state finance statutes (1861-65), 101,
102, 110–12
Constable, William, 16–17, 22, 25
Continentals (paper currency)
Congressional debate, 14–16
Duer's speculation in, 20, 21
Hamilton's proposal to redeem, 6, 7
speculation in, 8, 12–13, 14
continuous trading, 75, 148–9
contract, 33
Cook, Sir James, 154
Cooke, Henry, 103, 109–10
Cooke, Jay, 98, 103
battle with Morgan, 140
war bond sales, 103, 104–7, 108–9
Cooper, James Fenimore, 49, 79
Copperheads (southern sympathisers
in New York), 96, 98, 100
Coppinger, Joseph, 50
Corbin, Abel Rathbone, 127–8
and Gould's gold corner, 128–30
Corbin, Jennie (Virginia) Paine (née
Grant), 128, 130, 132
corporate charters, 37
Corre's Hotel, Buttonwood Agreement
meeting, 27, 28
Cortelyou, George B., Treasury
Secretary, 167
cotton trade, 47–8
contraband, 125
price falls, 53
'country players', purchase of war
bonds, 107–8
Craigie, Andrew, 14, 16–17, 199n

credit
    and appearance, xiii, 144–5
    assessment of, 55
    expansion of, 56
    pyramiding of, 77–8
    restrictions on, 174–5
credit, letters of, 137
Credit Mobilier scandal, 140
credit-rating agencies, 90–1
crime, fear of, 88
'crop theory' (Gould's), 127, 128–9,
    131
Croton Water System, 87
Cruger, Henry, 26
cultural institutions, 49–50
Curb Market, 50–1, 74–5, 149, 191,
    213*n*
    expansion of, 147–8, *148*
    indoor trading, 75, 149
    pad shovers, 148, *148*, 157
    runners, 148, *148*
    see also American Stock Exchange;
        Open Board of Brokers
currency
    Continentals (paper), 6
    dollar as world reserve, 189
    Hamilton's new, 7
    national paper 'greenbacks' (from
        1862), 105–6, 110
    Second National Bank's control of
        bank notes, 55
    state banks, 101, 102
    tax on state bank notes (1865), 102,
        110, 111
    see also money question
Curtis, William E., 144
customs revenues, 60
Cutler, Rev. Manasseh, 21

Daily Advertiser (New York), 29, 199*n*
David Goesbeck & Co., 157
Davis, Jefferson, 94
de Peyster, Frederick, 196*n*
debts, and over-extended trusts, 166
Delmonico's restaurant, 100, 121, 157,
    210*n*
Democratic Party, 94, 100
    New York (Tammany Hall), 116
Dennie, Joseph, *Port Folio* magazine, 54

department stores, 89
dependence on Wall Street, 135
DePeyster, Abraham, 4
Dickens, Charles, in Philadelphia, 69
Dispensary for Poor Women and
    Children, 88
Dodd, Samuel C.T., 141
Dongan, Thomas, Governor of New
    York (1680s), 4
dot.com mania (1990s), xiv, 165, 166,
    193
Dow, Charles, 159, 215*n*
Dow Jones Index, 159, 215*n*
draft (Civil War)
    exemptions, 98
    riots (1863), 98–100, *99*
Drew, Daniel, 24, 113–15, 157, 210*n*
    bankruptcy and death, 123
    control of Erie Railroad, 119–24
    and railroad stocks, 116–17
    rivalry with Vanderbilt, 113, 114,
        115
Duer, William, 12, 20–1, 27
    and Buttonwood Agreement, 27
    and national bank scheme, 21–2
    and Pintard, 22–5, 199*n*
Dun and Bradstreet, 90–1
Dutch East India Company, 2, 12
Dutch West India Company, 2, 3

Eacker, George I., 35
Eastman, Arthur M., 101
Eccles, Marriner
    banking reforms, 185–6
    Chairman of Federal Reserve, 186
economy
    1834 slump, 64
    dominance of agriculture, 77
    global, 187–90
    inland, 37, 43–4
    national, 135
    see also trade
Eddy, Thomas, 49
Edison Electric Illuminating Co., 136
Edison, Thomas Alva, 130, 136
elections
    1832 presidential (Jackson), 62
    1860 presidential (Lincoln), 93
    New York mayoralty (1834), 66

electricity, 178–9
Embargo Act (1807), 36, 37
Emerson, Ralph Waldo, 116
Enlightenment, the, and republican
   ideals, 31–2
Enron, 186, 193
Erie Canal, 41, 42–5, *44*
   financial leverage, 46–9
   tolls, 44–5
Erie Railroad, 113, 114–15, 141
   battle for control, 119–24
evangelical movement, 89–92
   revival in 1857 panic, 92
Evans, George Henry, 88
Examiner (Virginia), 109

farmers
   credit requirements, 77–8
   and Gould's 'crop theory' of gold,
      127
   and money question, 175, *176*
   and Populist Alliances, 175
Farmers Alliance, 175
Federal Deposit Insurance Corporation,
   184
Federal Hall, Wall Street, 9, 30
   sub-treasury office, 68, *69*, 99
Federal Reserve, 55, 61, 112, 185–6
   defaults (1929), 181
   established (1913), 173, 176–7
Federal Trade Commission, 184
Federalist Papers, Hamilton's contribution to, 5
Field, Cyrus, 157
financial crises
   1790-92, xiv, 5
   1833-37, 67–9, 78
   1894-95 gold, 144
   1907 dollar, 164, 165–8
   1907 gold, 144–5, 162
   1929 Crash, 162, 179, *180*, 181
   1987 October, 187
   2002, 187
   domino effect in, 77–8, 179, 181
   effect of telecommunications on, 81,
      158–9
   episodic ('creative destruction'),
      164–5, 193
   see also panics

financial trusts, 135, 160
   expansion of, 164, 165, 166
   Morgan's use of, 140–1, 160, 165,
      166, 170–1
Finney, Charles, evangelist, 89–90
First National Bank, 53
First Savings Bank, 49
Fisk, Jim ('Admiral' and 'Colonel'), 24,
   98, 113, 126
   and 1871 Orangeman parade, 131
   character and career, 124–6
   and Erie Railroad stock, 119, 121,
      122–3
   and Gould's gold corner, 128, 129,
      130–1, 151
   murder (1872), 132
   and Victoria Woodhull, 152
Fletcher, Duncan U., Senator, 183
Forrest, Edwin, actor, 83–4, *85*
Fortune magazine, 163
Fowler, William, 108, 115, 121, 122
France, 6, 36
   banking houses, 142, 144
Franks, David, and Rebecca, 9
Fremont, Major General John C., 101
Fulton, Robert S., 46
funding and assumption scheme
   (Hamilton's), 6, 12, 16, 20

Gallatin, Albert, Treasury Secretary, 38,
   64, 65
Garrison, William Lloyd, 91
gas lighting, 49
Gentleman Bankers Code, 141–2, 143,
   160, 164, 171–2
   challenged, 173–4
   Jack Morgan's defense of, 183
Germany, 164
   banking houses, 142, 144
Gerry, Elbridge, 15
Ghent, Treaty of (1814), 42
Girard, Steven, 38
Glass–Steagall Act (1933), 184, 185
global finance, 187–90
globalization, 163, 190
   and supranational actors, 190
Gold & Stock Telegraph Co., 157
Gold Exchange, 74, 130
Gold Room, 130–1

gold markets
    'crop theory', 127, 128–9, 131
    Gould and Fisk's manipulations,
        124, 126–31, 151
    instability of, 105–6, 133, 144
    and money supply, 165–6
gold standard (hard money), 174, 175
Goluchowski, Count, 164
Gomez, Isaac M., Buttonwood
    signatory, 9, 10
Gould, Jay, 119, 121, 122–3, 125
    attempt to corner gold market,
        126–31, 151
    crop theory, 127, 128–9, 131
Government Bond Department, 149
Graf, Lya, 183–4
Graham, Elizabeth, 26
Graham, Sylvester, 91
Grant, Ulysses S., 102, 113, 117, 132–3
    and Gould's gold corner, 128,
        129–30, 151
    as President, 124, 127–30
Grant, Virginia see Corbin, Jennie
    (Virginia)
Great Britain, 36, 38, 46
    capture of New Amsterdam, 2–3
    as source of capital, 38, 42, 72, 138
    US capital investment in, 164
    see also London
Great Northern Railroad, 141
Greeley, Horace, 91, 93
    New York Tribune, 83, 104
Green, Edward H., 155
Green, Hetty, 154–7, 156
Gropper, William, New Masses, 180
Guaranty Trust bank, 168
guild organization, of Buttonwood
    Agreement, 8–9

Hamilton, Alexander, xiii, xiv, 4–5, 87
    assessment of, 19–20, 197n
    commercial ideals of, 31, 32
    and Duer, 22, 24, 66
    and exchange of information, 7,
        12–13, 17–18
    funding and assumption scheme, 6,
        12, 16, 20, 29
    killed in duel, 35
    and national bank, 20–7, 66

    as policy maker, 12, 14–16, 196n
    project, 6–8
    propensity for personal feuds, 33–4
    quarrel with Burr, 34, 35, 87, 197n
    Report...for the Support of the Public
        Credit, 6, 20
    statue, 51
    see also Bank of New York
Hamilton, James, 52, 103
    and Andrew Jackson, 52–3, 58, 59,
        65–6
    banking policy, 57–9
    concept of narrow banking, 57, 68
Hamilton, Philip, 35
Hapgood, Norman, 173
Harburg, E.Y., 193, 216n
Harlem and Hudson Rail Line, 119
    stock trading, 116–17
Harper's Weekly, 173
Harriman, Edward, railroad battle with
    Morgan, 142–4
Hart, Bernard, Buttonwood signatory,
    9, 10, 196n
    and NYS&EB, 39, 75, 205n
Hart, Henry, 196n
Harte, Bret, 196n
Hazard, Ebenezer, 199n
health
    fashions, 91
    public, 83
Heath, William, pad shover, 157
Henry, Michael D., 26
Herald (New York), 100
historiography, 5–6
Hobart, Judge, 27
Homestead Act, 111
Hone, Philip, 66–7, 68, 72, 86
    and Astor Place Riot, 84
    hotels, 88
Howland, Abby Slocum, 154
Hughes, Ball, 51
Humanitarian (journal), 154
Hume, David, 32

immigrants, 4, 47, 82
    associated with car bombing (1920),
        178
    as curbstone brokers, 75, 147–8
    and public school movement, 88

on Wall Street, 9
see also Irish immigrants; Jews
incorporation, regulation of, 37
Independent Treasury Act (1839), 68, 101
industrial trusts, 165
information, privileged, and Hamilton's project, 7, 12–13
Initial Public Offerings (IPOs), 193
insurance industry
Federal Deposit Insurance, 60
fire, 71
underwriting cargoes, 47
Inter-Allied Stabilization Fund, 187
international economy, and globalization, 190
International Monetary Fund, 188
International Workingmen's Association (IWA), 153
Interstate Commerce Act (1887), 160, 169
investment bankers, private, 136
Gentleman Bankers Code, 141–2, 143, 160, 164, 171–2
investment banking, 42, 144, 184–5
Irish immigrants
as curbstone brokers, 75, 147, 213n
influence of, 94

Jackson, Andrew, President, 51, 52
and 1819 panic, 54
and 1832 presidential election, 62
and independent treasury, 68
and James Hamilton, 52–3, 65–6
message to Congress (1829), 59–60
opposition to central bank, 56–7, 59–61, 62–3, 65–6, 105
Specie Circular, 67
Jefferson, Thomas, President, xiv, 14, 202n
and Hamilton, 15–16, 33
neutrality policy (1807), 36
opposition to national bank, 20
and Pintard, 26, 29
republican ideals, 16, 31–2, 49
Jersey Central Railroad, 141
Jevons, William Stanley, 77
Jews
among Buttonwood signatories, 9–10

as Curb Market brokers, 147, 213n
influence as bankers, 142–3
prejudice against (on Wall Street), 75, 147, 179, 213n
Johnson, Seth, 199–200nn
Jonathan's Coffee House, London, 10
Jones, Eddie, 159
Journal (New York), on Hamilton, 19–20
journalism
financial, 159
see also newspapers
J.P. Morgan and Company, 138
and banking reforms, 184–5
car bomb (1920), 177–8, 178
judicial system, corruption in, 120–1, 132
Judson, Edward Z.C. ('Ned Buntline'), journalist, 84

Kellum, John, architect, 145
Kennedy, Joseph, 178
Keynes, John Maynard, 188, 189
Kieft, William, Governor of New Amsterdam, 194n
Knickerbocker Trust, 166
Knickerbockers, 113, 117
Knights of Reliance, 175
Knox, J. Armory, The Man from the West, 108, 209n
Kuhn, Loeb & Co., 142–3, 212n

labor, division of, 32
Lamar, Gazaway Bugg, 94
Lamb, William, 201n
Lamont, Thomas W., 173–4, 185
land speculation, 4, 48, 67
and Central Park, 87
payment in specie, 67
Lawrence, Augustus H., Buttonwood signatory, 10
and NYS&EB, 39
Lawrence, Cornelius, 66
Lawton, William, 201n
Le Roy, Herman, 14
Lee, General Robert E., 98, 106, 117
Lee, Henry ('Light Horse Harry'), 17–18
Leef, Charles, 183–4
Leffingwell, Russell, 182, 185

Legal Tender Act (1862), 102, 105, 106
legalism, 40
legislation *see* regulation
Lehigh Valley Railroad, 141
letters of credit, 137
Levy, Jules, 126
Lex Mercatoria, xiv, 31
Life magazine, 163
limited liability
  stock, 2
  of trusts, 141
Lincoln, Abraham, President
  1860 election, 93
  Emancipation Proclamation (1863),
    98, 100
  inauguration, 95
  relations with Wall Street, 95, 97–8
  and war finance, 100–1, 103
Lincoln, Mary (née Todd), 151
Lindbergh, Charles A., Sr, 168
Lindsay, Vachel, *180*
Little, Jacob, stockbroker, 75–6
Livingston, Walter, 22, 46
London, City of
  financial links with, 38
  Stock Exchange, 10
  trading companies, 12
  view of Civil War, 142
Louisiana, bond issues, 41
Louisiana Purchase, 54
Louvre, Salon Carré, 78, 79
Luce, Henry, 163, 164
Lyman, George T., 102–3, 109

McClane, Louis, 65
McClellan, George C., mayor of New
  York, 167
Mackay, Charles, *Extraordinary Popular
  Delusions and the Madness of
  Crowds* (1841), xiii
McKeen, Joseph, 88
Maclay, W., Senator, 198*n*
Macomb, Alexander, 22, 25–6
Macready, William, English actor, 84
Macy, R.H., department store magnate,
  97
Madison, James, President, 202–3*n*
  and Continentals crisis, 14–15
  opposition to national bank, 20
  and Pintard, 29

Magnetic Telegraph Co., 79
Main Street(s), 165
  and 1929 crash, 179, 181
  opposition to Wall Street's
    dominance, 143–4, 145, 160,
    167–8, 172
  political voice, 164
  public buying of war bonds, 107–8
  relations with Wall Street, xii, xiii,
    108–9, 133, 174–5, 192–3
  role of, 192–3
  soft-money policy (economic
    growth), 174–5
Manassas (Bull Run), first Battle of, 97
Manhattan
  deep-water ports, 36
  great fire (1835), 51, 71–2
  name, 86, 194*n*
  urban planning, 49, 71–2, 82
  see also New York
Manhattan Bank, 72
Manhattan Company (and Bank),
  34–5, 200*n*
Mansfield, Josie, 132, 151
  mistress of James Fisk, 126, 152
  and Victoria Woodhull, 151
market trends, analysis of, 76
markets, cornering, 76, 126–8
Marshall, John, Chief Justice, 26, 29
Martin, James, 154
Marx, Karl, Victoria Woodhull and, 153
mathematics, probability statistics, 159
Medberry, James, 114, 133, 147
membership (of Wall Street), as closed
  club, 27, 73, 74–5, 146–7
Mercantile Agency (later Dun and
  Bradstreet), 90–1
merchant bankers
  British, 136
  Jewish bankers' origins as, 142–3
Merchants' Bank, 22, 72
Merchants' Exchange Building, 50, 51,
  70, 213*n*
  fire (1835), 51, 71
mergers, into industrial trusts, 165
'Million Bank', 22
Mining Board, specialized exchange,
  74
Minnegerode, Meade, 125–6

Minturn, Robert Browne and Anna
    Mary Welden, 207*n*
Mirror (New York), 51
Mississippi, bond issues, 41
Mitchell, Charles, 179
monetary policy
    and Bretton Woods system, 187–8,
        189–90
    Open Market Committee control of,
        186
money question, gold standard or
    economic growth, 173–7, *176*
money supply, and 1907 crisis, 165–6
Money Trusts, 168, 172
Morgan, Drexel and Company, 138
    see also J.P. Morgan and Company
Morgan, J. Pierpont, 38, 98, 135,
    138–42, *139*, 179
    and 1907 dollar crisis, 164, 165–8
    backing for Edison, 136
    Civil War profiteering, 101
    as *de facto* central banker, 144–6,
        164, 165, 168
    death, 172–3
    and Gentleman Bankers Code,
        141–2, 160, 164, 171
    Harriman and Schiff's assault on,
        142–4
    home at 219 Madison Avenue, 136,
        138
    private telegraph, 102
    and Pujo hearings, 169–73
    railroad interests, 138–41, 212*n*
    use of trusts, 140–1, 160, 165, 166,
        170–1
Morgan, Jack (John Pierpont), 172–3,
    179
    and Senate Subcommittee on
        Banking and Commerce, 182–4
Morgan, Junius Spencer, 101, 138, 143
Morgan, Louisa, 172
Morgenthau, Henry, Jr, 186
    Treasury Secretary, 187–8, 189
Morrill land grant Act, 111
Morrill tariff, 95
Morris Canal & Banking Co., 76
Morrison, John, 32
Morse, Samuel F.B., 49, 100
    as painter, 78–9, 81, 206*n*

'Peace Society', 95
telegraph, 79, 81
The Marquis of Lafayette, 78, 79
Mount, J.R., 51

Narragansett Steamship Company, 126
'narrow banking', Hamilton's concept
    of, 57, 68
NASDAQ exchange, 146
National Bank, 21–2
    effect of lack of on war financing,
        38, 100–1, 105–6
    Hamilton's concept of, 20–7, 57, 173
    Jackson's opposition to, 56–8, 59–61,
        65–6, 105
    and money question, 174–7
    Second National Bank's *de facto*
        position as, 55, 173
    Tibbets' proposal for, 60–1
    see also Federal Reserve
National Banking Act (1863-4), 102,
    110–11, 112
National Bankruptcy Act, 111–12
National Biscuit, 165
Necker, Jacques, 32
Netherlands
    origins of stock trading, 2
    Revolutionary war debt, 6
New Amsterdam, Dutch colony of, 1,
    2, 9
New Deal, xv, 181–2, 186–7
New Orleans, 97
New York, xiv, 3, 4
    Central Park, 82, 87–8, 207*n*
    growth of, 3–4, 84–5
    harbour, 60, 87, 195*n*
    interests and Civil War, 94–6, 100
    proposal for independence as city-
        state, 94, 95
    public transport, 86–7
    southern sympathisers in, 96–7
    suburbs, 82, 88
    traffic congestion, 81, 86
    urban improvements, 29–30, 49–51,
        87–8
    urban planning experiments, 81–2,
        84–5
    see also Manhattan; Wall Street

New York Central Railroad, 114, 119, 141
New York city government (Tammany Hall), urban planning, 87–8
New York Clearing House, 102
New York and Harlem Railroad, 86–7
New York Historical Society, 30
New York Institute of Learned and Scientific Establishments, 49–50
New York Stock Exchange, xii, xiv, 145, 213n
  and 1929 crash, 179
  centennial (1892), 28
  membership (selling of seats), 146–7
  merger with Open Board and Government Bond Department, 149
  trading posts, 149
  transformation, 146–9
New York Stock and Exchange Board (NYS&EB), 39–40, 96
  changes name, 145
  closure (1873 panic), 140
  constitution, 39–40
  daily routine, 72–3, 74
  exclusivity, 74–5, 146
  Merchants' Exchange Building, 50, 71–2
  opposition to regulation, 67–8
  twice-daily auctions, 72–3
  see also New York Stock Exchange
New York Theological Seminary, 90
New York Thruway (over Erie canal), 44
New York Times, article on Gould's crop theory, 128–9
New York Tribune, 83, 93
newspapers
  and advertising, 104
  prelude to Civil War, 93
  proliferation of, 82, 204n
  share price listings, 81, 201–2n
Nicholson, James, 35
Ninth Regiment (Fisk's New York), 126, 131
North Dakota Church, Fulton Street, 92
Northern Pacific Railroad, 140, 141, 142
  Harriman and Schiff's attempted takeover, 143–4

office design, investment banking houses, 137–8
Ohio, bond issues, 41
Ohio Life Insurance and Trust Company, 67, 91
Ohio River, Erie canal and, 43
Olmsted, Frederick Law, 87, 97, 100
omnibuses
  fixed rail system, 86–7
  horse-drawn, 49, 86
Open Board of Brokers, rival to NYSE, 146, 148–9
  Long Room, 148–9
  merged with NYSE (1896), 149
Open Market Committee, 186
Orangemen's March (1871), 131
Other People's Money, 185

pad shovers, 148, 148, 157
Panama Canal, 165
panics
  1792, 24–6
  1819, 53–4
  1834, 64
  1857, 76, 91–2, 94
  1869 gold crisis, 130–1
  1873 railroad, 140
  1929 crash, 179
  domino effect in, 77–8, 179, 181
  see also financial crises
Paris Commune, 153
Park Theatre, 49, 83
Parker, Charles, semaphore alphabet, 80
Peabody, George, 138
Peace Convention (1863), 96
'Peace Society' petition, 95
Pecora, Ferdinand, Senate Subcommittee on Banking and Commerce, 182–3
Pennsylvania Avenue (Washington)
  and New Deal, 181–2, 186–7
  as political centre, 30, 135, 160–1, 164
  relations with Main Street, 186
  relations with Wall Street, xii–xiii, 30, 70, 91–2, 145
  role as referee, xiii, 159–61, 186–7
Pennsylvania Railroad, 119

'people's capitalism', 192–3
Petheram, John, 32
Petroleum Board, specialized exchange, 74
Philadelphia, 4, 50, 78
    stock exchange, 39, 46
    see also Chestnut Street
Philadelphia, National Bank, closure, 68–9
Philadelphia and Reading Railroad, 141
Pike's Opera House, Fisk's offices in, 125–6
Pintard, John, 12, 26, 27, 198n, 199nn
    agent for Duer, 22–5, 199n
    on commerce, 49
    patronage of arts, 79
    public works, 29–30, 49
Pintard, Lewis, 22, 29
police force, 87
populism, 160, 175
    see also class; farmers
Populist Alliances, 175
Port Folio magazine, 54, 55
poverty, in New York, 82, 83
Prime, Frederick, 87
Prime, Nathaniel, 38, 40–2, 48, 136
    and NYS&EB, 39, 40–1
    suicide, 42
Prime, Rufus, 87
Prime, Ward & King, 42
Prime's rate of interest, 41
prisons, 87
private bankers, Prime, 41
probability statistics, 159
public education, 30, 82, 87–8, 202n
    universities, 111
public health, 83
public opinion, and Civil War, 93
public relations campaigns, government war bonds, 104
public transport, 86–7
Pujo, Arsene, Hearings of the House Banking and Currency Committee, 169
Pujo hearings (Congress), 168–73
Pure Food and Drug Act (1906), 169

railroads, 45, 48–9, 113–15, 133, 212n
    effect on economy, 135

financing of, 42
freight rates, 160
J.P. Morgan's interests, 138–41
New York Central, 44
Northern Pacific, 140
over-capacity, 118, 139
rivalries, 115–18
transcontinental, 143
urban, 86–7, 116
registry of births and deaths, 29
regulation
    de-regulation (1980s), 186, 187
    federal, 175
    Roosevelt's banking reforms, 182, 184–6
    Roosevelt's New Deal and, 181, 186–7
    of sale of securities, 67–8
    theory of, 160–1
relationship banking, 141
Republican Party
    and Civil War, 94–5
    isolationism, 162
republicanism, traditions of, 31–2
Revolutionary War, bonds to replace debt, 1, 6–7
Reynolds, James, 18
Reynolds, Maria, 18
Ringling Brothers Circus, 183–4
roads, 37, 45
Robinson, Edward Mott, 154
Robinson, William, Buttonwood signatory and NYS&EB, 39
Rockefeller, John D., 98, 139, 143
Rogers, Isaiah, architect, 72, 73, 84
Roosevelt, Franklin D., President
    and Bretton Woods system, 187–8
    New Deal, xv, 181, 186–7
Roosevelt, Theodore, President, 165, 169
Rothschilds, 42
Russia, 164

Sackett, Edward, 106
St Louis Alliance, 175–6
Salt Lake City, 185
Sand, Georges, 153
Sanitary Commission, 97, 100
Santa Fe Railroad, 141

Schiff, Jacob, 135, 142–4, 179
Schiff, Morti, 143
schools *see* public education
Schumpeter, Joseph, 165
secession, 93
Second Bank of the United States
    re-chartered (1816), 39, 42
    re-chartered (1836), 52, 61–2
Second Free Presbyterian Church, 90
Second National Bank
    as bank for federal government, 55
    Chestnut Street, 50, 53, 60, 69–70
    demise, 69–70, 76
    Jackson and, 57–8, 59–61
    and Nicholas Biddle, 54–7
    Wall Street opposition to, 60, 61
Securities and Exchange Act (1934),
    184
Securities and Exchange Commission
    (SEC), 184
securities trading, 67–8, 70, 195n
    buying long, 76, 117
    continuous, 75, 148–9
    daily settling of accounts, 77
    NYS&EB auctions, 72–3, 149
    price indexes, 159
    railroads, 48, 115, 116–18
    selling short, 75–6, 116–17
    specialized exchanges, 74, 75, 148–9,
        213–14n
    see also investment bankers; specula-
        tion; stock
Seixas, Benjamin, Buttonwood
    signatory, 9–10, 27, 200n
Seixas, Gershon Mendes, Rabbi, 10
Seixas, Nathan, 75
Seixas, Rebecca, 10, 196n
self-regulation, xiv, 1, 68, 186–7, 189
semaphore, 78, 80
Senate, Subcommittee on Banking and
    Commerce, 182
Seton, William, 24
Shattuck, Peaslee and Co., 104
Sherman Anti-Trust Act (1906), 169
Sherman, Roger, 15
shipping, transatlantic, 47–8, 143
slavery
    abolitionism, 91

Lincoln's Emancipation
    Proclamation (1863), 98, 100
    see also Civil War
Smith, Adam, 32
Smith, Hugh, Buttonwood signatory
    and NYS&EB, 39
social reform movements, 88
Society for the Diffusion of Political
    Knowledge, 100
sociology, 154
soldiers, compensation for war duties,
    12–13
South Sea Bubble (1720), 19, 203–4n
Southern Railway, 141
Southern States, links with Wall Street,
    96–7
space, effect of telegraph on, 81, 158
speculation
    after Revolutionary War, 7–8, 29
    and panics, 19
    see also financial crises
spiritualism, 150–2
Standard Oil, 165
Stanton, Elizabeth Cady, 153
state governments
    debts, 67
    and public policy, 160
state-chartered banks, 55, 63, 111,
    201n
    growing number of, 67, 202n
    paper currency, 101, 102, 110, 111
steamboats, on canals, 46–7, 202n
Stevens, Simon, 101
Stewart, Alexander, 280 Broadway
    store, 89, 97, 145
stock, 2, 118
    manipulation, 119, 120, 121
    watering, 120
    see also gold; railroads; securities
        trading
stock prospectuses, 136, 193
stock tickers, 135, 157
    gold, 130
stockbrokers
    licenses, 23
    professional, 75–7
    role of, 11–12
    women, 152–3
Stokes, Edward S., 132

Strickland, William, 54
Strong, Benjamin, 100
Strong, George Templeton, 78, 83, 88, 100
  on evangelical revival (1857), 92
  on Fisk, 125, 126
  on Lincoln, 97–8
  on Wood, 96
Stuyvesant, Peter, Governor of New Amsterdam, 1, 2–3
suicides, 166
  Prime's, 42
Sun (New York), 152
Sweden, 164
Sweeny, Peter B., 116
symbolism, of Wall Street, 192

Tammany Bank, 22
Taney, Roger, Treasury Secretary, 63
Tappan, Arthur and Lewis, evangelicals, 90–1
Tax on State Bank Notes Act (1865), 102, 110
Taylor, George Rogers, 43
Taylor, Zachariah, 97
technology, 157–9, 206*n*
  and 1920s bull market, 178–9
  computerization, 189, 191
  engineering, 45
  see also telecommunications; telegraph
telecommunications, 158–9, 189, 191
telegraph, 135
  effect on trading, 78–9, 81
  Morgan's private, 102
  transatlantic, 81, 157
  wires, 159
telephone, 135, 158, 179
textile industry, uniforms, 97
theaters, 83
  and Astor Place Riot (1849), 83–6
Thomas, Ransom H., 167
Thompson, Euclid, 49
Thompson, Jeremiah, 47
Thompson, Jonathan, 84
Thwaites, Reuben Gold, 54
Tibbets, Elisha, proposal for national bank, 60–1
time, effect of telecommunications on, 81, 158–9

Time magazine, 163
toll roads, 37
Tontine Coffee House, 10–11, *11*, 50, 71, 196*n*, 213*n*
Tracy, Charles, 144
trade
  embargo (1807-12), 36–7
  through American ports, 36
  see also canals
trade union movement, 135
trading post, 75
transparency
  in Bretton Woods system, 188
  principle of, 184
transport
  public, 86–7
  see also canals; omnibuses; railroads; roads
Treasury, xii, 68
  dependence on Morgan, 167–8
  as lender-of-last-resort, 177
  and problem of war financing, 101, 102–3
  sub-treasury offices, 68, *69*, 99
  see also Federal Reserve
'Tri-Insula' (New York city-state), 94
Trinity Church, Wall Street, 4, 89, 213*n*
trust
  anti-trust law, 169–70
  see also financial trusts
Tuckerman, George, 55
Tulipomania (Holland 1637), 19, 119
turnpikes, 37
Twain, Mark, 132
Tweed, William M. ('Boss'), 116

underwriters, investment bankers as, 136
Union Bank, 72
Union Carbide, 165
Union Pacific Railroad, 142
United Copper, collapse of, 166
United Fruit, 165
United States
  the American Century, 162–4, 187
  isolationism, 162, 177, 178
  and World War I, xv, 177, 178
  see also US Government

United States Bank, 72
  failure of, 179
Untermyer, Samuel, colloquy with
  Morgan, 169–72
Upjohn, Richard, architect, 89
urban improvements, 29–30, 49–51
  see also architecture; civic works
U.S. Gazette, 63
US Government
  dependence on Morgan's credit
    reputation, 144–5
  public expenditure projects, 202–3n
  Second National Bank as depository
    for, 55
  and theory of regulation, 160–1
  see also Congress; New Deal;
    Pennsylvania Avenue; Treasury

value, dependent on confidence, 137
Van Buren, Martin, Governor of New
  York, 52, 57, 65, 68
van Twist, Anna, 155–6
Vanderbilt, Cornelius ('Commodore'),
  113, 115, 154
  backing for Victoria Woodhull, 150,
    151–2, 153
  and control of Erie Railroad, 119–24
  railroad stock trading, 116, 117
  rivalry with Drew, 113, 114, 115
  spiritualism, 123–4, 151–2
Vanderbilt, Sophie, 151
Vanderbilt, William, 154
Varrick, Richard, mayor of New York,
  23
Vaux, Calvert, 87
Vauxhall Gardens, 83, 84
Verplank, Giulian, 66, 96

Wadsworth, Jeremiah, 15, 26
Walker, Benjamin, 22
Wall Street, 3–4, 81, 195n
  anniversaries, 28, 191
  anti-regulation stance, 162, 181–2
  appropriation of economic power,
    135, 139
  brokering (NYS&EB), 39–40
  brushwood barrier/fence, 1, 3, 194n
  capital exports, 163–4, 177
  character of, xii–xiii, 190–3

  and Civil War, 97–100, 101–2
  and creation of Federal Reserve,
    176–7
  and Harlem Railroad, 86–7
  influence of evangelical movement
    on, 89–92
  internationalism, xiv, 162, 177
  and National Bank Act (1863-4),
    110–12
  opposition to Bretton Woods, 189
  post-Civil War cynicism, 133–4
  and rebuilding after 1835 fire, 71–2,
    73
  relationship with Main Street,
    xii–xiii, 30, 91–2, 107–9
  relationship to Pennsylvania
    Avenue, xii–xiii, 30, 135, 186
  repository of choice, 76–7, 174
  and Roosevelt's banking reforms,
    182, 184–5
  support for hard money (gold
    standard), 174
  see also Morgan, J. Pierpont; New
    York Stock Exchange
Wall Street Journal, 159, 172
Wall Street in Paradise (satire), 134
War of 1812, xiv, 36, 37, 38, 39
war financing
  government bonds, 102–3
  lack of national bank and, 38, 100–1,
    105–6
Ward, Ferdinand, 132
Washington Consensus, 163
Washington, DC see Pennsylvania
  Avenue
Washington, George, 26, 29, 30
water supplies
  Burr's purification scheme, 34–5, 71,
    87, 200n
  Croton Water System, 87
Webster, Daniel, Senator, 62
Western Union Telegraph Co., 81, 157
Whig party, 66
White, Harry Dexter, 188, 189
White, Robert, 84
Wilkeson, Sam, publicist, 104
Wilks, Mr and Mrs M.A., 156
Willing, Thomas, 19, 198n
Wilson, Woodrow, President, 163

women
  as clients, 152
  and social reform movements, 88
  on Wall Street, 149–57
women's rights movement, 153, 156
women's suffrage, 150, 153
Wood, Fernando, mayor of New York,
  93–4, 95, 96
  Peace Convention (1863), 96
Woodhull, Canning, 150
Woodhull, Claflin and Co., 152–3
Woodhull and Claflin's Weekly, 150, 153
Woodhull, Victoria, 150–4
  in England, 153–4

radical politics, 153–4
runs for president, 150, 154
spiritualism, 151–2
Vanderbilt's support for, 150, 151–2,
  153
World Bank (International Bank for
  Reconstruction and
  Development), 188
World (New York), 100, 109
World Trade Center, 11 September
  2001 attack, 191
World War I, financing of, xv, 177
World War II, America and, 163, 187
WorldCom, 186, 193